Firestorm at Gettysburg
Civilian Voices

Firestorm at Gettysburg
Civilian Voices

Jim Slade and John Alexander

Schiffer Military/Aviation History
Atglen, PA

Acknowledgements

There are many to whom the authors of this book owe special thanks for their inspiration and assistance. First, there was Becky Lyons and Mark Nesbitt of Gettysburg who teased us, more than twenty years ago, with a few stories of heroic survival by townspeople. Colonel Jacob Sheads inspired us, and Dr. Charles Glatfelter of the Adams County Historical Society encouraged us.

Efforts to collect and preserve civilian narratives began in the mid-1940s when Dr. Robert Fortenbaugh started the Adams County Historical Society Library. Concurrently, Robert L. Brake is another of the early researchers to whom we owe gratitude.

History consultant Elwood W. Christ must be singled out as particularly helpful and constructive. We also extend thanks to historian and author, Timothy Smith, whose special interest in the townspeople will no doubt bring to light more exciting discoveries in the future. Dave Hedrick, with the Special Collections at Gettysburg College, Craig Caba, Gregory Coco, E.F. Conklin, Peter Monaghan, Clair P. Lyons, Carolyn Durboraw, Bonnie Weatherly, R. William Bean, Evelyn Hughes, and Sarah Mummert proved most helpful. Michael Winey and Randy Hockenburg at the U.S. Military History Institute demonstrated superhuman patience with a couple of journalists plowing ground on historian's turf. And the staff of Carlisle Camera gets special thanks for helping solve a difficult problem on very short notice.

The authors.

For Mary Alice and Sheila, who endured the Firestorm, too.
And for Jeff, who rekindled it.

Book Design by Ian Robertson.

Printed in China.
ISBN: 0-7643-00618-9

We are interested in hearing from authors with book ideas on related topics.

Published by Schiffer Publishing Ltd.
4880 Lower Valley Road
Atglen, PA 19310
Phone: (610) 593-1777
FAX: (610) 593-2002
E-mail: schifferbk@aol.com
Please write for a free catalog.
This book may be purchased from the publisher.
Please include $3.95 postage.
Try your bookstore first.

Table of Contents

Reference Calendar, 1863
Monday, June 15 – Sarah Broadhead begins her diary.
Tuesday, June 16 – New rumors spread each day.
Wednesday, June 17
Thursday, June 18
Friday, June 19
Saturday, June 20 – Rebels reported at Chambersburg.
Sunday, June 21 – Rebels seize Fairfield, eight miles away.
Monday, June 22 – Large Confederate force seen in mountains west of Gettysburg.
Tuesday, June 23 – US Cavalry scouts in Gettysburg.
Wednesday, June 24
Thursday, June 25
Friday, June 26 – Early's raid.
Saturday, June 27
Sunday, June 28 – U.S. Cavalry passes through Gettysburg.
Monday, June 29 – Cavalry engages Rebels at Hanover.
Tuesday, June 30 – U.S. Cavalry takes position in Gettysburg.
Wednesday, July 1 – Battle begins, Union retreats through town.
Thursday, July 2 – Battles at the Peach Orchard and Culp's Hill.
Friday, July 3 – Pickett's charge.
Saturday, July 4 – Lee withdraws.
Sunday, July 5 – Meade sends troops to follow Lee.
Monday, July 6 – Cleanup begins.
Tuesday, July 7 – Additional medical assistance arrives, Meade leaves Gettysburg.
Wednesday, July 8
Thursday, July 9 – Railroad repaired, more supplies pour in.
Friday, July 10
Saturday, July 11
Sunday, July 12
Monday, July 13 – Lee's army crosses the Potomac at Williamsport, unmolested by Union forces.
Tuesday, July 14
Wednesday, July 15 – Sarah Broadhead sets her pen aside.

Preface

"Between January and April, 1863, (General Stonewall) Jackson had his Chief Engineer, Major Hotchkiss, prepare a remarkable map of the country from Winchester to the Susquehanna, compiled from county maps of Maryland, Virginia and Pennsylvania. It was on a large scale and noted farm houses with names of occupants."

– Memoirs, General E. P. Alexander, C.S.A

Fifty-four year old Abraham Lincoln, an Illinois lawyer, won the Presidential election of 1860 with a majority of the electoral votes. As soon as he was inaugurated, March 4, 1861, in Washington, DC a half-dozen southern states made plans to secede from the Union. When Fort Sumter was fired upon Lincoln's call for 75,000 volunteers was enthusiastically received in the north. However, the President had difficulty finding capable generals to execute the war. Union victories were infrequent. On January 1, 1863 Lincoln signed the Emancipation Proclamation. It freed slaves in areas held by the rebels and authorized the creation of Black military units. On May 4th Lincoln learned of General Joseph Hooker's indecisiveness at Chancellorsville and of still another Confederate victory in the field. *Courtesy Library of Congress.*

Robert E. Lee had tried once before to carry the fighting north of the Mason-Dixon line and had failed, driven back in September of 1862 by Union forces who met him at Antietam creek, Maryland. But the stakes were too high to back away; victory in the north could turn things around, perhaps win foreign recognition for the Confederacy, and give Lee the strength to march on Washington itself. So, after months of planning, and after final consultations with Confederate President Jefferson Davis and his cabinet, Lee turned north again.

In the early morning of June 3rd, 1863, the first elements of a mighty Confederate force left the vicinity of Fredericksburg, Virginia, for the Shenandoah Valley. Reports of their departure sparked panicked debate between then-Union Commanding General Joseph Hooker in Fredericksburg, and his superiors in Washington over whether to challenge the Confederates directly or to launch a counter-offensive on Richmond. Hooker felt that an assault on the Confederate seat of government would force Lee to reverse course and race to its defense. President Abraham Lincoln finally decided the issue, ordering Hooker to give chase, but to keep his army positioned between Lee and Washington, to screen off and protect the US capitol. Hooker lost the debate and, subsequently gave up his job.

Lee's plan was to cross the Blue Ridge and turn north. So, in stifling dust and summer heat, the miles-long Rebel army worked its way up the farm roads of Virginia's Shenandoah Valley to Winchester, where it brushed aside Federal opposition. Then, crossing the Potomac above Martinsburg, it moved inexorably through Williamsport and Hagerstown, Maryland, to Greencastle, Chambersburg, and Carlisle, Pennsylvania, living off the lush countryside as they marched. Some lead elements reached as far north as Harrisburg, Lee's initial goal, and engaged Federal units there, marking the deepest penetration of the north ever accomplished by a massed Confederate force.

But while at Chambersburg, Robert E. Lee was informed that the main body of the pursuing Federal Army, led by its newly-appointed Commander, George Gordon Meade, was at Frederick, Maryland, and that portions of the Federal force were blocking passes through the mountains to the Shenandoah Valley. Fearful that his supply lines might be cut behind him, Lee wheeled his army to the east from Chambersburg and to the south from Harrisburg, hoping to arrest the Union advance. A quick look at a modern roadmap will show why Gettysburg ultimately became their place of engagement; the town was caught squarely in the middle.

The encounter that followed became Gettysburg's firestorm; a rushing, sweeping, not-to-be-denied firestorm which enveloped the tiny town, consumed anything in its way, and moved on.

More than 170-thousand Union and Confederate troops met at Gettysburg, and some 2500 townsfolk were swallowed up in one of the most decisive...and devastating...battles of the American Civil War.

Well over a century later, the citizens of Gettysburg have been all but forgotten, their stories yet to be told in any detail. Virtually every major book and article about that famous battle focuses on the military, on the strategy, on the officers and their men. However, when one examines the wealth of material the townspeople and their descendants left, the examiner gains a new perspective of the battle and of the military occupation of this small, crossroads town.

Although the local population had been aware of the oncoming Rebel force for weeks, no one knew where it would pass, and few had a chance to flee. When the Confederate and Union armies both arrived in Gettysburg, the people were left to their own devices.

Many of the heroic stories of this book are told by women and children. As they did upon receiving previous rumors of raid or invasion, many businessmen and bankers shipped their goods and money to York or Philadelphia. Many military-age men were in the armies. Others left with horses and livestock they knew would be confiscated if left behind. But the majority – an undetermined number of civilian men, women and children – spent three long days in or near their homes and even longer nights in cramped cellars subject to military whim. Those older men who stayed with their families still lived in fear of arrest. The women did not know what to expect for themselves or for their children. In most cases, the 'enemy' behaved decently – not many friendships, but a certain degree of respect, developed. However, there was never doubt that either army would do whatever was deemed appropriate or necessary. In the case of the Confederate soldier camped in the town's streets, that usually meant taking anything edible or 'rideable.'

It is our intention to recreate a six month period of these people's lives with their own words. We will follow them from the rumors and fears of June through the somber yet inspirational dedication of the National Cemetery in late November 1863.

We come to this work as journalists, not historians. In that role, basing our book entirely on diaries, narratives, manuscripts and other published or unpublished accounts, we hope to convey the emotional experience of the townspeople equally with the historic circumstance, breathing new life into the Gettysburg drama.

As for the officers and soldiers, we will attempt to demonstrate their interaction with the townspeople. Sometimes, soldiers will provide interior detail. But primarily we will unfold the story as the citizens of Gettysburg themselves experienced it; that is, from the distance of their rooftops, street corners, porches and cellars, and later through close-up encounters with the wounded and dying who were brought into their homes. And we will unfold it in their own words.

The townspeople got a lot of information hearsay. They knew few of the technicalities of the Fishhook, the salients, the line of march or cannon positions that we read about today. For them, the soldiers were simply everywhere – in their houses, occupying their businesses, shelling their homes and barns, trampling their crops and raiding their cellars. It was a blur of men, horses, wagons and cannon, dust, mud and heat. It was a deafening roar of exploding gunpowder and the chilling wail of dying men. And after the fight had exhausted itself, it was the muffled squeak of wagon wheels and thousands of feet shuffling away in the night. Then, for weeks after, there was the intermingled stench of death and burnt gunpowder, the mountains of limbs, the unburied dead, and the horribly wounded...an estimated ten to twenty wounded for every man woman and child of Gettysburg.

In some ways, what was left remains today. The citizens of Gettysburg and Adams County, Pennsylvania, might be justified in claiming that the region never fully

Fifty-five year old Jefferson Davis of Mississippi, a former US Senator, soldier, and plantation owner, was elected President of the Confederate States of America February 9, 1861 – some six weeks after South Carolina became the first state to secede from the Union. He was inaugurated in Montgomery, Alabama, Capital of the Confederacy, February 18, 1861. On April 12, 1861 Confederate guns fired on the federal outpost at Fort Sumpter located off the coast of Charleston, South Carolina, beginning the American Civil War. *Courtesy Confederate Veteran Magazine.*

Fifty-six year old General Robert E. Lee was a Virginian whose father was a hero of the American Revolution. Lee had been educated at the US Military Academy at West Point. When Civil War became evident President Lincoln offered him field command of all Union forces. Lee declined. On April 23, 1861 he accepted the position of Commander-in-Chief of the military and naval forces of Virginia. He was military adviser to President Jefferson Davis. After five major victories during the first year of the war Lee suffered a major setback at Antietam. But after decisive Confederate victories at Fredricksburg, Stones River and, most recently, at Chancellorsville Lee determined the time was right for another invasion. *Courtesy Massachusetts Commandery of the Military Order of the Loyal Legion of the United States and the US Army Military History Institute, Carlisle, Pennsylvania.*

"Stonewall" Jackson was "the missing man" at Gettysburg. Educated at the US Military Academy at West Point, "Stonewall" earned his nickname at the first battle of Bull Run, Virginia. General Robert E. Lee relied more on Jackson than any of his other Generals and Jackson never disappointed him. His field strategies brought victory upon victory. Ironically, at Chancellorsville, Jackson and his escort were in advance of his men on a flanking maneuver when they were mistaken for a detachment of Union soldiers. Jackson was killed. Lee grieved. He missed Jackson at Gettysburg, for many believe had he not died the results in Pennsylvania would have been different. Thomas Jonathan Jackson was 39 when he was killed in service to the Confederate States of America. *Courtesy Massachusetts Commandery of the Military Order of the Loyal Legion of the United States and the US Army Military History Institute, Carlisle, PA*

recovered from the great battle. Farmers were ruined by the two army's passing. Businessmen, homeowners and churches spent years seeking compensation from the Federal Government.

Most tragically, a memory of unspeakable horror was seared into Gettysburg's collective memory. As a result, the people in these pages seemed to have a passionate need to write or otherwise tell their experience. Taken separately, the stories are interesting reading. Placed in a chronological blend, they are compelling. In some cases, the official record may be slightly adjusted or improved for the reader by these narratives because in the melee, a soldier fighting for life itself saw only a particle of the event. The broader description given by wide-eyed civilians can provide context.

The modern reader should be cautioned: the people in *Firestorm at Gettysburg* are real; the times were chaotic and people saw their world differently. Some of their language may be offensive to today's society, but it is their language and they had reason for it. We have not changed their words to suit current sensibilities, nor should we.

It must also be understood that time can dim or smooth memory in the speaker's favor. We will leave it to the reader to decide which comments are self-serving and which are brutal fact. It is sufficient to say that, on balance, we found that most of the accounts square nicely with those of their neighbors.

We have made no effort to pretty up or "adjust" the narratives; in some cases we have dropped tangential or irrelevant comments, but these rare "edits" have been done only in the interest of clarity. To arrange the narratives in a chronological flow that meshes with their neighbor's observations, we have broken them into minute by minute accounts, but in no case have we changed or taken their words out of context.

As authors, we have tried to keep our voices out of the citizens' stories. We have confined ourselves to introductions, transitional explanations, parentheses (rarely), captions and footnotes. In fact, we are tempted to apologize for such heavy use of footnotes, but felt that was more desirable than interjecting ourselves in a way that would disturb the story's flow. All we can promise is our good intentions: that each footnote will help the reader better understand the situation and who these people were.

Additionally, we have included a running chronology of events on the battlefield to keep the reader aware of what the townspeople are describing at the moment.

But whatever device the mechanics of book-writing force upon us, a mosaic human experience rises from these narratives that casts new light on a pivotal episode in one of America's greatest national tragedies.

There has never been a battle to rival Gettysburg on American soil, and yet the words of the citizens who lived through it, who lost much and gave much, who nursed and cared for the wounded, and who buried the dead, have remained unassembled and unpublished far too long.

In absorbing and then threading these stories together, we came to feel a kinship, admiration and personal concern for a group of people we had never met or considered...until now. *This is their book.*

General George Gordon Meade, 58, born in Spain while his father was in service to the US Navy, was a civil engineer by profession. He served with distinction on the staffs of Generals Taylor and Scott in the Mexican War. Meade began the Civil War by commanding a brigade of volunteers and after General Hooker's indecisiveness at Chancellorsville he now found himself in command of the Army of the Potomac en route to check Lee's invasion of the North. *Courtesy Massachusetts Commandery of the Military Order of the Loyal Legion of the United States and the US Army Military History Institute, Carlisle, Pennsylvania.*

The 30th Pennsylvania Infantry, also known as the 1st Pennsylvania Reserves, counted many men and boys from Adams County and Gettysburg among its ranks. When this photograph of the camp was taken at Fairfax Courthouse, Virginia, June 4th, 1863, some of Lee's Army was already in Culpeper and the rest was en route. A month from now the 30th Pennsylvania Infantry will have successfully helped extinguish a firestorm that was to engulf Company K's hometown of Gettysburg. *Courtesy Massachusetts Commandery of the Military Order of the Loyal Legion of the United States and the US Army Military History Institute, Carlisle, Pennsylvania.*

Gettysburg and Some of Her Citizens – An Introduction

Gettysburg's economy was built around the carriage industry, but farms and warehouses were also important. The Gettysburg Railroad was very good for business as it made getting local products to new markets easier. **Robert McCurdy** and **Josiah Diehl** had just opened a large new warehouse near the railroad tracks several weeks before the battle. McCurdy was President of the Railroad. He was a well known and respected businessman on both sides of the Mason-Dixon line.

Charles Boyer helped his father **William** run the family grocery store on the Diamond (the town's square). Father and son businesses were fairly common. **Samuel Buehler** and his son **Alexander** operated Buehler's Book and Drug store. It was close to Pennsylvania College and a favorite gathering place of students. Some of the more affluent farmers had homes in the city. Tenant farmers were in charge of day to day operations.

Mary McAllister supported herself by re-selling to the townsfolk bacon and other cured meats that she obtained from area farmers. She lived with sister **Martha** who was married to **John Scott**. Scott, with his oldest son **Hugh**, operated a telegraph office. It is very likely that the sisters had a garden as most townsfolk did, and that they stored and preserved vegetables and other foods as the processes of that day permitted. The income Martha's husband John made from the telegraph office would have contributed to the family income, also.

Speaking of processed food, in 1835 **Professor Michael Jacobs**, at Pennsylvania College, was one of the earliest successful experimenters in this country in canning vegetables. He developed his technique after reading about both the French process for preserving fruit by canning and a similar process the English had developed for extending the life of meat safely.

One of the more controversial US politicians of the time, **Thaddeus Stevens** lived in Gettysburg for 25 years, and with **George Arnold** established the Gettysburg Iron Foundry in 1837. Arnold was one of Stevens' early business associates who became one of the town's most influential citizens. Several years before the war Stevens, who had moved from Gettysburg, was elected to the US Senate. A staunch opponent of slavery, he wielded great power, and chaired the Ways and Means Committee during the Civil War.

George Arnold remained a life long resident of Adams County. At the time of the battle Arnold was an officer of the Farmers & Mechanics Savings Institution that he helped to found in 1857. He also had a clothing store and real estate holdings. Arnold was described as an ardent Unionist and active in politics. In the summer of 1862, in his 60s, Arnold traveled to Harrison's Landing, Virginia, to help care for wounded from the Peninsula Campaign.

Early on the morning of the first day seventeen year old **Amelia Harmon**, who lived with her aunt at the old McLean estate off Chambersburg Pike, was among the first to have her home consumed by the firestorm. The Confederate Louisiana Tigers set fire to the stately brick McLean-Harmon mansion, partly from battle-lust and partly because Union soldiers had briefly taken a stand from inside the house before retreating. Amelia and her aunt were forced to set out on foot, among flying bullets and cannonballs.

John Burns, a veteran of the War of 1812, was a cantankerous former constable who decided to take up arms and go up against the rebels personally. A cobbler at town council President **David Kendlehart's** boot and shoe shop, Burns had nothing but unkind things to say about his fellow townsmen whom he considered cowards for not helping out the army.

John Will, in his 20s, helped his father **Charles** run the Globe Inn when he was not calling on **Martha Martin**, whom he married a few months after the battle. The Globe was mostly a tavern at the time, across York Street from the Tyson Brothers Photographic Gallery. **James Gettys**, who founded the borough, had built the Globe in the 1790s. Traditionally, it served as local headquarters for the Democratic party

in Adams County. As an enterprising capitalist, young John did a booming business with quite a few of the Confederate soldiers, and his experiences will be shared with you.

David McConaughy, a life-long resident whose father had been a Gettysburg minister, was an attorney and also a staunch Republican. He stayed in the county during the battle, as did a few other leading citizens, but understandably laid low to avoid capture. Capture by the Confederates was a real threat to civilians in Gettysburg. Male residents who chose not to flee the area before the battle were at risk. At least eight or nine Gettysburg area men were taken prisoner, for reasons unknown, and marched to southern prisons.

McConaughy had been a member of the 1860 National Convention which nominated Abraham Lincoln for President. He helped organize, and was a Captain in, the Adams Rifles, a local militia. Upon the June 1863 invasion, McConaughy offered his services to the government and was assigned to the secret service. There is substantial confirmation that McConaughy supplied, and persuaded friends to supply, intelligence up to the time of the battle. Afterwards, General Meade thanked him for his effort.

One of McConaughy's close friends and business associate was attorney **David Buehler**. Mr. Buehler was also the town postmaster. Before he became an attorney, he edited The Sentinel newspaper for a dozen years. His brother **C.H. Buehler** (Captain of the Gettysburg Independent Blues, another local militia), also worked with Adams Sentinel publisher **Robert Goodloe Harper** before going into other business.

Fighting with Harper for the hearts and minds of Adams County's citizens was **Henry J. Stahle**, who owned The Compiler. Stahle was a Democrat, but loyal to the Union. Stahle described David McConaughy as "a cold-hearted personal and political enemy."

Another prominent Democrat you'll meet is **Dr. J.W.C. O'Neal**. Dr. O'Neal was persuaded to move from Baltimore to Gettysburg because the town Democrats wanted to strengthen the party. The town already had several doctors, including the Horner Brothers, **Dr. Charles Horner and Dr. Robert Horner.** Some of the Democrats in county government enticed O'Neal to town by promising him the county Alms House and prison patients. The 42 year old O'Neal had just moved his office from the David Wills building on the Diamond to the northeast corner of Baltimore and High Street, where two other doctors also hung out their shingles.

The outspoken O'Neal was not liked by everyone. **David Wills** may have been among them. Wills was a prominent Republican attorney who frequently sparred for power with another Republican attorney, David McConaughy. President Lincoln stayed at Wills home on the Diamond, or town square, when he came to dedicate Soldier's National Cemetery in November. Wills would certainly have objected to Dr. O'Neal's political views, but that may not have been the reason O'Neal moved his office. O'Neal's sympathy for the southern cause did force him to switch to the Reformed Church because his defense of slavery made him unwelcome at the Gettysburg Presbyterian Church.

Jane Smith and her mother, **Mrs. William Smith,** lived in the home of Mrs. Smith's parents, **Mr. and Mrs. John S. Crawford,** in a sturdy brick house north and east of the town, out near the Alms House. A cousin fresh out of school, **Anna Mary Young** was also living there. Mr. Crawford departed for safer refuge and took with him a valuable horse which he had kept saddled for two days in preparation for a hasty getaway. The women, however, were trapped precariously between the lines during the first day of the firestorm. Wounded and dying Union soldiers filled their house for days. Among them was young **Brigadier General Francis Barlow** who, early on the first day of fighting, had been left on the field for dead.

Another of the stalwarts in this human tragedy is a woman named **Sarah Broadhead**. Her husband **Joseph** came to this country with his parents as a child from England. He was an employee of the

Gettysburg Railroad. As the firestorm swept in and began its consumption, Sarah endured. She and her child and several of her neighbors, including **Jacob and Elizabeth Gilbert**, anxiously spent long dark hours in the cellar of harness maker **David Troxel.** She kept a diary. You will see the strength of this woman, and of several other women whom, we believe, behaved extraordinarily in the midst of the mud, blood, and mayhem.

Elizabeth Thorn and her husband **Peter** were born in Germany. Before the war Peter Thorn had been responsible for Evergreen Cemetery. He, his wife, their children and her parents lived in the Evergreen Gatehouse. However, at this time Peter was off in the service of his adopted country. Elizabeth was six months pregnant when the firestorm erupted and began to swirl all around her. Her three children and her elderly parents looked to her to keep them safe.

Salome "Sallie" Myers was a young school teacher who still lived at home with her family on the north side of West High Street, just off Baltimore Street. Her father was a Justice of the Peace. When the wounded and dying began seeking shelter in the homes and buildings of Gettysburg, "Sallie" Myers put the nursing skills she had been taught to good use. When the brother of a soldier who had died in her care came to claim his body after the battle, they fell in love. "Sallie" became **Mrs. Harry F. Stewart.**

A friend of "Sallie" Myers was **Alice Powers**. She and her four sisters (all in their twenties) taught school. No one could have been more proud of his daughters than **Solomon Powers**, the only stonecutter west of the Susquehanna River. He had his own profitable business on High Street that provided the capital to give his daughters a fine education. Miss Alice, who taught in one of the country schools in 1863, was home for summer vacation as were all the teachers and students of the public schools. She and her sisters, Sallie Myers, and several other women who lived nearby spent what seemed like a lifetime caring for the wounded and dying inside the Catholic Church. Like so many hundreds of other residents, they were fighting against being consumed by the firestorm.

Alice's older sister **Jane Powers McDonnell** was married to one of the civilians seized by Confederates on July 1st, but **Henry McDonnell's** fate was not as severe as some other male townsfolk. A Confederate officer ordered him released July 4th, and he was able to rejoin his wife and two small children. Some of the captured men from Gettysburg spent years in southern prisons, and one died before being paroled.

As the Union forces moved through the streets of Gettysburg to engage the Confederates on McPherson's Ridge, **Henrietta Weikert Shriver** grabbed up her two small children and ran next door to butcher **James Pierce's** house. Pierce thought it would be a good idea to send his oldest daughter **Matilda** with Mrs. Shriver out of harm's way. Mrs. Shriver's father, **Jacob Weikert**, had a large farm a few miles south of town off Taneytown Road. It was at the base of two large knolls known as "The Round Tops." **Tillie Pierce**, only 17 at the time, wound up in three days of hell.

Henry Eyster Jacobs, 18, had graduated from Pennsylvania College the year before and was now a student at the Lutheran Theological Seminary. He lived at home on West Middle Street with sister **Julia**, 16, and brother **Luther**. As the first day's fighting wound down the Confederates established a line of defense right down Middle Street. The Jacobs, all other residents of Middle Street and streets to the north were behind Confederate lines for three days.

Henry's father, **Dr. Michael Jacobs**, was a professor at Lutheran Theological Seminary. Both Henry and the Professor kept extensive journals of their experiences, and to them we are grateful. Dr. Jacobs was a pathfinder in meteorology and frequently lectured on the subject. He was also quite interested in electricity. Among the apparatus he devised for class demonstration was a small metal track that extended around the room. On it was a metal car. Before he demonstrated it to his class, he brought son Henry (then 9) over to the college. When the Professor connected wires from a battery with the track the car ran around the room. He said "Henry, remember this, this will be the motor power of the future."

Another professor, **Dr. Martin Luther Stoever** married into the McConaughy family. He lived with wife **Elizabeth** and the children on south Baltimore Street. They leased a portion of the first floor of their residence to **J.L. Schick** for his dry goods business. It was the Stoever's who befriended **New York Times Correspondent Samuel Wilkeson** after the battle when Wilkeson found the body of his oldest son, artillery **Lieutenant Bayard Wilkeson**, among those who had been killed in the first day's fighting out near the Alms House.

Eighteen year old **Daniel Alexander Skelly** had just returned from West Point as the forces from both sides were closing in on Gettysburg. Local Congressman **Edward McPherson** had obtained a temporary appointment for him, but young Dan apparently failed to meet academic requirements. He was returning home to his job at the Fahnestock Brothers General Merchandise Store. Skelly's father was one of the town's tailors.

Johnston Skelly, Daniel's father, had apprenticed **Jennie Wade's** father, **James** years before. James Wade, who had a terrible reputation and a temper to match, was imprisoned in solitary confinement in 1850. He was declared insane two years later and committed to the insane ward at the Alms House.

On June 26, when **General Jubal Early** and his forces rode through Gettysburg, Jennie Wade was with sister **Georgeanna McClellan** who was giving birth. She was still at her sister's house near Baltimore Street and the Baltimore Pike when killed by a sharpshooters bullet.

Charles Tyson and his brother Isaac had come to Gettysburg to open a photography studio in 1859. A few years later Charles met, and only months before the battle, married **Maria Griest** from nearby Biglerville. Many of the photographs that you see in this book were taken by the Tysons, or by one of their competitors. It is surprising that a rural community like Gettysburg had so many people engaged in what was then a relatively new profession.

The morning of the battle was a busy day for Charles Tyson. He spent that morning taking portrait photographs of Union soldiers who lined up in his studio as their units headed into battle!

Albertus McCreary, about 15 in 1863, and a couple of other young boys – **Charles McCurdy** whose father Robert was President of the Railroad, and **Gates Fahnestock**, both 10 – provide for us a description of the fighting, the sniping, the scampering, and the shelling as could only be described through the wonderment and awe of children who saw more in three days than most adults experience in a lifetime. Gates' father **James**, and two of Gates' uncles, owned the Fahnestock Brothers General Merchandise Store one block south of the Diamond. The store's rooftop observation deck provided citizens and officers with an unobstructed view of the terrain west and south of town.

Much has been made over the years of young **Wes Culp** leaving Gettysburg to join the Confederacy and returning to be killed in the battle. Wes was not the only resident or former resident of Gettysburg to return in service of the Confederacy. Virginia's **Lieutenant J.F. Crocker**, a former student at Pennsylvania College, was wounded at Picket's Charge and captured. Afterwards, on his word of honor, he freely walked the streets of town renewing old acquaintances!

These are not all the people who were engulfed in and survived the firestorm. You will meet others as their remarkable stories unfold in their words to create a rich tapestry that is a testament to the human spirit.

Battle Chronology
July 1-4, 1863
The Battle of Gettysburg[1]

Wednesday, July 1st

5:30 a.m.: Corporal Alphonse Hodges, 9th New York Cavalry, USA, discovers Confederate troopers advancing along the Chambersburg Pike, a mile and a half west of Gettysburg. Unwittingly, they exchange the first shots of the Battle of Gettysburg as Hodges alerts his fellow pickets. At this time, the main body of General Robert E. Lee's Army of Northern Virginia is to the west and north of Gettysburg, moving toward Harrisburg. Lee himself is on horseback near Cashtown, among foot soldiers of Longstreet's division. His newly-appointed Union counterpart, General George Gordon Meade, is encamped south of Gettysburg near Taneytown, Maryland. Neither commanding general expects or wants an engagement at this point; both are simply trying to concentrate their forces.

But along Seminary Ridge, it has already begun.

10 a.m.: Union Major General Abner Doubleday's I Corps arrives to relieve the Union Cavalry, which has been engaged with elements of Major General Henry Heth's Confederate division since the opening shots. Heth has since brought artillery into play. Brigadier General John Buford's Cavalry spreads east to hinder two divisions of Lieutenant General Richard S. Ewell's corps, now approaching from the north and northeast on the Carlisle and Harrisburg Roads.

10:30 a.m.: Major General John F. Reynolds sends a rider to a division of Major General Oliver Howard's XI Corps at Horner's Mills, calling them forward to assist. Reynolds is killed minutes later.

Noon: Lee reaches the field.

12:30 p.m.: The Union reinforcements summoned by Reynolds arrive.

2 p.m.: The main column of the Union XI Corps positions itself. One division digs in south of town on Cemetery Hill, two others hurry to the open fields north of Gettysburg to back up the cavalry that is watching Ewell's progress. Confederate Major General Robert E. Rode's division of Ewell's corps attacks and is repulsed by the augmented Union force, but not before gaining good ground. At the same time, Lieutenant General A. P. Hill increases pressure against I Corps at McPherson's farm, forcing the Union troops back to the Seminary. Watching the fight evolve, Lee senses confusion in the Federal ranks and orders his officers to press on, thus ensuring a full-scale battle.

2:30 p.m.: Jubal Early's division reaches Gettysburg, launching an attack from the northeast against Howard's right flank, causing Federal troops to begin a disorganized retreat through the town. Early's troops capture hundreds of Yanks in the chaos. To the west, A. P. Hill's soldiers push the Union I Corps off Seminary Ridge, leaving the Federal troops in danger of being cut off by Rodes. After murderous fighting, the remainder of I Corps reaches and takes position on Cemetery Hill.

4:30 p.m.: Concluding that Gettysburg will be the ground for engagement, Meade sends orders from Pipe Creek for all corps to march on the town. Lee orders Ewell to attack Cemetery Hill if he can. But Ewell feels his forces are in no condition to continue, demurs, and waits for Johnson's division to reach the field and reconnoiter. By the time Ewell has sufficient numbers to move ahead, the night is gone and he holds back.

In the background during the afternoon and night of the first day: Numerous divisions of both sides continue to arrive, building the opposing forces steadily as they funnel into the rear. By evening, an estimated 35,000 Confederate troops are at Gettysburg, in contrast to some 25,000 Union soldiers. But that will be the last time Lee's army can claim superior numbers. Within hours, three more Union divisions arrive.

Midnight: Meade reaches Cemetery Ridge, finding his army in a good defensive position.

Thursday, July 2nd

By daylight, Meade counts as many as 46,000 men. Lee has approximately 40 to 45,000 available, although neither commander has any knowledge of the other's real strength. By late afternoon, Major General John Sedgwick's division of 15,000 men arrives from Manchester, Maryland to add to Meade's strength. After discussion in which Longstreet tries unsuccessfully to persuade Lee to wait for Meade to attack, Lee orders Ewell to threaten the Union right flank, Longstreet the left. Hill will keep the Union center occupied with an artillery barrage. It looks good on paper, but Lee gets poor cooperation from his officers and the morning passes quietly. On the Union left, Major General Dan Sickles sees what he thinks is a better position about three-quarters of a mile to his front and...on his own initiative...sends a reconnaissance group to check it.

1 p.m.: Never one to doubt himself, Sickles moves his entire corps forward, leaving Little Round Top unoccupied and exposing Hancock's left. Luckily the Confederates are slow to respond. Longstreet waits for Hood's incoming troops to reinforce him. When they arrive, they are given a 30 minute rest. Then Longstreet takes 3 1/2 more hours to organize his forces.

4:30 p.m.: Longstreet attacks. Long on good intentions but short on reconnaissance, he runs directly into one of Sickle's divisions. The fight is bloody, and the Union line is badly damaged...The outcome would be much worse for the Union except for Brigadier General Gouverneur K. Warren, USA, who sees that Little Round Top is undefended and calls in troops to defend it. The fighting, encompassing the Wheat Field, Plum Run, Devil's Den and the slopes of Little Round Top, lasts four hours. Losses are heavy on both sides, the Rebel line has advanced, but Meade plays a good tactical game, and the Union position holds on Cemetery Ridge. However, the day isn't over. Ewell's front extends for two miles through the town, curving around and behind Culp's Hill to a spot just a mile behind Meade's headquarters. In fighting Longstreet, Meade moved two divisions of Slocum's force to his left to cover the hole created by Dan Sickle's adventuring. As a result, the Union right flank is guarded by a single brigade. It was only because Brigadier General Henry Hunt's artillery covered that thinly-protected zone that Ewell did not attack at the same time as Longstreet. In fact, he didn't move until Longstreet's battle was ending and by then it was getting dark.

Twilight: Two of Jubal Early's brigades struck Cemetery Hill, reaching the crest to meet Howard's XI Corps. Hancock sent a Federal brigade to help, and with later backing from other units of the XI and I Corps, the Rebels were pushed back. Meanwhile, Johnson's Confederate division rushed the east side of Culp's Hill; but, the defenders, in trenches and behind stone walls, were able to drive most of Johnson's people back. Ironically, one of Johnson's Confederate brigades did get into unoccupied trenches above Spangler's Spring, directly behind the Union right rear, but they didn't realize their advantage until daylight. Before that time, Meade ordered Slocum back to his original position, bringing the Union right flank back to full strength, and evicting the Rebel trench holders. Looking to the next day, Meade told his commanders that if Lee should attack again, it would be at the center of the Union line.

Friday, July 3rd

Lee wanted to begin the decisive battle in "the early gray of morning." As Meade predicted, Lee planned an assault on the Union center. To do it, he would begin with an artillery barrage followed by an attack by Major General George E. Pickett's division of Longstreet's corps plus elements of all three of A.P. Hill's divisions, making a combined marching force of more than 13,000 men. Longstreet argued against it vehemently, citing the Union strength he had observed first hand the day before. But Lee would not be persuaded. What he did not know was that Meade had repositioned his artillery during the night so it could provide a tremendous crossfire over the center of the line. Concurrently, he had improved his firing positions on all higher elevations to cover an expected assault on Culp's Hill. Both sides were planning to bring the affair to a conclusion.

4:30 a.m.: Union artillery opens on Johnson's position on Culp's Hill. Because of the steep terrain, Johnson advances to escape and runs into Union troops anxious to recover the trenches he has just evacuated. Artillery fire is so heavy it denudes Culp's Hill of trees. The fighting in that sector lasts for 7 hours and Johnson is pushed back.

11 a.m.: The bloodied Confederates withdraw to their lines within the town, and the Union line is fully restored.

1:07 p.m.: Two Confederate guns signal the start of a bombardment of the Union line on Cemetery Ridge. One hundred forty Rebel guns begin firing along a two mile front. Eighty Federal pieces return the compliment, beginning a duel unlike any ever seen or heard in North America. It lasts nearly two hours.

About 3 p.m.: During a lull, Confederate Colonel E.P. Alexander sees eighteen Union guns being withdrawn, and signals Pickett to seize the opportunity to advance. Pickett gains permission from a reluctant Longstreet and rides to the center of a 13,000 man line. Because the Union guns at the center were loaded with canister, those batteries kept silent until the Confederate line reached the Emmitsburg Road. Then, II Corps opened, joining crossfire already coming from Little Round Top and Cemetery Hill. Only a few hundred Rebels reached the Union center. More than 7,000 lay dead or wounded behind them. Longstreet was right. It was sheer suicide.[2] Meeting those who returned, General Lee told them, "This was all my fault. It is I that have lost this fight, and you must help me out of it the best way you can." Meade does not counterattack.

Evening of July 3rd: Lee pulls in his lines from left and right, expecting an attack the following morning. He recalls Ewell's divisions from Culp's Hill and the town, and Longstreet's from around Devil's Den, meanwhile preparing for the march back to Virginia. If there is to be any more fighting, it will be up to Meade to start it.

Saturday, July 4th

Heavy rain turns the roads to mud, slowing the progress of wagon trains loaded with wounded and supplies as they struggle out the Chambersburg Road. Some 4,000 Union prisoners are taken with the retreating Confederate army down the Fairfield Road. Rebel cavalry ride guard along both routes.

Sunday, July 5th

Finally convinced that Lee has pulled up stakes, Meade sends a Cavalry brigade toward Chambersburg and starts Sedgwick's corps along the Fairfield Road to watch the retreat.

July 7th

Meade leaves Gettysburg, turning his force west at Frederick, Maryland. They catch up with the Confederates days later near Williamsport, Maryland, where they have taken up defensive positions waiting for the flooded Potomac to recede.

July 13th

Lee crosses the river without incident.

July 14th

Lincoln agonized over Meade's failure to go for the jugular. He wrote a letter to Meade, in which he said, in effect:
"I do not believe you appreciate the magnitude of the misfortune in Lee's escape. He was within our easy grasp, and to have closed upon him would in connection with our other late successes[3] have ended the war."
Mindful of the success Meade did achieve, the President never sent the letter.

NOTES

1. Sources include: Adams County Historical Society; National Military Park Archives, Gettysburg; *Gettysburg, the Long Encampment*, by Jack McLaughlin; *Gettysburg!*, Edward J. Stackpole, *The Civil War Times*; various others.
2. Stackpole.
3. Grant at Vicksburg.

Prologue

"The month of June, 1863, was an exciting one for the people of Gettysburg and vicinity. Rumors of the invasion of Pennsylvania by the Confederate army were rife..."

– Daniel Alexander Skelly

In truth, Gettysburg had been on edge for months. The war always felt close; the Mason-Dixon line was just a few miles south. In September of the year before, residents had listened attentively to the rumble of cannon at Sharpsburg, Maryland, as they "put period" to Robert E. Lee's first attempt at an invasion of the northern states. If Lee had won the battle of Antietam Creek, well then...Gettysburg was just across the border.

While not all the world's roads led to Gettysburg, most roads of any consequence to the region led through it. No fewer than ten highways met there, each leading to another important town. If you paste the Gettysburg map to the face of a clock, the Carlisle Road is at 12 o'clock. At 1 o'clock is the road to Harrisburg; the York Pike is 2 o'clock. At 4 is Hanover Road and at 6 o'clock, Baltimore Street. Emmitsburg road is positioned at 7, Fairfield Road is at 8. At 10 o'clock is the Chambersburg Pike, and

This photo was taken some seventy-five years after James Gettys decided to build a tavern here and lay out a borough in the 1780s. He had sound reasons for settling here. He could offer refreshment and lodging to travelers on the turnpike between Philadelphia and Pittsburgh and points in between. Gettys' borough grew rapidly. By the summer of 1863 it was the seat of the Adams County government and home to some 2,500 residents, many of them immigrants from Ireland, Scotland, France, or Germany. *Courtesy Adams County Historical Society.*

Thaddeus Stevens, 71, a Vermont native, had moved to Gettysburg soon after graduating Dartmouth College in 1816. Stevens and George Arnold had several businesses together, and the two shared similar political views. Stevens background in law ideally suited him to run for the Pennsylvania legislature, which he did. He was elected to Congress in 1849. *Courtesy Adams County Historical Society.*

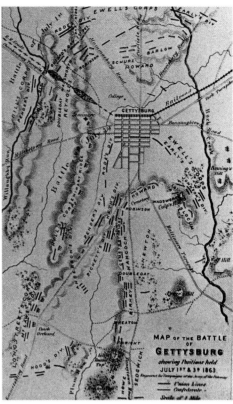

While not all the world's roads led to Gettysburg, most roads of any consequence to the region led through it. No fewer than ten highways junctioned there, each leading to another important town. So, it was logical to believe that Gettysburg would see at least part of the two great armies that were moving into south-central Pennsylvania that summer. *Courtesy Massachusetts Commandery of the Military Order of the Loyal Legion of the United States and the US Army Military History Institute, Carlisle, Pennsylvania.*

Mummasburg Road sits at 11. Given that perspective, it was logical to believe that Gettysburg would see at least parts of the two great armies that were moving into south-central Pennsylvania that summer.

Gettysburg was, and still is, the Adams County seat. A pretty little town with brick row houses in the center and large, comfortable homes on the outskirts, Gettysburg had dirt streets and paved sidewalks in 1863. The tree-lined avenues gave it a sleepy, comfortable atmosphere. But looks are often deceiving; Gettysburg was a busy place.

Around 2,500 people lived there, taking part in a diverse economy. As is the case today, there was a strong Dutch, German and Scots-Irish heritage. The 1860 census shows that about 8 percent of the town's residents were black or mulatto. An unknown number of them were most certainly runaway slaves, and it is acknowledged that Gettysburg was a station on the Underground Railroad that assisted blacks in their journey to freedom.

Gettysburg was the commercial center of a large farming region, there was an iron works, a foundry, a stove factory, a brickyard, a tannery, and there were stone and marble cutters. Eleven carriage makers created work for wheelwrights, trim shops, canvas shops and even for silversmiths, who furnished plating for the vehicles.

At the time of the great battle, Gettysburg was served by seven churches, nine law firms, a fair-sized college and a seminary. The town had a brisk mercantile trade, including dry goods, general merchandise, cobblers, butchers and grocers. The largest store in Gettysburg was the Fahnestock Brothers General Merchandise Store, located one block south of the central Diamond (town square) on Baltimore Street. Smaller specialty merchants competed throughout the central part of the city.

There was at least one telegraph office, and the town was the terminus of the Gettysburg Railroad, which was indispensable to the economy.

There were two newspapers, the Republican Adams Sentinel and the Democratic Gettysburg Compiler, who competed vigorously and vociferously in a hotly divided political environment. Republicans were adamantly pro-Union, Democrats were more liberally disposed toward the south, and had a strong organization in Gettysburg.

George Arnold, 63, was one of Gettysburg's most prominent business men. He had been a friend and business associate of Thaddeus Stevens for years. Arnold had various real estate holdings, had established an iron foundry in 1837, and the Farmers & Mechanics Savings Institution in 1857. Arnold was active in local Republican politics and an ardent "unionist." *Courtesy Adams County Historical Society.*

The rolling countryside, whitewashed fences, painted barns, flowing wheat, and bountiful orchards belied the tension building among the residents in town and on the farms. The armies were out there. The question of where they would eventually collide was the source of much anxiety. *Courtesy Massachusetts Commandery of the Military Order of the Loyal Legion of the United States and the US Army Military History Institute, Carlisle, Pennsylvania.*

In short, Gettysburg was a place of substance, so its anxious citizens had all the more reason to believe that they would host the military juggernaut at one time or another. To what end, they could only speculate.

And they did speculate.

CHARLES M. McCURDY[1] was the 10 year old son of Gettysburg Railroad president, Robert McCurdy. They lived on the town's west side, at 26 Chambersburg Street:

"From the beginning of the war we had been expecting Rebel raids. We lived only a short day's drive from the Potomac, which seemed to be the dividing line between north and south. Although Maryland had not seceded, many of her men were in the southern army and sentiment for the south was strong. We knew that there were certain brilliant Confederate cavalry officers who loved to do spectacular things, who wore plumes

Cavalry scouts of both armies roamed the countryside looking for fresh horses. Quartermaster scouts scoured the region for livestock. This photo was taken of cavalrymen who stopped at a house near Gettysburg. Whenever civilians heard of an approaching army they often tried to hide their animals for fear they would be taken. Twelve year old MARY ELIZABETH MONTFORT, of Gettysburg, described in her diary the lengths to which a neighbor went to keep his milk cow from falling into the hands of the Confederate invaders: "Lem Snyder brought a pail of fresh milk to the house. Lem explained to Mother when he heard the Rebels coming into town he took Bessie and tied her in the parlor. She's been there ever since." *Courtesy Massachusetts Commandery of the Military Order of the Loyal Legion of the United States and the US Army Military History Institute, Carlisle, Pennsylvania.*

The Globe Inn was built in the 1790s by town founder James Gettys and was the first brick structure in the area. Adams County farmer Charles Wills purchased it in 1860. Wills and 25 year old son John operated it. *Courtesy Adams County Historical Society.*

in their hats and affected a dress that revealed a love of romantic exploits. A raid into rich and opulent Pennsylvania, which the war had only enriched, would not only add to their renown for daring deeds but would yield a more substantial reward in horses and supplies badly needed by the enemy. Amateur scouts patrolling the roads that led to the river would now and then produce hostile troopers from very unlikely sources. Then would come the wild dash for the valley and the cry 'The Rebels are coming.'"

And then an exodus would begin. Hotel keeper, JOHN C. WILLS often saw Maryland and Pennsylvania farmers "stampede" through Gettysburg:

"While standing in front of the Globe Hotel,[2] it was a sight, at night in the moonlight, to see them going through the town with horses, with teams, a number of the wagons being loaded with goods, a number of them going southward. A majority of them going eastward to York County and into Lancaster County, to places of safety."

Twenty-one year old SALLIE MYERS completed her first term as Second Assistant to the Principal of the Gettysburg school on May 31st, 1863. As a teacher and life-long resident, she was well "tuned" to the village:

"The sentiment in Gettysburg was strongly Union, but at the same time we had in the community a good many Democrats, or 'Copperheads' as we called them, who naturally affiliated with the South. They were not very open in upholding the Southern cause, but just seemed to think the South was right, and we often squabbled on that subject.

"It was early in June that we had the first reports that the rebels were coming. Naturally, the people of the town became terribly excited and business was at a standstill. Bankers sent their money away. Merchants sent their goods to Philadelphia and other places for safety. Day after day the people did little but stand along the streets in groups and talk. Whenever someone heard a new report all flocked to him. The suspense was dreadful. Of course, there was no social life in the town at the time, though the young folks would meet and sing patriotic songs."[3]

"We had a vague idea that the Rebels were a dreadful set of men, and we didn't know what horrid things they might do. So we mostly kept in our houses out of their way."[4]

SARAH M. BROADHEAD[5] started a diary on Monday, June 15, 1863, because she was "bored, filled with anxieties and apprehension." Fortunately for us, she kept writing until July 14th, bracketing the firestorm at Gettysburg.

Salome "Sallie" Myers, 21, was a Gettysburg school teacher. On May 31, 1863 she finished her first term as assistant principal. Her father was a justice of the peace who had served in the 87th Pennsylvania Volunteers until discharged for disability. Sallie had four younger sisters and an older brother, Jefferson. The family attended the local Methodist Church and lived on West High street. *Courtesy Adams County Historical Society.*

Joseph Broadhead, 32, was English by birth. He had come to the US with his parents as a child. A one-time express agent Broadhead was now an engineer with the Railroad on the Gettysburg to Hanover route. He was also active in the local militia. *Courtesy Adams County Historical Society.*

Jefferson Myers, 23, was Sallie Myers' older brother. Jeff had been a member of the 1st Pennsylvania Reserves, but was discharged for disability. He had just married Annie Culp in May and was working as a printer. Both Jeff and his father are believed to have left town during the battle. *Courtesy Adams County Historical Society.*

Sarah Broadhead, 30, lived with her husband Joseph and daughter Mary in the last block of Chambersburg Street before it divided into Chambersburg Pike and the Hagerstown Road. From her two-story brick home she could see the sweeping view of Seminary Ridge. Her brother, Paul, was serving in the army. She would see him in a few days. Diagonally across the street, a few houses to the west, lived John Burns – a cantankerous cobbler and one-time constable. *Courtesy Clair P. Lyons.*

Mrs. Broadhead's British-born husband, Joseph, was an employee of the railroad which operated between Gettysburg and Hanover, and a Lieutenant in the Gettysburg Zouaves, a local militia. The Broadheads and their 4 year old daughter, Mary, lived at 217 Chambersburg Street, within a mile of the Lutheran Seminary.

Thirty years old at the time of the battle, frail in appearance, Sarah Broadhead was a person of strong character who, like many other townswomen, swallowed her fears and stepped in where she felt needed. We will follow these women carefully and with appreciation throughout this book.

"June 15, 1863: To-day we heard that the Rebels were crossing the river in heavy force, and advancing on this State. No alarm was felt until Governor Curtin sent a telegram, directing the people to move their stores as quickly as possible. This made us begin to realize the fact that we were in some danger from the enemy, and some persons, thinking the Rebels were near, became very much frightened, though the report was a mistake."

TILLIE PIERCE,[6] the 15 year old daughter of butcher James Pierce, lived at 301 South Baltimore Street, along one of the main roads from the Maryland border:

"Upon the first rumor of the rebel invasion, Major Robert Bell, a citizen of the place, recruited a company of cavalry from the town and surrounding country. A company of infantry was also formed from the students and citizens of the place which was mustered into Colonel Wm. Jennings' regiment of Pennsylvania Emergency Troops."[7]

According to Tillie, many of the town's older men formed a 'home guard' of their own.

"They were armed to the teeth with old, rusty guns and swords, pitchforks, shovels and pick-axes. Their falling into line, the maneuvers, the commands given and not heeded, would have done a veteran's heart good."

But in reality, nothing could have made the townspeople feel more secure. The region's population was aware of the Southern army's invasion, but had no way to predict where it would go, or what it would do. Anything unusual made them "jump":

SARAH BROADHEAD:

"June 16: Our town had a great fright last night between 12 and 1 o'clock. I had retired, and was soundly asleep, when my child cried for a drink of water. When I got up to get it, I heard so great a noise in the street that I went to the window, and the first thing I saw was a large fire, seemingly not far off, and the people were hallooing, "The Rebels are coming and burning as they go." Many left town, but, having waited for the fire to go down a little, I returned to bed and slept till morning. Then I learned that the fire was in Emmettsburg, ten miles from here just over the Maryland line, and that the buildings were fired by one of her townsmen. Twenty-seven houses were burned, and thirty-six

William Culp enlisted in the 87th Pennsylvania with "Jack" and Charles Skelly, Billy Ziegler, and Billy Holtzworth. William is the older brother of Annie, Julia and Wes Culp. Wes went south with his employer before the war. Now, Wes is in the Army of the Confederacy. The Culp brothers' regiments had just faced each other at Winchester, Virginia.

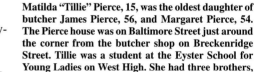

Matilda "Tillie" Pierce, 15, was the oldest daughter of butcher James Pierce, 56, and Margaret Pierce, 54. The Pierce house was on Baltimore Street just around the corner from the butcher shop on Breckenridge Street. Tillie was a student at the Eyster School for Young Ladies on West High. She had three brothers, James 27, William 22, and Franklin 14. *Courtesy Adams County Historical Society.*

families made homeless, all effort to stop the flames being useless, as, owing to everything being so dry, they spread with great rapidity."

SALLIE MYERS' diary:

"Wednesday, June 17. I am getting very tired of all this fuss consequent upon border life though the numerous reports do not alarm me. On the contrary I am sometimes quite amused by seeing the extremes to which people will go. I pity the poor darkies. They seem perfectly bewildered.

"Thursday, June 18. The rebels are coming. That again is the latest."

SARAH BROADHEAD:

"June 19: Another excitement to-day. The 87th Pennsylvania Volunteers is composed of men from this and adjacent counties, one company from our town being of the number. Word came that the captain, both lieutenants, and nearly all the officers and men had been killed or captured.[8] Such a time as we had with those having friends in the regiment! At 10 o'clock, it was rumored that some of the men were coming in on the Chambersburg pike, and not long after about one dozen of those who lived in town came in, and their report and presence relieved some and agonized others. Those whose friends were not of the party, were in a heart-rending plight, for these returned ones could not tell of the others; some would say, This one was killed or taken prisoner, and others, We saw him at such a place, and the Rebels may have taken him; and so they were kept in suspense.

William T. "Billy" Ziegler was among those taken prisoner at Winchester, Virginia, when his good friend "Jack" Skelly was wounded. Charles Skelly and Billy Holtzworth were also captured. It is said that Wes Culp visited the wounded Skelly in the Confederate hospital, and also got a chance to see his other captured boyhood friends. Jack Skelly had gone south with Wes before the war, but returned home when the fighting started. Legend has it that Skelly, knowing his wounds were very serious, gave Wes a message for his mother, should his friend's unit wind up anywhere near Gettysburg.

Samuel H. Buehler's Book and Drug Store, in the first square of Chambersburg Street, had been a fixture in the community almost as long as Pennsylvania College. His store was a popular gathering place for the college students. In recent years, Samuel had been grooming his son Alexander to take over the business, so he was working less and his son was working more. On this day everyone who comes into Buehler's Store talks about the fact that Lee's Army is in Maryland and headed this way. *Courtesy Adams County Historical Society.*

Pennsylvania College students found it difficult to concentrate on their studies. Discussing the rumors and distant mountain campfires that flickered like stars in the night sky, some of them joked about their options: flee town or form up. They formed up. Twenty-one Pennsylvania College students were joined by sixty-two others in an "emergency militia." *Courtesy Special Collections, Gettysburg College.*

College President Dr. Henry L. Baugher, who had lost a son at Shiloh the year before, counseled discretion and advised what he called the "embryonic heroes" to immediately return to their college duties. His words fell on deaf ears. These were desperate recruits who wanted so much to be like other local groups that had formed in defense of their homes and farms. *Courtesy Special Collections, Gettysburg College.*

Professor Frederick A. Muhlenberg, who had been offered command of the "college militia" declined on grounds that school duties made it impossible. When the group assembled on the town square Professor Muhlenberg spoke to them on the importance of a faithful discharge of duties, and inspired them to do honor to the state, the college, and themselves. *Courtesy Special Collections, Gettysburg College.*

"June 20: The report of to-day is that the Rebels are at Chambersburg and are advancing on here, and refugees begin to come in by scores. Some say the Rebels number from twenty to thirty thousand, others that Lee's whole army is advancing this way. All day we have been much excited."

SALLIE MYERS:

"June 20. Some Cavalry from Philadelphia who armed & equipped themselves came tonight. They are entirely and altogether volunteers.[9]

"June 21. For the first time for more than 2 years I have been alarmed and excited. The Rebels have taken possession of Millerstown, about 8 miles from here, or rather Fairfield, which is its proper name.

"Evening. Had no preaching. Rev. Eisenberg has "skeedaddled." The town is pretty clear of darkies. They have nearly all left. I pity the poor creatures. Darkies of both sexes are skeedaddling and some white folks of the male sex."[10]

SARAH BROADHEAD:

"June 22: The report now is that a large force is in the mountains about eighteen miles away, and a call is made for a party of men to go out and cut down trees to obstruct the passages of the mountains. About fifty, among them my husband, started. I was very uneasy lest they might be captured, but they had not gone half way, when the discovery was made that it was too late; that the Rebels were on this side of the mountain, and coming this way. Our men turned back, uninjured, though their advance, composed of a few men, was fired upon. About seventy of the Rebels came within eight miles, and then returned by another road to their main force. They stole all the horses and cattle they could find, and drove them back to their encampment. We did not know but that the whole body would be down upon us, until 11 o'clock, when a man came in and said that he had seen them, and that they had recrossed. I shall now retire, and sleep much better than I had expected an hour since.

"June 23: This has been the most quiet day since the excitement began. I expect news to-morrow, for it has been too quiet to last long.

"June 24: As I expected, the Rebels have, several times, been within two or three miles, but they have not yet reached here.[11] Two cavalry companies are here on scouting duty,[12] but they can be of little use, as they have never seen service. Deserters come in every little while, who report the enemy near in large force. This morning early a dispatch was received, saying that a regiment of infantry was coming from Harrisburg. We do not feel much safer, for they are only raw militia.[13] The train bringing them came within ten miles, when it ran over a cow, which threw the cars off the track. No one was hurt, and they are now encamped near the place of the accident. The town is a little quieter than on yesterday. We are getting used to excitement, and many think the enemy, having been so long in the vicinity without visiting us, will not favor us with their presence. They have carried off many horses. Some, who had taken their stock away, returned, supposing the Rebels had left the neighborhood, and lost their teams."

Not surprisingly, TILLIE PIERCE wrote that the town's black population were certain the Confederate troops had "an especial hatred toward them, and believed that if they fell into their hands, annihilation was sure." With each new rumor, they ran: "These folks mostly lived in the southwestern part of the town, and their flight was invariably down Breckenridge Street and Baltimore Street, and toward the woods on and around Culp's Hill...men and women with bundles as large as old-fashioned feather ticks

Confederate General Jubal Early had excellent intelligence. When the small "emergency militia" that included the Pennsylvania College students persuaded Col. W.W. Jennings to allow them to join his Regimental Organization of 743 men, Early sent White's battalion of cavalry, General Gordon's Brigade, to "amuse and skirmish with them." Early's force of six to seven thousand men made plans to come up from the rear, flank Jennings' main contingent, and capture the whole force. *Courtesy Massachusetts Commandery of the Military Order of the Loyal Legion of the United States and the US Army Military History Institute, Carlisle, Pennsylvania.*

John Hopkins, was not the Vice President of Pennsylvania College in 1862, but the title was bestowed upon him in the College album as a token of the affection students and faculty felt for "Jack," the longtime caretaker of the school. Of Gettysburg's 2,500 population, less than 200 were black. Most left town when they heard the Rebel Army was headed their way. Not much is known of those who dared to stay behind. A black woman named "Liz" didn't get out of town quickly enough. When Early's Cavalry rode into town she climbed to the cupola of Christ Lutheran Church where she hid for several days ... until it was safe to come down. Another free black, Owen Robinson, who lived – as did most of the black population – in the southwest part of town, left in such a hurry that he was afraid if he took his hogs they would slow him down, so he asked the McCurdy's to look after them. Hogs and chickens were among the first things confiscated by the invaders. *Courtesy Special Collections, Gettysburg College.*

J. Howard Wert, Class of 1861 Pennsylvania College, was a school teacher and sometimes civilian scout for the Union Army during the invasion. His father Adam, a veteran of the War of 1812, had a large farm just off Baltimore Pike. This photo, taken toward the end of the war, shows Wert in his lieutenant's uniform when he served with the 209th Pennsylvania Volunteers. *The J. Howard Wert Gettysburg Collection.*

across their backs, almost bearing them to the ground. Children also, carrying their bundles, and striving in vain to keep up with their seniors. The greatest consternation was depicted on all their countenances as they hurried along; crowding and running against each other in their confusion; children stumbling, falling, and crying."

But 'black flight' was not just a local phenomenon. Living at a major crossroads, residents of Gettysburg saw a great wave of black people wash north before the Confederate tide.

SAMUEL BUSHMAN was a clerk at the Farmer's and Merchant's Savings Institution, which faced the Diamond, Gettysburg's main square:

"Some would have a spring wagon and a horse, but usually they were on foot, burdened with bundles containing a couple of quilts, some clothing and a few cooking utensils. In several instances, I saw 'em trundling along their little belongings in a two wheeled handcart. Occasionally, there'd be one who was driving a single sheep or hog or a cow and a calf. They were a God-forsaken looking people. The farmers along the roads sheltered them nights."

SARAH BROADHEAD:

"June 25: To-day passed much as yesterday did. Every one is asking, Where is our army, that they let the enemy scour the country and do as they please? It is reported that Lee's whole army is this side of the river[14] and marching on Harrisburg; also that a large force is coming on here, to destroy the railroad between there and Baltimore. Our militia did not come to town, but remain encamped where they were yesterday."

Friday, June 26th

"During the week of June 26th, the railroad and telegraph had been destroyed and Gettysburg was cut off from the world and, figuratively, out of the Union. But not for long." – Professor J. HOWARD WERT

Numerous townspeople packed up and left Gettysburg in these uncertain days, but like many others, nineteen year old NELLIE AUGHINBAUGH's[15] mother was not among them, saying "if we all have to be killed, we would prefer to die at home." Nellie was learning the milliner's trade with eight or ten other young women at the Middle Street

This view is of Carlisle Street, looking north, from the town square. Robert McCurdy's new warehouse was just across the railroad tracks on the west side of Carlisle. A few houses further north, also on the east side, was the home of the Aughinbaugh family. *Courtesy Massachusetts Commandery of the Military Order of the Loyal Legion of the United States and the US Army Military History Institute, Carlisle, Pennsylvania.*

home of Mrs. Mary Martin, and on the morning of June 26th, they were trying to carry on as usual:

"Mr. Martin[16] rushed excitedly into the work room, exclaiming that the Rebels were coming and he needed all the lead spoons. Why? Well, with the Rebs coming, he said he was going to melt them down into bullets. 'They're at Cashtown now. Send the girls home." he told his wife. Several of the girls stopped immediately and left. I was working on a bonnet that Mrs. Martin, who was very particular, had made me rip twice that day and start over again, and I said, 'I'm not going home until I finish this bonnet, not if the whole Rebel army comes to town.'"

Nellie should have listened to Mr. Martin; she had no idea how prophetic her words would become.

Advancing the southern army, General Jubal Early's division of Ewell's II Corps was on its way to York Pennsylvania, to seize the bridge spanning the Susquehanna River. Early and other commanders had set a pattern, moving into a town, harassing the people, demanding tribute or ransom, collecting supplies for themselves and for the men who followed them. So, on Friday, June 26th, Jubal Early's troops swept into Gettysburg to "tree the town."

In the end, they would only meet frustration; merchants and bankers alike had shipped their goods to safety in response to Governor Andrew G. Curtin's warnings of the oncoming invasion. Nevertheless, June 26th brought the war to Gettysburg once and for all, presaging terrible events still to come.

Twenty-seven year old SARAH BARRETT KING lived on Gettysburg's east side, at the southwest corner of York and Liberty Streets. Her husband, 33 year old William, was at home with her and their five children when the Rebels made their first appearance at about 2 p.m.:

"After days of expectancy, Bell's Cavalry scouts brought in the word to Gettysburg that the Rebels were just a few miles west of town and a hasty departure was the advice of their Captain Bell...with the warning that every man should take care of himself and report in Harrisburg or Columbia.

"My husband, a sergeant in that company, was resting on a couch, having been thrown from a horse a few days before. I called to him, 'The Rebels are here...get up and get your horse ready, for you will only have a few minutes in which to escape.' In a short time, he and others of the company were going down the York pike hurriedly, as there was urgent business in that direction. They barely escaped."

Across Chambersburg Street from the Broadhead residence, photographer CHARLES TYSON and his new bride, MARIA, were absorbed in domestic chores, not suspecting they would soon have visitors:

William T. King, 33, was a Master Tailor by trade and, like many other male residents of Gettysburg, stood ready to defend homes and families. The 1860 Adams County Census reports that King and his wife Sarah, 27, had four children and were "not affiliated with a religious denomination or political party." *Courtesy Adams County Historical Society.*

When Robert Bell and Abigail King were married in 1853, and he settled into a job as a bank cashier in Gettysburg, Bell never suspected that by age 33 he would be leading the Adams County cavalry, a.k.a. Company B, 21st Pennsylvania Cavalry. *Courtesy Adams County Historical Society.*

The three bullet holes in King's sign were made by Rebels on horseback in hot pursuit of King and other local militia men. Another group of Rebel horsemen shot and killed 20 year old George Washington Sandoe as he rode south along Baltimore Street. Sandoe was the first Union soldier to die at Gettysburg. *Courtesy Adams County Historical Society.*

Charles Tyson and his brother Isaac operated a photography studio on York Street across from the Globe Inn. The Tyson Brothers Studio was one of three photography studios in Gettysburg. *Courtesy Adams County Historical Society.*

James McAllister, 77, owner of McAllister's Mill, south of town on the Rock Creek, was at his home on Baltimore Pike and saw George Sandoe shot from his horse. He rushed toward the Rebel Cavalrymen giving them hell for shooting Sandoe in the back when he had not been returning their fire. McAllister, his neighbor Adam Wert and several other influential townsfolk, were ardent abolitionists. McAllister's Mill had been a stop on the famous Underground Railroad for years, and only days before the battle members had helped a black family fleeing slavery move further north out of harms way. *Courtesy The J. Howard Wert Gettysburg Collection.*

The Female Institute, founded by the Rev. David Eyster, and sometimes called the "Ladies Seminary," has been run by Eyster's wife Rebecca since his recent death. It is located on the southwest corner of West High Street at South Washington. Previously, this building served as the original home of the Lutheran Theological Seminary (1826) and Pennsylvania College (1832). Today there is still an artillery shell lodged next to one of its second floor windows. *Courtesy The J. Howard Wert Gettysburg Collection.*

"My wife and I were putting down the last carpet in the front second-story room in our little house...when we heard an unusual noise, and upon looking out the turnpike toward Cashtown, we saw the advance of Ewell's Corps, consisting of numerous mounted men,[17] some with hats, some without; some in blue and some in gray.

"On, on they came, and as they dashed past the house and up into the town they rent the air with yells , at the same time discharging their carbines and pistols into the air."

NELLIE AUGHINBAUGH:
"I still intended to complete the bonnet. Once more, Mr. Martin came running in and, hurrying over to me, he grabbed my work from my hands and exclaimed: 'Go home, girl! The Rebs are at the edge of town.'

"I did. As I reached the center square, the Rebels were riding into it from the other direction with yells and cheers. I was frightened and ran all the way home. I had to cross the square and go down Carlisle Street. When I reached the house, Mother was standing in the doorway, ringing her hands.

"My God, Child, where have you been?

"Never in my life had I ever heard my mother use the Lord's name in that way and I always told her that she frightened me more than the coming of the Rebels because I thought she had suddenly lost her mind."

TILLIE PIERCE was attending 'literary exercises' at the Ladies Seminary on the southwest corner of West High and Washington Street as the rebel 'avalanche' descended:
"What a horrible sight! There they were, human beings! clad almost in rags, covered with dust, riding wildly, pell-mell down the hill toward our home! shouting, yelling most unearthly, cursing, brandishing their revolvers, and firing right and left."

Eighteen year old ANNA GARLACH lived at 323 S. Baltimore Street, the southern route out of town:
"A number of people were trying to save their horses and had taken them down the Baltimore pike. Word came that the Rebels were coming and down the road more riders went, going as fast as their horses could go! There was a mail carrier trying to save his mail. He dropped a pouch in front of our house...

"The Rebels later discovered the direction the men had gone with the horses and gave chase down Baltimore street."

In their wild run down Baltimore Street, the Confederate riders spotted one of Bell's Cavalrymen, Private George Sandoe. They caught up to him near his home south of the Cemetery, and when Sandoe resisted, killed him on the spot.

Sandoe was left where his pursuers found him, marked with the sad distinction of being the first soldier to die at Gettysburg.

SARAH BARRETT KING watched with her heart in her mouth as a unit of the Confederates chased her husband and other fleeing militiamen out of town to the east:

"My father was sitting by a window, busily engaged reading a daily paper, little dreaming the Rebels were so close by. I said to him, 'Here they come.' He asked, 'Who?' I answered, 'the Rebs, don't you hear the yell,' and he looked out and saw them in pursuit of Captain Bell. He said, 'Bring the children in and close the door.'

"I said, 'No, I want them to see all they can of this,' and remained on the porch of the house standing on the southwest corner of York and Liberty streets. My father went upstairs and got behind a high French post bedstead where he looked out a window in the direction of the race going on.

"I stayed on the porch and watched the party, listening to the yells and seeing them ride at their greatest speed after Captain Bell, whom they seemed very anxious to capture. Captain Bell was perfectly at home on his horse and was not uneasy, keeping at a very tantalizing distance, seemingly."

From her farmhouse three miles north, MRS. HARRIET BAYLY was listening closely to the sounds of the raid because her husband, JOSEPH, and 13 year old son, BILLY, had just fled east with their valuable horses.

"I heard firing apparently about half a mile from the house, which frightened me at the time, as I feared that my husband and his party had been overtaken."

It could have happened. At that moment, young WILLIAM HAMILTON BAYLY, "Billy", was riding across open fields toward Hanover:

"On crossing one of the roads radiating from Gettysburg, I noticed a horseman coming over the hill toward us and, being anxious for information about the enemy, I hung back and let my party go on, having every confidence in the fleetness of my mount. The horseman, covered with a rubber poncho splashed with mud, rode up to where my horse was standing, and I recognized him as a recruit in Bell's cavalry whom I knew. So I said, 'Hello, Bill! What's up?'

"Bill replied, 'If you don't get out of here pretty quick, you'll find out what's up. The Rebel Cavalry chased me out of town about 15 minutes ago, and must now be close on my heels.'

"My desire for information not being satisfied, however, I said, 'But where is the rest of your company?'

Anna Garlach, shown here holding her brother William, lived with her mother Catherine, father Henry, and three other children on South Baltimore Street. Mr. Garlach, 42, was a cabinet maker. *Courtesy Pat and Jamie Newton.*

William Hamilton Bayly, 13, was the oldest of the six children of Joseph, 54, and Harriet, 40, Bayly. The family's large farm, more than 300 acres, was some three miles north of Gettysburg. Joseph's mother Margaret, 60, and her sister Mary, 55, also had a house on the farm. According to the 1860 Adams County Census Corinna Black, 40, and her two daughters Sarah Jane Black, 22, a teacher and Elizabeth Black, 19, lived there, too. *Courtesy Special Collections, Gettysburg College.*

James Fahnestock, 37, along with his two brothers, ran Fahnestock's General Merchandise Store, located a block south of the square on Baltimore Street. Henry, 35, lived a block from the store on the southeast corner of West Middle and South Washington. James lived with his wife Sarah and five children – Charles 12, Gates 9, Anna 7, Samuel 5, and James, Jr. 3 – diagonally across from the store on the northeast corner of Baltimore at Middle Street. The youngest brother, 33 year old Edward, was a Lieutenant Colonel in the 165th Pennsylvania Infantry. *Courtesy Adams County Historical Society.*

Henry Eyster Jacobs was the 18-year old son of Pennsylvania College Professor Michael Jacobs. Henry had graduated Pennsylvania College in 1862 and was now a student at Lutheran Theological Seminary. The Jacobs' lived in a two-story brick home on the northwest corner of West Middle and Washington Streets. *Courtesy Special Collections, Gettysburg College.*

"'Oh, hell,' said the trooper, 'I don't know; they ran long before I did. But you git or you'll be got.'"

In the minor skirmish that followed, some five miles northeast of Gettysburg that morning, Colonel W. W. Jennings lost about forty of his pickets to General John B. Gordon's Confederate brigade. Soon after, near Bayly's Hill, White's Cavalry routed a confused regiment, captured every member of the so-called "Emergency Militia" formed by Pennsylvania College students. In disarray, the rest of Jenning's regiment took to the fields and woods to evade capture while pushing on to Harrisburg.

SUE KING BLACK lived on Bayly's Hill, and was close enough to see faces and name names of the fleeing students who were seeking refuge wherever they could find it:

"One of the boys hid under a bed where a Reb found him and asked if his mother knew he was out."

Many of the remaining militia escaped to Harrisburg or Columbia as ordered by Captain Bell; those who didn't...approximately 175...were marched back to town. But it didn't matter much to the Rebels; as Early's foot soldiers trooped in behind the cavalry, it became clear that their real interest was Gettysburg itself.

SARAH BROADHEAD, Chambersburg Street:

"They came in on three roads, and we soon were surrounded by them. We all stood in the doors whilst the cavalry passed, but when the infantry came we closed them, for fear they would run into our houses and carry off everything we had, and went up stairs and looked out of the windows. They went along very orderly, only asking every now and then how many Yankee soldiers we had in town. I answered one that I did not know. He replied 'You are a funny woman; if I lived in town I would know that much.'"

ANNA GARLACH's grandmother was teased a little, too:

"Some of them asked her what she thought the Rebels were like, whether they had horns. And she replied she was frightened at first, but found them like our own men."

Soon to be ten years old, GATES FAHNESTOCK was swept up by the excitement. He and his brothers and sister[18] ran to an upstairs window of their Middle Street home to watch:

"The boys looking through the slatted shutters on the second story saw and enjoyed it as much as a wild west show."

Most public officials left town, fearing arrest. The Western Maryland Railroad's telegrapher, Hugh D. Scott, fled also, because there were advance rumors that the Rebels

Dr. Charles Horner (Left) and his brother Dr. Robert Horner (Right), shown here in their later years, both remained in Gettysburg at the time of the battle. Charles married George Arnold's daughter, Kate. Dr. Robert Horner's wife, Mary, is believed to be the woman on whom the narrative of Jennie Croll is based. *Courtesy Adams County Historical Society.*

would 'draft' all telegraph operators. Before he signed off, Mr. Scott alerted fellow operators, George Grove and Daniel Trone in Hanover:[19]

"I will leave this place at once. This is my last message. A minute later, I will have my instrument under my arm ready to drive down the turnpike to York, for I do not want to be captured."

SARAH BROADHEAD:

"The Rebel band were playing Southern tunes in the Diamond. I cannot tell how bad I felt to hear them, and to see the traitor's flag floating overhead. My humiliation was complete when I saw our men[20] marching behind them surrounded by a guard. Last of all came an officer, and behind him a negro on as fine a horse as I ever saw. One, looking up and noticing my admiration of the animal, said: 'We captured this horse from General Milroy,[21] and do you see the wagons up there? We captured them, too. How we did whip the Yankees, and we intend to do it again soon.' I hope they may not."

SALLIE MYERS, W. High Street:

"We were not afraid, but it is exasperating that we are now under control of armed traitors."

HENRY EYSTER JACOBS:

"We sought an officer as soon as they took possession of the streets and inquired concerning the fate of the emergency regiment, and were taken to the students they had captured. Admitted within the guard, we were permitted to converse with our friends on the steps of Christ Lutheran Church."

JENNIE S. CROLL:

"They told us ladies that we might feed them. We thanked them for the privilege."

The Demands

"They gathered in the center of the town in the open square and called for town officials." – ALBERTUS McCREARY[22]

Lieutenant General Jubal A. Early, C.S.A., reportedly threatened to burn Gettysburg if it failed to provide money and supplies for his army.

According to 25 year old JOHN WILLS, Early sent the borough council a note 'previous to his coming' that he would want to see them and 'make a requisition.'

WILLS says Early rode to the town square, "The Diamond" at 4 p.m., inquiring for "the Mayor of your town":

"Word was at once sent to his (the Burgess') residence, north west corner of the Diamond. Mrs. Martin answered the call, saying that the Burgess, Robert Martin, and the Councilmen had left town. We reported this to General Early. He then inquired for – using his own words – 'the Commissioners of your town.' Knowing that Mr. Kendlehart was at home, we directed him to the residence of Mr. David Kendlehart, President of the town council."[23]

Will says Kendlehart promptly came to meet Early, standing directly in front of Early's horse while he listened to the Confederate General's 'requisition.'

Kendlehart's daughter, MARGARETTA, recorded that in addition to money, Early specifically demanded 60 barrels of flour, 7,000 pounds of bacon, 1,200 pounds of sugar, 600 pounds of coffee, 1,000 pounds of salt, 40 bushels of onions, 1,000 pairs of shoes, and 500 hats.

She wrote that her father told Early it would be impossible to comply.[24] He also gave the general a formal reply in writing:

Robert Martin, the Burgess of Gettysburg, and his father Ephiram ran a tailor's shop off the square. His mother taught millinary classes at their Middle Street home. His younger sister Martha was the fiance of John Wills whose father owned the Globe Inn. Martin, and several other council members, left town prior to the arrival of General Early. *Courtesy Adams County Historical Society.*

David Kendlehart, 50, had a prosperous boot and shoe business on the east side of Baltimore Street, a block off the square. When William McClellan resigned from the town council because of illness, Kendlehart took his place and was elected President, replacing Henry Rupp. Although Kendlehart was a Democrat, he is said to have had strong anti-slavery views. He was sent for, since the Burgess was out of town, to receive General Early's demands, which he rejected. Later that night Kendlehart slipped out of his Middle Street home and made his way to McAllister's Mill. He maintained a low profile during the battle. Sixty-nine year old John Burns, who lost his job as constable in the last election, was a cobbler for Kendlehart. *Courtesy Adams County Historical Society.*

General Early.

Sir.

The authorities of the Borough of Gettysburg in answer to the demands made by you upon the said Borough and County, say their authority extends but to the Borough. That the requisitions asked for cannot be given, because it is utterly impossible to so comply. The quantities required are far beyond that in our possession.

In compliance, however, to the demands, we will request the stores to be opened, and the citizens to furnish whatever they can of such provisions &c, as may be asked – further we cannot promise.

By authority of the Council of the Borough of Gettysburg, I hereunto as President of said Board, attach my name.

D. Kendlehart.

Later that night, a Confederate officer came looking for Kendlehart at his home, but by then, he too, had left town.

Bank Clerk SAMUEL BUSHMAN[25] could vouch personally for the absence of cash...and did:

"We had scares all along from the fall of 1862 until late in 1864, and we carried off the funds eighteen or twenty times. On several occasions I went alone, and there was once I took as much as one hundred and twenty-five thousand dollars. I'd drive with a horse and buggy by the old pike twenty-eight miles to York and then ship the fund by railroad to Philadelphia.

"We'd heard that Stonewall Jackson had threatened to lay waste the country when he got into Pennsylvania and not leave one brick on top of another.

"Just before the raid[26]...I went off with the bank funds, and when I returned, I found the Rebels in possession of the town. They took me to the bank and made me show 'em that we hadn't any money there, and one of 'em threatened to send me and the treasurer to Richmond. They had demanded that Gettysburg should give 'em twenty-five thousand dollars in money, ten thousand barrels of flour and a lot of other things, but they didn't get the money or much else in the town. The stores would have yielded them a lot of plunder if the proprietors hadn't guarded against that possibility by carrying just as small a stock as they could. However, the raiders went out into the country around and stole every farm animal that walked, and secured a great deal of corn, oats, hay, meat, etc. Their teams were going all the time, taking the stuff south into the Confederate lines."

SUE KING BLACK saw them first hand:

"The first we saw of them were half a dozen officers, all of them on fine sorrel horses. They rode up to the yard fence and asked for something to eat. Mother and I took them some bread, butter and a pitcher of water.

"One of them said, 'Why, Madam, you are scared; when we came over here they expected to see us with horns.' And he told me: 'The ladies here have two sides to their aprons and turn out the side of whichever party was there.' That wasn't true. I had a Union apron, but lent it to Mary Miller at Boyers, but the Rebs got it when they ransacked the Boyer house, but there weren't two sides to it. As the Boyers left their house, the Rebs took possession of it and did all kinds of mean tricks. They carried window shades, pictures, etc. up to the woods. They used the dough tray to feed their horses and a drawer of the sideboard to mix dough.

"They opened a jar of black cherries, poured it down the stair steps, then cut a chaff bed open and spread it over them. Then they wrote on the wall: 'Done in retaliation for what was done in the south.'"

"There was a hill back of us from our barn to the school house. They rode to our barn, carried hay and all kinds of feed to their camp. Three of them brought a three bushel bag of flour from Boyers to get mother to bake; she baked them short cake. The men waited on the porch for them.

"While there, a tall fellow with a little piece of red flannel pinned on his coat and a darkey at his heels, came blustering into the yard, said he was going to search the house. The man on the porch said, 'You better go slow or I will report you.' The house wasn't searched.

"The man waiting gave Mother a 50 cent silver piece for baking and gave me a big bunch of silk skeins, all colors. He offered me more, but I wouldn't take it. I counted a hundred who came into the yard, got tired counting, and quit."

Other squads worked their way through the town. Some black residents who did not flee the Rebels were rounded up and marched off, although a few managed to escape. A number of black townspeople were hidden by white friends until the crisis passed.

Houses were searched...whether the owners cooperated or not. CHARLES TYSON chose to cooperate:

"We had taken the precaution to lock the front door and yard gate, and were looking out through the venetian shutters - seeing but unseen. We heard them trying the door, and heard one fellow spell out from the door-plate 'T-Y-S-O-N; wonder who the devil he is,' and at the same time began chopping on the step or door, and I said to my wife: 'There's no use trying to keep them out if they want to get in; I will go down and open the gate.'

"I did so, and said to them: 'You look warm and dry; we have a well of good cool water in here; come in and refresh yourselves.' They came right along without a second invitation, and then they wanted bread and butter, but we told them we did not have enough to commence on and they were satisfied far more easily than I expected; were very polite and gentlemanly. One, a German, asked where Joe Hooker was;[27] said they were after him, and would have him if they had to go to Philadelphia for him."

But not all of them behaved themselves. SARAH BARRETT KING:

"It was said that a man who once worked at blacksmithing in Gettysburg was one of those who piloted them and it was reported that this same man went to the home of Adam Doersom, Sr., and made a demand for money and even tortured the man who had befriended him, for this same fellow had worked for Mr. Doersom years before that time and lived in his family, worthy people who were kind to all.

"Soon, a thorough canvass had been made of the town and Early's Division of Ewell's Corps were going into camp in the northeastern portion of the town a short distance away from my home with their plunder. Some of the men had a pile of hats on their heads looking comical, strings of muslin and other goods trailing on the ground, the blankets, quilts and shawls were piled up on their horses, shoes tied to the stirrups, altogether forming a laughable picture. For once they were having a good time and the miserable appearance of the many certainly indicated that it would be appreciated.

"Some of the less fortunate had brimless or crownless hats, shoes not worthy of the name, and one poor fellow had only one leg covered because his pantaloons were of the one legged style. That was the fashion with some.

"I was on the porch when Early's Division passed by. To be candid, they had my sympathy. I was reminded of Falstaff's recruits – ragged and with a look of hunger in their eyes – telling plainly of suffering and privations endured beyond description. As they marched by, some of them would talk to the children. One of them said to my son, 'Bub, would you like to shoot a Rebel?'"

By that time, ten year old CHARLES McCURDY was circulating freely among the troops on Chambersburg Street:

"Across the street from our house a little man named Phillip Winter kept a cake and candy shop. He was only about 5 feet high, so very quiet and unobtrusive, minding only his own small affairs, that the children, who were his chief patrons, called him Petey Winters. Only the very forward ventured to address him in this familiar way for he had a quiet dignity that resented the use of this diminutive.

"His specialties were molasses taffy, sticks of which homely confection stuck on bits of brown paper, he sold for a penny – and large round formidable looking ginger cakes of great substance and lasting quality, which could be had for the same modest sum.

"When it definitely was known that the Rebels were coming, Mr. Winter locked his front door, closed his wooden shutters, fastening them with diagonal iron bars, and retired to the privacy of his apartments in the rear of his shop. But the invaders learned that behind these iron bars there was a stock of sweets. Mr. Winter was brought to the front, his door was opened, and soon a perplexed little man was overwhelmed with orders. No penny sales of molasses taffy now. Hilarious boys in gray were giving him a new idea of trading. He was doing the business of his life, handing out candy in exchange for Confederate money. One big trooper came out of the shop with his hat full of candy and seeing an expectant looking small boy gazing enviously at his store, gave me a handful."

Charles said he remembered the trooper for the rest of his life, thinking of the southerner as a 'kindly youth' for the rest of his life.

SARAH BARRETT KING:

"I had a visit from two of these soldiers, asking me to sell them bread and butter. They did not come in company, first one then the other. I did not sell, but gave one a loaf of bread, then the other part of my very small quantity of butter, telling them to divide.

"They crossed the street, sitting on a porch to eat their bread and butter. The lady of the house heard one say, 'I think the people of this place are very kind considering we came here to kill off their husbands and sons.'

"In the evening a cavalryman rode up to the house and called to me. He said he wanted his horse shod and that I should tell the blacksmith to come out. There was a blacksmith shop to the rear of our home. I told him there was no blacksmith here and I knew nothing of his whereabouts. Well, he said, if I could get in the shop and get shoes, I would shoe the horse myself. I said to him, do as you please, I am not concerned in the shop or its owner.

"In a few minutes, I saw he had forced a window and my son, a boy of four years, was holding the window up with the soldier's carbine, evidently feeling very important. I went out and objected. The soldier answered, 'No danger, I've got the shoes and am sorry the blacksmith is not here. I would like to pay him for them.'

"I said, 'Leave the money with me. If you are anxious about it, I know where he lives and will send it to him.'

"He got out his pocketbook, searched it and there was nothing to be found. He laughingly said, 'I brought the wrong pocketbook.' I said, 'It was the blacksmith's loss for evidently you are very anxious to pay him.'

"He said, 'Why are you women so afraid of the Rebels?'

"'Why,' I said, 'that is news to me, I did not know they were.'

"He added, 'General Lee ordered us to treat the women with respect, not like your men treated our women in Winchester.'

"I said, 'Your women spat upon our men, some from this town, in Winchester, and Virginia had no better men, and when women resorted to such insults they deserved all they got.'

"I asked him, 'Where are you going?'

"'Oh,' he said, 'to Bunker's Hill, and we will not leave one stone on another there.'

"I answered, 'Before many days you will wish you were across the Potomac.'

"'Well, it might be,' he replied, and lifting his hat said, 'Good bye'."

The Rebel army did not invent the practice of "requisitioning" goods and supplies. Armies have always done it to one degree or another, and Union soldiers were no different. Seven year old HARRY ERNEST TROXEL's[28] older brothers discovered that for themselves when their father sent them off to hide the family's best horse:

"The boys hitched into a buggy and drove off as fast as they could go. They wanted to get on the other side of the Susquehanna River. There we thought they'd be safe. It was a forty mile ride and they hadn't been gone a great while when some of the

Rebels came galloping down the street...a whole lot of 'em. They were after the people who were flying with their stock.

"Just one square above us lived a butcher who had a little Dutch feller by the name of Charlie Supann working for him. He sent Charlie off with his horse before our boys got started, but they overtook Charlie out here by the tollgate house. Charlie was drivin' along pretty leisurely, and they told him he'd better hurry.

"'But my orders are not to drive fast,' he said.

"Well, our boys went on and left him behind and the Rebels caught him and took his horse. While they were parleying with him our boys hurried along as fast as they could and they escaped. They got to the big covered bridge at Columbia over the Susquehanna, and they told us afterward that people were going through there with their horses just like a cavalcade...chasing through one after the other all the time. At the far end were some Union officials stopping every one that had a good horse, and if the horse suited them, they'd take it and give in return a slip of paper entitling the owner to pay from the government.[29]

"Right in front of our boys was a young feller on an awful nice horse and the officer said, 'Is that a good riding horse?'

"'Yes,' the feller says, 'Father keeps him for that.'

"'Then you jump right off,' the officer said. 'He's just what I want.'

"Next he spoke to our boys and asked if theirs was a riding horse.

"'No, you can't do anything with her for riding,' they said.

"'Then get out of this,' he told 'em. 'We don't want her.'

"They were lucky to get across the bridge when they did, for the pursuing Rebels were close behind and the Federals burnt part of the bridge just before the enemy got there to keep them from going farther.

"Our boys were now strangers in a strange country. But they soon located on a farm with a man who was starting harvesting and they got right out in the harvest field, and went to work."[30]

There was always strong political division in Gettysburg. With the war at high ebb, the Republican faction actively promoted patriotism and support for the Union, and inferred without hesitation that Democrats were southern sympathizers.

JOHN WILLS was the son of CHARLES W. WILLS, proprietor of one of Gettysburg's best known hotels, the Globe Inn, which, in addition to housing the traveler and keeping a friendly bar, was Democratic headquarters of Adams County. Needless to say, the Will were strong Democrats.

The Confederates were clearly aware of local politics. Wills tells stories of men he took for Rebel spies staying at the Inn well before the time of the battle. During Early's meeting with Burgess David Kendlehart, Wills struck up a conversation with one of Early's aides, who tacitly admitted coming to the Globe three weeks before. The aide paid for dinner with a silver quarter, as Wills remembered. At any rate, it appears the Rebels felt kindly toward the Globe, whatever the Wills' real political sentiments may have been. That may be why John had no trouble getting permission from the raiders to unload a railroad car:

"An individual car was run by George Strickhouser to and from Baltimore, hauling freight and goods for merchants and citizens and also for the Globe Hotel, where he was boarding. We had in that car for the Globe Hotel six barrels of whiskey, forty bushels of potatoes, three barrels of sugar, one barrel of syrup and one tierce of hams and shoulders of cured meat.

"We called on General Early and asked him to give us a guard while we were getting these goods out of the car and removing them to the cellar. He kindly furnished them, saying 'we will protect private property.' After having removed the goods from the car, they set fire to several company freight cars which were standing on the tracks and run them down the track to Rock Creek.

But the day wasn't over for the Wills and their Confederate guard:

Daniel Alexander Skelly, was one of seven children of Master Tailor Johnson Skelly and his wife Elizabeth. They lived on West Middle Street near the Fahnestock Store. Eighteen year old Daniel's recent appointment to the U.S. Military Academy at West Point by Congressman Edward McPherson had not worked out to his satisfaction. So, in late June of 1863, he returned to Gettysburg and found more than his old job as clerk at Fahnestock Brothers General Store waiting on him. *Courtesy Adams County Historical Society.*

"Now these Confederates, remembering well where we put the whiskey, late in the evening a Confederate officer with three Confederate privates came to the hotel and compelled my father to open the cellar doors and roll out three barrels of whiskey. They left, taking the whiskey with them to camp, the officer saying he would return later and pay for it.

"About eleven o'clock that night, the officer came to the hotel and drew up an order on the Confederate government which father refused to accept, saying 'I want good money.'

"The Confederate replied: 'In two months our money may be better than yours as we may remain in your state an indefinite time.' The order was all he (father) got."

So, the locals had a lot to talk about while they waited for the "other shoe to drop." And there was ample warning that it would drop soon.

DANIEL ALEXANDER SKELLY was eighteen:

"We knew the Confederate Army, or a part of it at least, was within a few miles of our town and at night we could see from the housetops the campfires in the mountains 8 miles west of us. We expected it to march into our town at any moment and we had no information as to the whereabouts of the Army of the Potomac. We little dreamed of the momentous events which were soon to happen right in our midst."

The Gettysburg Compiler:

"It cannot be possible that a great battle between the two contending armies can be avoided much longer. It may occur at any moment and in our own county. Let our ladies go to work at once and prepare lint, bandages and other articles that may be useful in the hospital."

Saturday, June 27th

The Diary of SARAH BROADHEAD, Chambersburg Street:

"June 27: I passed the most uncomfortable night of my life. My husband had gone in the cars to Hanover Junction, not thinking the Rebels were so near, or that there was much danger of their coming to town, and I was left entirely alone, surrounded by thousands of ugly, rude, hostile soldiers, from whom violence might be expected. Even if neighbors were at hand, it was not pleasant, and I feared my husband would be taken prisoner before he could return, or whilst trying to reach me. I was not disturbed, however, by anything except my fears, and this morning when I got up I found that the Rebels had departed, having, on the night of the 27th,[31] burned the railroad bridge over Rock Creek, just outside of the town, and the cars that had brought up the militia and had torn up the track and done other mischief. I became more uneasy about my husband, and I went to see some of the railroad hands to find out what I could relating to him. They told me that he had been captured and paroled[32] and that he had gone to Harrisburg; so I feel easier, and hope to rest to-night. Three of our scouts came in this morning just after the Rebels left, and report a large force of our soldiers near, making all feel much safer."

SARAH BARRETT KING:

"While sitting around that day on our porch, waiting for something to happen, we saw coming down York street, riding leisurely, a party on horseback in chaplain's uniform, looking as though he was more than pleased with his surroundings. Perhaps he was thinking of going on to Washington or Bunker's Hill, when some one called 'Halt.'

"He did not halt, but just jogged on. Then a leaden voice spoke.[33] I suppose it was more persuasive, as the party stood still.

"It seems some one carried word to the Eagle (hotel) that a Rebel chaplain was passing through. George Guinn, home on furlough, rose to the occasion and made his capture. I believe they found papers on him of some import. He was paroled and allowed to go home. Chaplain McGill, living near Frederick, I heard was the name of the party."

JOHN WILLS and his father took advantage of the lull to get a few things in the ground:

"...My father took the precaution to save some our supplies and eatables. Late at night, none of the family knowing it, with our colored help we removed sugar, hams and shoulders, some potatoes and boxes of groceries to a loft above the rear of the building. Then we dug a trench in the garden. Into this we put two barrels of each, whiskey, brandy and gin. On this we placed boards and covered over the ground. Then we planted this all over with cabbage plants."

The Old Farmer's Almanac often advises planting "by the light of the moon."

Sunday, June 28th, 1863

SARAH BROADHEAD:
"June 28: Sunday. About 10 o'clock a large body of our cavalry began to pass through town, and we were all busy feeding them as they passed along. It seemed to me that the long line would never get through. I hope they may catch the Rebels and give them a sound thrashing. Some say we may look for a battle here in a few days, and others say it will be fought near Harrisburg. There is no telling where it will be."
SALLIE MYERS:
"Sunday, June 28. We feel safe now as the Artillery & Infantry are not very far off. We did not have Sunday School this afternoon – too much excitement. We were too glad to see our noble looking Union troops. Quite a contrast to the dirty mean looking rebels who call themselves Southern Chivalry."

There were church services, however, in nearby Fairfield. As students at the Lutheran Seminary, MARTIN LUTHER CULLER and a friend were asked to go to Fairfield to substitute for Dr. E. S. Johnson, who could not be there. Culler's friend performed the morning services. Culler planned to preach in the evening, but never got the chance:
"Just as the morning service was being concluded, the Confederates dashed into the village. The people did not wait for the benediction.

"Just after the noon hour we walked to the east end of the town where the Confederates were encamped. While we were looking at them, at what we thought a safe distance, two Union scouts rode up on the opposite side of a hedge-fence, completely hidden from their enemies. Having discharged their carbines at them, they dashed away unobserved toward Emmitsburg. Of course, the rebels returned the fire in the direction of the smoke from the carbines. Their bullets flew too dangerously near us, causing us to run for safety into the nearest house. But we were pursued by the enemy, charging us with having fired the shots at them. They were very angry, thrust their revolvers in our faces, arrested us as prisoners of war, and marched us out of the house.

"We stood under arrest until their captain approached, whom I saluted, and ventured to tell him that he men were laboring under a very grievous mistake. To his credit, be it said, he listened very graciously to what I had to say.

"After he had politely heard my version of the shots fired and why we ran, he answered: 'Your story seems plausible, but I do not know whether it is true of not.' He hesitated. The suspense was painful, for we did not know what he order would be.

"I resolved upon a 'coup d'etat.' I said: 'Captain, you do not arrest ministers of the gospel, do you?' He at once said: 'Are you men ministers?' I think it was the truth when we said we were. We have come there to preach and we were students for the ministry.

"Feeling a little more at ease with this courteous captain, I said to him: 'Do you see that brick church yonder? There we were holding religious services this morning. This man whom you see with me was preaching. You men rushed into town and disturbed our worship. Now you occupy the town and this hinders me from preaching the splendid sermon which I intended to preach this evening.'

"He smiled and said: 'Many things are permissible in time of war which would not be in time of peace.'

"I knew we had won the day. He said, 'No, we do not arrest ministers of the gospel unless they are bearing arms. Where do you live?' When told, he said: 'You had

(Right) The Adams County Jail, on East High Street, was temporary home for several suspected Confederate spies. They were held only until they could be turned over to the professional army. Among the spies held briefly was one captured by Private Thomas Smith with Company A 7th Michigan Cavalry. When Smith's company came into town, June 29th, he was granted permission to visit friends. However, in the middle of the night the company sergeant received word to pull out. He left a note at the hotel for Private Smith. The next day when Smith went to the hotel he learned of his dilemma: his unit was gone and rebels may be headed for town. A friend lent Smith some civilian clothes just in case…

Captain John Myers, 80, and a veteran of the War of 1812, is believed to be the one who tipped Smith to a man he suspected of trying to get Union troop information out of children playing in the school yard. Smith chased down the man, who was unarmed, and brought him back into town at gun point. Private Smith turned him over to Sheriff Adam Rebert and deputy Zack Myers.

The man insisted he belonged to Colonel White's Guerrillas and was a scout, not a spy. However, Sheriff Rebert found enough papers hidden in one of his boots to condemn him. Private Smith said his goodbyes and headed out to rejoin his unit. About five miles south of Gettysburg he ran into General Buford's Cavalry. Buford halted his command long enough to ask Smith where he belonged.

THOMAS SMITH: "As I was feeling quite happy I told him I belonged to the army. He asked what army. Union, of course. He called out 'you are a rebel lying son of a bitch for I am further advanced than any man in the Union army!' I then told him I had held Gettysburg for the last two days single-handed. He was unimpressed, telling me to consider myself under arrest."

As Buford's cavalry rode into the town square, the Sheriff, who was still there with the prisoner and a dozen men, turned the man over to the General. Buford recognized him at once as a man who'd been in his camp the night before claiming to be a union citizen. Buford then asked to see the citizen who captured the spy. Smith concludes his story:

THOMAS SMITH:

"I rode up from behind and saluted. He seemed upset: 'Why in hell didn't you tell me before? Says I: 'General, why in hell didn't you give me a chance?' General Buford then ordered me released from arrest and ordered me to remain with him 'til the arrival of my command.' The spy gave the name of Will Talbott, 35. He was dressed in a dark broadcloth suit, wore broad brim black slouch hat, and had no arms with him of any kind."

Young Mary Montfort wrote in her diary a few days before the battle, "a Union Chaplain turns out to be a rebel spy. They pulled some papers out of his boots and marched him down the street barefoot. He was a rebel spy taking news to the enemy. When a war is going on you can't believe anything you see or hear." Whether she was describing the Smith incident is simply conjecture. However, there were quite a few Confederate scouts and spies circulating throughout the Pennsylvania countryside during the invasion. Some of them were caught and spent time in the Adams County Jail. *Courtesy Adams County Historical Society*

better go home.' Then said I, 'Do you order us to do so?' His answer was: 'I have no right to give such an order.'

"When he desired to know whether the horse we drove was a good one, our reply was: 'It is old, blind and poor in flesh. We are Yankees enough to know better than venture anywhere near your army with a good horse.'

"He took a hearty laugh and assured us that we might drive home undisturbed with such a horse."[34]

Monday, June 29th, 1863

SARAH BROADHEAD:

"June 29th: Quiet has prevailed all day. Our cavalry came up with the Rebels at Hanover, fourteen miles from here, and had quite a spirited fight, driving them through the town. Their infantry had reached York and had taken possession, as they did here, and demanded goods, stores, and money; threatening, if the demand was not complied with, to burn the town. Dunce-like, the people paid them $28,000, which they pocketed, and passed on to Wrightsville. A company of our militia, guarding the Columbia bridge over the Susquehanna, retreated on the approach of the Rebels, and fired the bridge, which was entirely consumed, preventing the enemy from setting foot on the east bank, and ending their offensive movements for a time."

But from the top of a hill sheltering her family's farm north of Gettysburg, HARRIET BAYLY could see that their troubles were only beginning.

"Looking west at night we could see camp fires along the mountain side eight miles distant, and it seemed as though the enemy were there in force."

WILLIAM HAMILTON BAYLY:

"It was rumored that the main army[35] was on the other side of the mountain advancing up the Cumberland Valley…"

In fact, both forces were massing nearby. On the evening of June 29th, the center of the US Army of the Potomac settled on PETER KOONS' Middleburg farm near Taneytown, Maryland, about fifteen miles south of Gettysburg. Newly-appointed commanding General George Meade's headquarters tents were pitched on the farm, creating a spectacle the Koons family would never forget because, where a General pitches a tent, a city rises. Koons' son, 19 year old JAMES, described it:[36]

The 150th Pennsylvania "Bucktails" Regiment, as it appeared in northern Virginia just a few weeks before marching northward to stem Lee's invasion. They will be involved in the first days fighting at Gettysburg. *Courtesy Massachusetts Commandery of the Military Order of the Loyal Legion of the United States and the US Army Military History Institute, Carlisle, Pennsylvania.*

An encampment of the Army of the Potomac. It is difficult to visualize the enormous numbers of men, material and supplies when we talk about the involvement of the two armies en route to Gettysburg. Massive troop movements on both sides are taking place. The armies are composed of companies which make up regiments. Several regiments make up a brigade, and three or four brigades make up a division. There are approximately three divisions per Corps. The Confederate Army strength, as it moves into Pennsylvania, is estimated at 75,000. The strength of the Union Army, as it concentrates its Corps to defend against the invasion, is put at 97,000 men. *Courtesy Massachusetts Commandery of the Military Order of the Loyal Legion of the United States and the US Army Military History Institute, Carlisle, Pennsylvania.*

At Gettysburg the Confederate Army had 287 guns, the Union 362 guns. General Robert E. Lee had 69 batteries of field artillery. General George Meade had 65 batteries of field artillery. *Courtesy Massachusetts Commandery of the Military Order of the Loyal Legion of the United States and the US Army Military History Institute, Carlisle, Pennsylvania.*

Ammunition trains are necessary to support the field artillery. If the train isn't nearby it's always given right of way to move forward. The lines of supply are critical for both armies. A major battle could erupt at any time because neither army is certain of exactly where the other is. *Courtesy Massachusetts Commandery of the Military Order of the Loyal Legion of the United States and the US Army Military History Institute, Carlisle, Pennsylvania.*

Another key component of an advancing army is the ambulance train. It must be at the ready to transport the wounded. *Courtesy Massachusetts Commandery of the Military Order of the Loyal Legion of the United States and the US Army Military History Institute, Carlisle, Pennsylvania.*

This wagon park is part of the Quartermaster Department. These wagons are used to haul the equipment for field repair shops. The supplies necessary to build bridges and new wagons must be transported along with the men and materials to make and repair boots, saddles, harnesses, and wheels. The wagons also must carry enough food to feed an army. *Courtesy Massachusetts Commandery of the Military Order of the Loyal Legion of the United States and the US Army Military History Institute, Carlisle, Pennsylvania.*

Whenever something breaks or a new piece of equipment is needed it has to be taken care of right away. Repair shops and forges are an integral part of an army on the move. The "smithy" keeps the horses shod and limbers, cassions, and artillery operational. With so much traveling and so much fighting there is always work for carpenters and wheelwrights. Rocks and ruts take their toll on wagon wheels. What they don't damage, the enemy's artillery does. *Courtesy Massachusetts Commandery of the Military Order of the Loyal Legion of the United States and the US Army Military History Institute, Carlisle, Pennsylvania.*

The Cavalry has been described as the eyes and ears of the Army. Its officers were generally more dashing, more cavalier, than their infantry or artillery counterparts. Reporters loved to write about the exploits of "Kil" Kilpatrick, George Custer, and JEB Stuart – who even now is off raiding the Maryland countryside instead of scouting for his commander-in-chief who has already crossed into Pennsylvania. Stuart is still hours away from Gettysburg. He has been slowed by the capture of a Union Supply Train, June 25th, just outside Rockville, Maryland. The 400 prisoners, 900 horses and mules, and more than 100 wagons (and several minor skirmishes with Union Cavalry outfits) add frustration to Stuart's elation because it is slowing his effort to re-join Lee. *Courtesy Massachusetts Commandery of the Military Order of the Loyal Legion of the United States and the US Army Military History Institute, Carlisle, PA.*

"Every field was occupied, excepting those in wheat uncut, although on both sides of the main road was an additional road through the uncut wheat used by the cavalry as the main road was filled with infantry for miles.

"In one field, blacksmith shops were run all night, in another field was General Meade's headquarters tents with the pay-master's wagon. He, the pay-master, in paying bills, used a pair of shears to clip from the sheets the money wanted, whether one, five, ten or hundred dollar bills. Each till contained a certain amount of sheets from a one dollar bill up, and all the pay-master had to do was pull out a sheet and clip off the amount wanted."

SALLIE MYERS diary:
"Monday, June 29. ...we may expect a battle both near and soon. God help us! for surely our cause is one of justice and humanity."

Tuesday, June 30th, 1863

MRS. HARRIET BAYLY:
"The whole air seemed charged with conditions which go before a storm; everybody anxious, neighbor asking neighbor what was going to happen and what will we do if the worst should happen?"
Union officers on the Koons farm were asking themselves the same questions. JAMES KOONS:
"Engineers and officers of headquarters, together with my father, Peter Koons, went in the rear of the barn on the hill and examined a large map.

"My father gave to the engineers the situation of every hill, ravine and crossing, every turn made in the creek's course for about four miles, as a battle ground...which map is in the records of the Army of the Potomac on file in Washington, D.C. He was well known as a Union man and, as such, the officers above-mentioned, could easily make known their business; they told him a battle would take place north of here. When, they did not know, but if beaten, here on Pipe Creek would be the stand made to cover Washington.

"He was cautioned not to disclose what took place on the hill until the war was over and he never told it to anyone until that time; then he said if General Meade would have been whipped at Gettysburg, we would likely have had to make a sudden move; he then told his family about the map made on the hill and the part he had been requested to act in it."
SARAH BROADHEAD:
"June 30: – My husband came home last night at 1 o'clock, having walked from Harrisburg, thirty-six miles, since 9 o'clock of yesterday morning. His return has put me in good spirits. I wonder that he escaped the Rebels, who are scouring the country between here and there. Fatigue is all the ill that befell him. This morning the Rebels came to the top of the hill overlooking the town on the Chambersburg pike, and looked over at our place. We had a good view of them from our house,[37] and every moment we expected to hear the booming of cannon, and thought they might shell the town. As it turned out, they were only reconnoitering the town preparatory to an advance if no force opposed them. We were told that a heavy force of our soldiers was within five miles, and the Rebels, learning that a body of cavalry was quite near, retraced their steps, and encamped some distance from town. It begins to look as though we will see a battle soon, and we are in great fear. I see by the papers that General Hooker has been relieved, and the change of commanders I fear may give great advantage to the enemy, and our army may be repulsed."

Dr. Michael Jacobs, 55, was a professor of mathematics and natural philosophy at Pennsylvania College. He was much more comfortable teaching his students in the field than in the confines of a classroom. Jacobs lived with his wife Julia and four children (Henry, 18, was the oldest) on the northwest corner of West Middle Street at South Washington. The professor was used to making daily weather observations and recording the information in his journal. He saw no reason to deviate from that routine because of the inconveniences swirling around him. *Courtesy Special Collections, Gettysburg College.*

When General John Buford and his Cavalry rode down South Washington Street into Gettysburg scores of residents stopped what they were doing and came to watch the parade. They were so relieved to see blue uniforms that they didn't seem to mind the dust and flying debris kicked up by the three brigades of cavalry, accompanied by artillery pieces, and wagons. Groups of young women even serenaded the soldiers. A few of them grabbed up small flags to wave. *Courtesy Massachusetts Commandery of the Military Order of the Loyal Legion of the United States and the US Army Military History Institute, Carlisle, Pennsylvania.*

Emma Aughinbaugh, 17, her sisters Ellen 19 and Martha 12, heard the commotion of the Cavalry's arrival from their home, north of the square on Carlisle Street, and went running across the blocks to greet the soldiers, too. That scene was no doubt repeated throughout the town as residents began to breath a sigh of relief. Their protection had arrived! *Courtesy The J. Howard Wert Gettysburg Collection.*

Gettysburg College Professor MICHAEL JACOBS lived directly south of the Broadheads at the corner of Washington and West Middle streets:

"Our garret window afforded a clear view of the Chambersburg Road, leading up to the Blue Ridge, eight miles away. I went up to the garret, taking with me the small telescope which was used in the astronomical department of the college, a powerful glass. I could see on the top of the hill west of the town a considerable force of Confederates who had come down from the mountains. On the summit stood a group of officers, sweeping the horizon with their field glasses. Back of them, but largely hidden by the shoulder of the hill, my glass enabled me to distinguish men both of infantry and artillery commands.

"Suddenly, the officers on the crest of the hill turned and rode back, and almost on the heels of the retreat, a roar of shouting arose from the streets below me. I hurried downstairs and saw General John Buford's (Union) cavalry division, including two brigades, riding into Gettysburg from the Taneytown Road, on the south. He flung one of his brigades directly north, along Washington Street; the other he dispatched to the west along the Chambersburg Road."[38]

TILLIE PIERCE:

"A crowd of 'us girls' were standing on the corner of Washington and High Streets as these soldiers passed by. Desiring to encourage them who, as we were told, would before long be in battle, my sister started to sing the old war song 'Our Union Forever.' As some of us did not know the whole of the piece we kept repeating the chorus."[39]

SALLIE MYERS:

"How they dashed by! Their horses' feet seemed shod with lightning. Along the street we stood – all the girls and women of the town. We had prepared food in advance, and had baskets and trays in our hands. They came by, snatching in their hasty passage whatever they could lay their hands on – sandwiches, pieces of pie, cold meat, bread, cakes, cups of coffee and bottles of water.

"The eyes of the soldiers blazed, they smiled and some joined in the song. It was the last song many of those brave men ever heard, and the bite we gave was the last many ever ate."

Professor J. HOWARD WERT:
"General Buford was not in town five minutes before he had orders printed up by sending compositors to the office of the Star who quickly had in type the orders which were placarded over town:
'Sale of spiritous liquors of any kind in this town during its occupation by the troops is strictly prohibited. Any violation of this order will be promptly and severely punished. The giving away of liquor will be punished the same as if a sale.'"

Wert wrote that the only drink available in Gettysburg that night was from the cavalry which had confiscated Maryland applejack which they put in their canteens against a time of need. "Some of the soldiers," he wrote, "helped out the thirsty citizens."

Dr. JOHN WILLIAM CRAPSTER O'NEAL[40] harbored southern sympathies. He had moved to the Pennsylvania town from Maryland to open a medical practice. It is only fair to point out that Dr. O'Neal was not alone in those feelings; the southern cause was upheld in many parts of the north. A fair number of young men went south from Gettysburg to join the Confederate army. As we will see later, some returned to fight in the great battle, and then visited friends and relatives when the fighting died.

As part of his scheduled rounds on June 30th, Dr. O'Neal had appointments with an injured Rebel infantryman in a barn along the Mummasburg Road, and then with William Myers, a sick man who lived at Bream's Mill.[41] The last visit took him out the Chambersburg Pike, giving him the unique experience of watching Buford's cavalry arrive in Gettysburg from the Rebel's point of view:
"I went up to the turnpike and at the old Herr tavern on the pike encountered a body of men coming down the pike from the direction of Cashtown under command, as I later learned, of General Pettigrew.[42]

"I was halted and questioned by General Pettigrew and his staff, first as to my business. I had my saddle bags with me containing my medicine case and this visiting list...in my pocket and with the help of the two I managed to convince them that I was a practitioner of medicine. Pettigrew was at length satisfied and said I might go and attend to my business.

This tattered flag belonged to 17 year old Emma Aughinbaugh. She grabbed it as she and her sisters ran from their house to join the townsfolk who waved flags, sang songs, and cheered the arrival of General John Buford's Cavalry as they rode through Gettysburg. *Courtesy The J. Howard Wert Gettysburg Collection.*

Dr. John William Crapster O'Neal, 42, a graduate of Pennsylvania College, was practicing medicine in Baltimore on the eve of the Civil War. He also sat on the school board. However, public disturbances in Washington and a fear of them spilling over into Baltimore caused him to seek a quieter, safer, environment for his family. At first he moved his family to Hanover, Pennsylvania, the hometown of his wife, Ellen. However, in nearby Gettysburg, Democrats looking to strengthen the county party leadership promised O'Neal the patients at the county Alms House and the Adams County prison if he would relocate there. O'Neal accepted their offer. The doctor was outspoken and his tongue frequently got him into trouble in a town where sympathies were divided. His defense of slavery and alignment with the southern cause did not make him welcome at the Gettysburg Presbyterian Church, so he switched to the Reformed Church. *Courtesy Adams County Historical Society.*

"I rode on towards Bream's Mill and had not ridden 200 yards when an orderly came galloping after me and calling on me to stop. Pettigrew re-examined me, asking whether there were any Yankees in town, when I left town and whether I had any newspapers. I answered as best I could saying I had no information of any forces being in town when I left and added 'General, if I did have any matter of information I couldn't give it to you for I'm a medical practitioner and not an informant.'

"Finally Pettigrew said I could go back, but not forward, through the lines. I thought best to stay with them, having been examined and given comparative liberty. I feared to leave them because the next party to examine me might take me along as a prisoner and the plight of my family in Gettysburg caused me some uneasiness.

"After some conversation between officers on the pike before the tavern we advanced to the toll gate house kept by the Johns girls and as we were passing through gates about a half dozen mounted men appeared. General Pettigrew turned to me and said 'I understood you to say there were no Yankees in town. There are mounted men pointing and are evidently from the town.'

"I was confused and could give no reasonable account, simply saying there were no forces of any kind of town when I left and what there was now I didn't know.

"General Pettigrew ordered the advance to fall back, which they did to the tavern. This was about 10 o'clock in the morning."[43]

While Pettigrew and Dr. O'Neal reversed course, General Buford began securing the approaches to Gettysburg until the larger Union force could arrive.

Luckily, Dr. O'Neal found a friend from Baltimore among the physicians traveling with Pettigrew's soldiers and was taken safely in tow. But he was still a long way from home.

DANIEL SKELLY:
"About 4 o'clock, I stood on the Cobean corner of Chambersburg street[44] while General Buford sat on his horse in the street in front of me entirely alone, facing to the west and in profound thought.

"It is possible that from that position he was directing, through his aides, the placing of his two brigades of cavalry (Gambles' and Devin's) to the west and northwest of the town."

Professor MICHAEL JACOBS:
"I took the telescope to the Lutheran Theological Seminary on Seminary Hill, west of the town, and went up to the observatory, where the whole horizon could be brought into view. I began a careful examination of the mountains to the west, where the Blue Ridge describes a semi-circle. Wherever the mountainsides held clearings, smoke curled upward. About the fires, I could see men walking, attending to camp chores, cooking – all the activities of an army held in leash. They showed as clearly as though they were not more than a couple of hundred yards away. And below me, within easy eyeshot, were both of Buford's Federal brigades. The tide of war was for the hour halted under my very eyes."

General James J. Pettigrew, CSA, 35, commanded a regiment under Henry Heth's division of A.P. Hill's corps. Pettigrew was a North Carolinian and a graduate of the University of North Carolina. He had settled in Charleston, South Carolina. A lawyer by profession, he also served in the South Carolina legislature. His orders on this day were to see what he could see and to avoid a fight. The legend that Pettigrew was coming in search of shoes is puzzling. The Confederates had good intelligence from their spies and sympathizers in the area, and should have been aware that Gettysburg had no more cobblers than any other small town. General Early had learned days before that merchandise in the stores had been moved to Harrisburg and Philadelphia. *Courtesy Massachusetts Commandery of the Military Order of the Loyal Legion of the United States and the US Army Military History Institute, Carlisle, Pennsylvania.*

Brigadier General John Buford, 37, was born in Kentucky, but moved to Illinois in the 1840s. His cousin, Abraham Buford, was a General in the Army of the Confederacy. On the morning of July 1st 1863 Buford knew his regiment would be the first line of defense in any confrontation with the Confederates. He knew other detachments were hours, if not days, away. So, he ordered his cavalrymen to dismount, and to dig in as infantrymen. They must hold position until Reynolds' I Corps arrives. *Courtesy Massachusetts Commandery of the Military Order of the Loyal Legion of the United States and the US Army Military History Institute, Carlisle, Pennsylvania.*

NOTES

1. From *Gettysburg, A Memoir* by Charles M. McCurdy. Published in 1929 by Reed & Witting Co., Pittsburgh.

2. Throughout this book, John Wills will call the Globe a "Hotel," although Gettysburgers called it an Inn until the 1890s. Mr. Wills' did not dictate his narrative, "Reminiscences of the Three Days Battle of Gettysburg at the Globe Hotel," until well after the turn of the century. By that time, he would have adopted the popular lexicon himself. Will helped his father manage the Globe from 1860 to 1864.

The authors do not intend to knowingly change any of the words written or spoken by the Gettysburg citizens. That is also why we will refer to Mr. Will as he gave his name in his memoirs; with an "s". When his father bought the Inn, the family's name, painted on the building's signboard, was Will.

3. From an interview with the Philadelphia North American, July 4, 1909.

4. This paragraph comes from Clifton Johnson's *Battleground Adventures*, published in 1913. Mr. Johnson wrote a whole book of interviews at Gettysburg without once identifying the people he interviewed. It was a "Victorian conceit" which invariably causes gas pains and rolling eyes among researchers. In this interview, he identified Sallie Myers simply as "The School Teacher." We have made every effort to unveil Mr. Johnson's modest conversationalists, not always succeeding as well as we would like.

5. In other books, Mrs. Broadhead is identified as Sallie Robbins Broadhead. Sallie is the diminutive of Sarah and Robbins was her maiden name.

6. Tillie Pierce described her experiences in *At Gettysburg, or What a Young Girl Saw and Heard of the Battle*, published by W. Lake Borland, NY in 1888. The book was published under her married name, Tillie Pierce Alleman. As is the case with many of these accounts, a full copy of Mrs. Alleman's memoir is in the archives of the Adams County Historical Society. It was first excerpted by the authors when they began this research in 1977.

7. The Gettysburg Times: "Citizens of Gettysburg volunteered to become members of a 'company of infantry' to be raised under the call of the Pennsylvania Governor on 16th of June, 1863. They formed on the 20th to serve during the present emergency."

Colonel W. W. Jennings recruited a regimental organization of 743 men from the region.

Against the advice of the president of Pennsylvania College, Dr. Henry Louis Baugher, twenty-one of the college's students joined with sixty-two local citizens as part of an "emergency militia." Dr. Baugher counseled discretion and advised those he called the "embryonic heroes" to return to their studies immediately. His advice was probably more heart-felt than the students realized; he had lost a son at Shiloh the year before.

8. She is referring to the 87th's participation in a battle at Winchester, Virginia, on the previous Sunday. The 87th was "regular army", not militia.

9. In his account, John C. Wills observed these troopers as extremely well groomed, expensively outfitted with white shirts and cuffs. His implication was that they were more "dandies" than professional soldiers.

10. Young to middle-aged men often feared being taken prisoner. Some were. Likewise, all Blacks feared enslavement...or worse.

11. These were scouts, combing the countryside for knowledge of the Federal army's movements, and for food and supplies to send back to the main force of the Rebel army.

12. US Cavalry.

13. These also were volunteers, called up for 'temporary duty' by Governor Andrew Curtin when the Confederate invasion became imminent. Until the battle of Gettysburg took place, Governor Curtin had trouble keeping his restless volunteers from packing up and going home.

14. The Potomac River.

15. As remembered by her daughter, Louise Dale Leeds.

16. Ephriam Martin, a tailor who operated a shop just off the Diamond with his son, Robert, who was also the town Burgess.

17. Elijah White's cavalry, under command of Jubal Early.

18. Twelve year old Charles, eight year old Anna, five year old Samuel and three year of James, Jr.

19. This account appeared in the Gettysburg Compiler on October 20, 1909.

20. Captured militia, many of them students at the college.

21. Major General Robert H. Milroy, USA, whose garrison at Winchester, Virginia, was overrun by Jubal Early's cavalry division of Lt. General Richard S. Ewell's Confederate II Corps on June 15, 1863. Milroy escaped, but the Rebels captured 4,000 Union soldiers and took 25 cannon. Milroy was held in contempt by Ewell's troops, who hoped to capture him.

22. From Albertus McCreary's *Gettysburg: A Boy's Experience of the Battle*. Fifteen year old Albertus lived with his father, 59 year old David McCreary, and six brothers and sisters at the corner of West High and South Baltimore streets.

23. 110 Baltimore Street.

24. Mercantile and bank goods had already been shipped to safety in places as far away as York and Philadelphia.

25. Bushman is another of the persons interviewed but unidentified by Clifton Johnson for his book, *Battlefield Adventures*, published in 1913. Through meticulous research, Bushman was identified by Gettysburg historian, Tim Smith.

26. June 26th.

27. Hooker was still in command of the Union Army of the Potomac at this time. But, smarting from defeat in Virginia and from the apparent lack of confidence among his superiors in Washington, Hooker asked to be relieved of his command. His resignation was accepted and General George Gordon Meade took charge on June 28th, two days after these events transpired.

28. Another interview from Clifton Johnson's *Battlefield Adventures*. Once again, we thank Gettysburg historian Tim Smith for an important identification.

29. This was the common practice on both sides. Often, though, the Rebel soldiers would try to pay in Confederate money, and that wasn't popular among the Pennsylvania farmers.

30. From Clifton Johnson's *Battlefield Adventures*.

31. She is referring to the part of the night between midnight and dawn of the 27th. The Gettysburg raid occurred on the 26th.

32. In addition to his employment with the railroad, Joseph Broadhead was a member of the militia.

33. A warning gunshot.

34. Related to the Gettysburg Compiler, July 19, 1911.

35. Confederate army.

36. James Koons, writing in the Carroll Record of Taneytown, 1895.

37. 217 Chambersburg Street. The house still stands.

38. Professor Jacobs noted: "His arrival had ended the facile control of the territory by the Confederates and the troops I had described from the garret window were a force under General Pettigrew of North Carolina, on their way to Gettysburg to procure shoes and some other supplies."

39. In addition to Tillie, the group was identified as Salome "Sallie" Myers, Jennie Myers, Susie Myers, Alice Powers, Florie Culp, Mary Culp, Sophia Culp, Dora Fleming, Anna Garlach, Sally McClellan, Belle McElroy, Ann Jane Powers, Amanda Reinecher, Carry Young, Irene Weisich, Mary Kendlehart and the Zeigler girls.

After the battle, soldiers told Tillie they remember the singing and said it was "good" but they would have "liked to have enjoyed more than the chorus."

40. According to a family history, Dr. O'Neal was a staunch Democrat; a southern sympathizer, or "Copperhead."

41. The request for a visit may have been a setup by a political rival anxious to steer the doctor toward Confederate lines. Dr. O'Neal said it later occurred to him that he was "sent for not so much to see the man as to get me into trouble." And, he added, "I had a time of it before I got home."

42. Brigadier General James J. Pettigrew, CSA.

43. Dr. O'Neal's account appeared in the Gettysburg Compiler on July 5, 1905.

44. Southwest corner of Chambersburg and Washington Streets.

Wednesday
July 1, 1863

"On Wednesday, July 1, the storm broke."

– Sallie Myers

MRS. HARRIET BAYLY:
"I hurried through with my morning work and went to a point on the farm from which the mountains for many miles are visible, and which also overlooks the valley in which the town lies.

"I found several of the neighbors, who were as anxious as I to see what was going on, at a blacksmith shop near this point. Everything, however, was quiet and not a soldier in sight; in fact, the stillness was oppressive."

SARAH BARRETT KING:
"I heard two cavalrymen talking that morning and one of them said, 'Well, the ball is about to open.'"

"The entire period of the invasion is remarkable for being one of clouds and, for that season of the year, of low temperature. All through the first day, the entire sky was covered with clouds, viz., cumulostratus at 7:00 a.m. and 2:00 p.m.; and cirrostratus at 9:00 p.m. A very gentle breeze (2 miles per hour).
Thermometer readings:

7:00 a.m.	2:00 p.m.	9:00 p.m.
72	76	74

– Journal of Professor Michael Jacobs
Courtesy of the Gettysburg National Military Park

Willoughby Run is a slow moving creek located between McPherson's Ridge and Herr Ridge a mile-and-a-half to the west of Gettysburg. The first shots of the battle were fired across it. *Courtesy Massachusetts Commandery of the Military Order of the Loyal Legion of the United States and the US Army Military History Institute, Carlisle, Pennsylvania.*

5:30 A.M. On the field: Corporal Alphonse Hodges, Company F, 9th New York Cavalry, Gamble's brigade, was dismounted while standing night picket duty near Willoughby Run, one and a half miles west of Gettysburg.

It was a worrisome business. Arriving the day before as commander of the advance unit of Meade's left wing, Brigadier General John Buford had spread his 1st Cavalry division along a sweeping line extending west and north of town to guard against Confederate movement along the roads approaching from those directions. Rebel infantrymen had been seen to the west the day before, but had pulled back quickly when they saw the Union advance.

It was understood that the main body of Lee's Army of Northern Virginia was camped near Chambersburg, 28 miles to the west, so Buford placed four dismounted

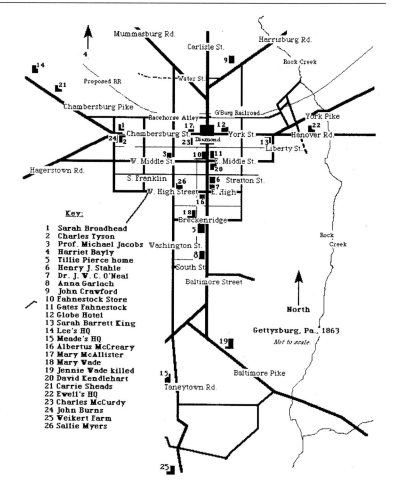

Key:
1 Sarah Broadhead
2 Charles Tyson
3 Prof. Michael Jacobs
4 Harriet Bayly
5 Tillie Pierce home
6 Henry J. Stahle
7 Dr. J. W. C. O'Neal
8 Anna Garlach
9 John Crawford
10 Fahnestock Store
11 Gates Fahnestock
12 Globe Hotel
13 Sarah Barrett King
14 Lee's HQ
15 Meade's HQ
16 Albertus McCreary
17 Mary McAllister
18 Mary Wade
19 Jennie Wade killed
20 David Kendlehart
21 Carrie Sheads
22 Ewell's HQ
23 Charles McCurdy
24 John Burns
25 Weikert Farm
26 Sallie Myers

James Gettys laid out his borough in a series of squares surrounding the "town square," referred to by town locals as "the diamond," where the four major roads came together. When the smoke cleared in late afternoon July 1st fully half of the town was behind enemy lines and the other half was caught in the crossfire. The firestorm that swept through Gettysburg was strongly felt by the residents within three miles in all directions. Most of the farms, homes and public buildings within this radius suffered occupation, some looting, and battle damage – including effects of being used as temporary hospitals.

General John Buford posted his artillery, under Calef, along McPherson's Ridge. From this point, looking west, Calef could see Marye's Confederate Battery on Herr Ridge in the distance. Willoughby Run is in the hollow. Heth's troops advanced from the field to the left. Shortly after 10:00 a.m. Buford sent a dispatch to Meade: "The enemy's force are advancing on me at this point and driving my pickets and skirmishers very rapidly."

squadrons across the Chambersburg Pike as guard until reinforcements came up. The rest, Devin's brigade, was deployed to the north near the Mummasburg Road.

The night had passed quietly, but now there was movement indeed.

In the day's first light, Hodges could just make out someone on the road about 500 yards away. Suspicious, he crouched and moved closer, hoping only to find some farmers getting the day started early. All such hopes vaporized when the unknowns opened fire. As he squeezed off return shots, Hodges called to his unit.

Although neither side fully understood what had just happened, the battle of Gettysburg was underway.

The Confederate troops were the advance of Brigadier General James J. Archer's brigade of Major General Henry Heth's division, Lieutenant General A. P. Hill's corps, now camped at Cashtown, 8 miles west. They did not know the full extent of Union forces in or near Gettysburg, and were anxious to get that information. The story goes that Heth's people were also in hopes of finding supplies, including shoes, in Gettysburg.

Truthfully, neither side knew much about the other's whereabouts or situation. When the shooting started, Generals Robert E. Lee, CSA, and George Gordon Meade, USA, were each miles to the rear, laboring to pull their massive armies together. Lee was riding with one of his chiefs, Lieutenant General James Longstreet, near Cashtown, Pennsylvania. Meade was in headquarters near Taneytown, Maryland, watching his army as it moved north from Frederick, five columns abreast along a fifteen mile front. Neither army was concentrated for an all-out fight, so neither commanding officer expected or wanted one at that particular time or place. But their plans didn't matter; fate would make the choice. As if drawn by some magnetic force, troops were converging on Gettysburg from the north, west and south, and as soon as they reached the crossroads town they would collide.

Aware that something important was happening, DANIEL A. SKELLY and a friend, Samuel Anderson, rushed out the Mummasburg Road to climb a tree and watch:

"We could then hear distinctly the skirmish fire in the vicinity of Marsh Creek, about three miles from our position, and could tell that it was approaching nearer and nearer as our skirmishers fell back slowly toward the town contesting every inch of ground. We could see clearly on the ridge about a half mile beyond us, the formation of the line of battle of Buford's Cavalry, which had dismounted, some of the men taking charge of the horses and the others forming a line of battle, acting as infantry."

Sporadic rifle fire continued for about two hours. Seventeen year old AMELIA E. HARMON[1] and an aunt lived in a large colonial mansion known as "The Old McLean Place."[2] The house was situated on a bluff overlooking Willoughby's Run, west of Seminary Ridge, placing them directly in the path of the Confederate advance. Corporal Hodges and other Union Cavalrymen were in the fields around them:

"We had decided to remain in the house even in the uncertain event of a battle, although most of our neighbors had abandoned their homes, for ours was of the old-fashioned fortress type with 18 inch walls and heavy wooden shutters. My Aunt and I were quite alone, our farmer having gone away with the horses in hope of hiding them in the fastness of the hills."

The "skirmish" rapidly changed character as reinforcements deepened the line, and the Rebels brought up artillery.

"At 9 AM came the boom of a cannon to the west of us. We rushed to the window to behold hundreds of galloping horses coming up the road, through the field and even past our very door.[3] Boom! Again spoke the cannon, more and more galloping horses, their excited riders shouting and yelling to each other, and pushing westward in hot haste, past the house and barn, seeking shelter of a strip of woods on the ridge beyond. But the ridge was alive with the enemy. A few warning shots from its cover sent them flying back to the shelter behind the barn, outbuildings, trees, and even the pump, seeking to hold the enemy in check.

"We did not know it then but we were in the very center of the first shock of battle between Hill's troops and the advance line of Buford's cavalry. Horses and men

Legend has it that General Henry Heth, CSA, was the only officer in the Army of Northern Virginia whom General Robert E. Lee addressed by his given name. Against Lee's orders, but with a wink from his commander A.P. Hill, Heth ordered two of his brigades to advance on the town and occupy it. Heth knew Union General John Buford's cavalry stood between his men and the town. The 38-year old Heth was severely wounded in that altercation. *Courtesy Americana Image Gallery, Gettysburg, Pennsylvania.*

General James J. Archer, CSA, commanded veteran troops of Alabama and Tennessee. The Princeton graduate and lawyer, moving his brigade south of Chambersburg Pike, was not prepared for what he encountered. *Courtesy Massachusetts Commandery of the Military Order of the Loyal Legion of the United States and the US Army Military History Institute, Carlisle, Pennsylvania.*

From the cupola of the Lutheran Theological Seminary General John Buford could see this view of the town when he looked east. When he looked west he could see the Confederate wave moving forward against the dismounted brigade of Colonel William Gamble along the east bank of Willoughby Run and toward Col. Thomas Devin's 2nd Brigade deployed north of the railroad cut. *Courtesy Adams County Historical Society.*

What few students remained at The Lutheran Theological Seminary were scattering into town, or heading into basement rooms. Lydia Catherine Ziegler's father, Emanuel, was steward of the Seminary. The fighting erupted before he and his family could make good their escape. *Courtesy Massachusetts Commandery of the Military Order of the Loyal Legion of the United States and the US Army Military History Institute, Carlisle, Pennsylvania.*

were falling under our eyes by shots from an unseen foe, and the confusion became greater every moment. Filled with alarm and terror, we locked all doors and rushed to the second floor and threw open the shutters of the west window. One glance only, and a half-spent minie ball from the woods crashed into the shutter close to my aunt's ear, leaving but the thickness of paper between her and death.

"This one glance showed us that a large timothy field between the barn and the woods concealed hundreds of gray, crouching figures, stealthily advancing under its cover and picking off every cavalry man who appeared for an instant in sight.

"An officer's horse just under the window was shot and the officer fell to the ground. 'Look,' we shrieked at him, 'the field is full of Rebels.'

"'Leave the window,' he shouted in return, 'or you will be killed.'

"We needed no second warning and rushed to the cupola. Here, the whole landscape for miles around unrolled like a panorama below us. What a spectacle! It seemed as though the fields and woods had been sown with dragon's teeth, for everywhere had sprung up armed men, where about an hour ago, only grass and flowers grew."

A woman identified only as THE COLORED SERVANTMAID[4] lived on the Chambersburg Pike, nearer Gettysburg. She and her employer chose to leave their home: "Mrs. Hartzell ran along with the little girl, and I gathered up the little three year old boy and hurried after her. We got up to the high ground and stopped to look back and, oh! there was the beautifulest sight...the Union army all in line of battle. The blue coats and guns and flags stretched away a long distance as fur as we could see.

"The Rebels fired the first shell and I pointed it out to the little boy way up in the air. After a while it busted. The Rebels fired twice before our people turned loose.[5] Then we ran, and I fell. Mrs. Hartzell thought I was shot. But we got safely to the house of an old gentleman named Chriss. He and his family and the rest of us went down in the cellar where we'd be mo' safer; and how that poor old soul did pray My laws! you never heard such prayin' in your life, and I think the Lord heard his prayers and took care of us."

Thirteen year old WILLIAM HAMILTON BAYLY, his brother, and a cousin were watching from that hilltop above the Bayly home north of town:

"We perched ourselves on the topmost rail of the road fence and drank in the melody of the battle.

"But our gallery seats, although good for the whole show, began to have features of discomfort when we noticed up the road, coming over the nearest hill, great masses of troops and clouds of dust; how the first wave swelled into successive waves, gray masses with the glint of steel as the sun struck the gun barrels, filling the highway, spreading out into the fields, and still going on and on, wave after wave, billow after billow."

Unaware of Billy's whereabouts, MRS. HARRIET BAYLY and an elderly friend ventured toward the Chambersburg road for a closer look:

"As if by magic, thousands of men rose from the earth in the direction in which we had been going, in the fields to the right and left of us, and my old friend and I made a hasty retreat for home, the roar of battle adding terror to our flight.

"Presently, we ran into a large body of Rebel cavalry and my companion was halted and put under arrest; he said to me, 'You hurry home as fast as possible. I am old and they won't keep me long.' The cavalrymen parted and I passed on between them. Occasionally, some one would say, 'Madam, where are the Yankees?' Or, 'How many Yankees are there out there?' to which I replied as I hurried along, 'Go on and you will soon find out, I did not stop to count them.'

"An officer said to me, 'Madam, you are in a very dangerous position,' a statement which I did not dispute."

DANIEL SKELLY was still in his tree-top:

"Shot and shell began to fly over our heads, one of them passing dangerously near the top of the tree I was on. There was then a general stampede toward town and I quickly

Dr. S.S. Schmucker, President of Lutheran Theological Seminary, had left town with his family before the fighting started. His home and yard took quite a beating from the musket and cannon fire, and from the occupation of Confederate soldiers who also used it as a makeshift hospital. *Courtesy Abdel Ross Wertz Library Archives Lutheran Theological Seminary, Gettysburg, Pennsylvania.*

Like Dr. Schmucker and many other residents of Adams County and Gettysburg, Seminary Professor Dr. Charles Krauth took his family to safer quarters before the fighting. The Krauth house was also occupied by the Rebels and used as a hospital. *Courtesy Abdel Ross Wertz Library Archives, Lutheran Theological Seminary, Gettysburg, Pennsylvania.*

This field is among those contested on the morning of the 1st with Reynold's I Corps fighting on the right. It is part of the farm property owned by Congressman Edward McPherson. *Courtesy Massachusetts Commandery of the Military Order of the Loyal Legion of the United States and the US Army Military History Institute, Carlisle, Pennsylvania.*

slipped down from my perch and joined the retreat to the rear of our gallant men and boys. I started for town on the old railroad but crossed from it over a field to the Chambersburg Pike on the east side of Miss Carrie Shead's School and when about the middle of the field a cannon ball struck the earth about fifteen or twenty feet from me, scattering the ground somewhat about me and quickening my pace considerably."

Thirteen year old LYDIA CATHERINE ZIEGLER lived on Seminary Ridge:

"A high fence surrounding our garden fell as if it were made of paper as men with picks and crowbars pressed against it.

"I slipped from our house to the edge of the woods back of the Seminary and was enjoying the awe-inspiring scene when a bullet blew so near that I heard its whizzing sound. I ran back to the house and the family went down to the cellar, none too soon. Two shells struck the house."

As was his habit, Pennsylvania College Professor Michael Jacobs had gone to his morning classes at 8 a.m. His son, eighteen year old HENRY EYSTER JACOBS,[6] reports that at 9, Professor Jacobs was visited by a Lieutenant Bonaparte of the US Signal Corps:

"Together, they went to the upper floor of the college, where my father pointed out the general contour of the country.

"A practical botanist and geologist, my father knew every inch of the territory for miles around, and he emphasized in the interview the importance to the Union forces of holding Cemetery Hill as the key to the situation."

DANIEL SKELLY:

"When we reached the pike, there galloped past me a general and his staff, who upon reaching the top of the ridge, turned into the lane toward the Seminary building. This was General Reynolds coming onto the field and going to the Seminary where he had an interview with General Buford (then on the cupola of the Seminary), before going out where the battle was then in progress. The time was about 9 o'clock or near it, and our infantry had not come up yet.

"I was not long in reaching town and found the streets full of men, women and children, all under great excitement."

At their home in the south-central part of town,[7] TILLIE PIERCE and her family were among the first to see the arrival of Union reinforcements:

"We hastened up what we called the side street,[8] and on reaching Washington Street, again saw some of our army passing.

"First came a long line of cavalry, then wagon after wagon passed by for quite awhile. Again we sang patriotic songs as they moved along. Some of these wagons were filled with stretchers and other articles; in others we noticed soldiers reclining, who were doubtless in some way disabled."

HENRY EYSTER JACOBS:

"Soon afterward, messengers came from General Reynolds, ordering all townsfolk to abandon their homes and retire to places of safety. We, with the rest, began preparations. But no one had departed when fresh orders came, countermanding the first. Gettysburg was quite well pleased. We could hear guns booming in the distance on the west, but nobody was alarmed."

"I made haste back home[9] and up to the garret. Along the Taneytown road, a large body of Union soldiers marched. My father joined me as I watched them. They were Reynolds' Corps, making quick time to the scene of action, systematically pressing onward in the most direct line possible.

"They quit the road for the fields, throwing ahead of them a body of 'Pioneers,' who tore down the post and rail fences and made free passage that brooked not a moment's delay. As soon as they reached the ground verging the rise of Seminary Hill, one third of a mile away, they formed in line of battle. Across the hill's summit every little while a shell sailed, until above the heads of the waiting men, it puffed into a white circle and then its detonation reached our ears. But now the town everywhere and all its environs seemed to be crowded with happenings, all disjointed, yet all having some obvious relation to the immense panorama of strife which was being unrolled."

Ten year old CHARLES McCURDY had stationed himself near the Union Cavalry's camp early that morning. Now, he began a retreat:

"I ran for the road and when I reached it found my father hurrying towards me.[10] Suspecting where I had gone, as soon as it was known that there would be a battle he had hastened out to find me. Now the cannonading became stronger. Several shells burst along the Chambersburg road, only a short distance to our right, and we ran for town as fast as we could go.

"By the time we reached home,[11] the battle was in full tide. There was heavy cannonading and the musket fire was continuous, making a rattling sound like heavy wagons being rapidly driven along a stony pike, or like hail falling on a tin roof.

"The streets were full of excited people hearing for the first time the dreadful and alarming sounds of battle, scarcely realizing that the greatest drama man can stage was being played at their doors.

"Union officers were advising people who lived on Chambersburg Street, running east and west, to go into the side streets where they would be out of line of the firing, and less subject to danger."

Edward McPherson, 33, had inherited a farm a couple of miles northwest of Gettysburg from his father but his interests weren't in farming. He had read for the law under former Gettysburg resident Thaddeus Stevens, tried his hand at journalism, and wound up in politics. McPherson, had spent most of his time in Washington, D.C. since his 1858 election to Congress, but he also had helped organize and recruit soldiers in his District. McPherson, a Republican, fell victim to the growing peace movement and was defeated in the elections of 1862. At the time of the battle McPherson's farm was the residence of John Slentz, 40. His wife Eliza, and their children sought refuge elsewhere during the conflict. *Courtesy Adams County Historical Society.*

Within minutes of the engagement of troops, the fields of McPherson's farm became covered with the dead and dying. These are Union men of the 24th Michigan Infantry, part of the famous Iron Brigade, killed shortly after they took the field, surprising the Confederate brigade commanded by General James Archer. *Courtesy Massachusetts Commandery of the Military Order of the Loyal Legion of the United States and the US Army Military History Institute, Carlisle, Pennsylvania.*

Sixty-nine year old Mary Thompson was a widow. She lived alone in a small stone house on Chambersburg Pike a few hundred yards west of Henry Dustman's farm.[1] On this morning Mary Thompson, in spite of a persistent rain shower, was in her garden picking peas when the shooting started. For a while she laid down in the pea patch to avoid being hit, but eventually was able to make her way back into her house. Mrs. Thompson's daughter-in-law (also named Mary) had moved in for a brief stay so the widow could help her give birth. She and her husband James lived across the road, but at this time he was in the Union army.[2] A baby girl was born June 30th.[3] When the house and yard became overrun with wounded and dying James' wife, toddler, and *day old* baby were forced to seek shelter elsewhere, possibly at the home of Hanna and Samuel Foulk just down the hill. It wasn't long before it, too, became filled with wounded and dying of both sides. *Courtesy General Robert E. Lee Headquarters Museum*

From this second floor window Samuel and Hannah Thompson Foulk could see the fighting on the campus of the Lutheran Theological Seminary. When it erupted they hurried their five children to the cellar. The recent rains had flooded most of it, so Hannah rounded up a couple of wash tubs and put the smallest of the children in them. When she had done all she could to insure their safety she went back upstairs to see what she could see. When the worst of the morning's fighting had ended, Hannah and Samuel braved picket and sniper fire, and set out to care for the wounded and dying. *Courtesy Adams County Historical Society.*

ANNIE YOUNG lived at the Crawford House, located on Gettysburg's northeast side, along the Harrisburg Road.[12] John Crawford had left on a valuable horse which he had kept saddled for two days in preparation for hasty flight. The Crawfords, who had three sons and two daughters, shared their home with Mrs. William Smith and her spinster daughter, Jane. Annie was a visiting relative:

"Immediately, you could see the housetops covered with ladies as well as gentlemen watching the battle. Our family repaired to the attic, and from the windows we could see the movements of our troops. It was not long until we very distinctly heard the mournful whiz of the Rebel shells as they came thick and fast through the woods just beyond us. But it was not until I saw the fences on our own premises torn down and cannon placed all around us, one battery just in our back yard, that I began to realize our danger. Then we shut up the house and went into the cellar, taking with us provisions to give our men, and rags for the wounded. Though the shells fell thick around us, shattering trees, knocking bricks out of the house, etc., Cousin Jennie stood on the cellar steps cutting bread, spreading it with apple butter and giving it to our poor men who had been marched double-quick for miles without any breakfast. The poor fellows were so grateful and would say, 'Courage, ladies, we'll drive the Rebs.'"

At that moment, HARRIET BAYLY was short-cutting across a high field some three miles north of town:

"Looking north and south the road and fields were full of soldiers in gray, all pressing forward toward Gettysburg.

From this high point, the greater part of the battle field was visible, but I was too excited to stop and take in the details. I have only the general impression of the smoke and dust, and masses of gray moving like waves or heavy shadows from clouds through the green fields; and the roar of battle beyond."

Engrossed in work at his second floor photography studio,[13] CHARLES TYSON may have been one of the few who did not know what was happening. When he went outside to get change for a customer, Tyson found panic in the streets:

"All the stores were closed and no one to be seen. I gave the man his money and he disappeared. Judge Russell turned the corner just then and I asked, 'What does this mean?' He answered, 'It means that all citizens are requested to retire into their houses as quietly and as quickly as possible,' and off he went, and off I went upstairs and gathered up a few valuables and started for home. By the time I reached the opposite side of the square, I met my wife, who was coming to see what had become of me."

SARAH BROADHEAD:

"What to do or where to go, I did not know. People were running here and there, screaming that the town would be shelled. No one knew where to go or what to do. My husband advised remaining where we were, but all said we ought not to remain in our exposed position, and that it would be better to go to some part of the town farther away from the

scene of the conflict. As our neighbors had all gone away, I would not remain, but my husband said he would stay at home."

Ten year old SADIE BUSHMAN was crossing an open field toward her grandparent's house when the battle took a personal turn:

"There came a screech and a shell brushed my skirt as it went by. I staggered from the concussion of it and almost fell when I was grasped by the arm and a man said pleasantly, 'That was a close call.'

"'Come with me, and hurry,' he added in a tone so commanding that I meekly followed.

"That man was Dr. Benjamin F. Lyford, a surgeon in the Union army.

"He led me to a place in a little valley where he had established an army corps hospital and then he put me to work. Wounded and dying men were then being carried to the place by the score. I was ready to faint at the sight, but the doctor, in his commanding way, gave me more fear of him than I had for the sight of the mangled and dying men about me, and I tremblingly obeyed him.

"As I reached the hospital tent, a man with a leg shattered almost to a pulp was carried in. 'Give him a drink of water while I cut off his leg,' was the command I got. How I accomplished it, I do not know, but I stood there and assisted the surgeon all through the operation."[14]

Steadily, more and more Union troops moved up to shore the line. SAMUEL BUSHMAN:

"They went through the streets in the double-quick step, which is next thing to a run. Some of them had marched thirty-two miles. It was very hot weather, and they'd thrown away much of their clothing. Often, they had very little on but their pants, and went right into the engagement hatless, shirtless and shoeless. Some of them had welts around their bodies where they wore their belts, three inches wide of blood and gore."

Farmer, NATHANIEL LIGHTNER lived southeast of Gettysburg near Power's Hill. He and a friend had gone to town that morning, unaware of either army's presence. By the time he and William Young reached the vicinity of Seminary Ridge, they had all the information they needed. Turning to leave, they were caught in the tide:

"We had not got half-way back to town when we met other Union troops pouring along the road and through the fields, coming out every street and alley and open spaces of the town, all rushing pell-mell forward, without any apparent order, with fixed bayonets, eager-eyed, stripped, perspiring and panting in the hot sun. They cursed us for being in the way, butted us back, and would have run right over us if we had not dodged out of their way. We crawled through among them as well as we could, dodging behind posts and buildings and gaining a run of a few yards whenever we could. We got separated, and I don't know how Young got home.

"A mad rush of more troops, wagons and ambulances followed, filling up streets, orchards, fields and every place."

This photograph of Hanna Thompson Foulk was taken when she was 78, but in 1863 she was 42. Hannah lived with her husband Samuel, a blacksmith, and their children down the hill from her mother's stone house on Chambersburg Pike. Carrie Sheads, who lived nearby, and had a school for young ladies in her home, witnessed some of Hanna's heroics:

CARRIE SHEADS: "Only two families remained on the Ridge, on this road…my father's and that of Samuel Foulk, whose excellent wife gave to the defenders of our flag, all that they could furnish—both food, and bedding, and to her motherly care – -through her five children were in momentary peril, many a soldier owes his life."[4]

CATHERINE FOSTER,[5] another neighbor who lived closer into town, expressed a great deal of admiration for both Hannah and her mother, Mary Thompson.[6]

CATHERINE FOSTER: "Old Lady Thompson…never deserted her house. Her house and lot were filled with wounded and dying during the first day. She remained to care for them, and had a daughter living at the foot of the hill, who baked up a barrel of flour into bread, which she carried up the hill to the wounded, and refused to cease doing so during the three days…until her clothes were perforated with bullets and yet she would not be dissuaded, said, "In God is my trust." All her clothes and bedding except those on her person were used in dressing the wounded and her carpet in wrapping the dead for burial.[7] Catherine Foster's desire to help almost got her killed on the first day. A shell struck the roof of the porch under which she had been standing, serving water to the soldiers, completely demolishing it. She was knocked backward by the percussion, into the house, otherwise she would have been crushed. A Regimental diary keeper, scurrying past, saw the incident and recorded her has having been blown to bits by an exploding shell. *Courtesy Evelyn D. Hughes*

The Fahnestock Brothers General Merchandise Store was the largest mercantile business in town. This photograph was taken a few years after the battle. Dan Skelly purchased the place in which he was a clerk at the time of the battle. Quite visible in this photograph is the observation deck on the back of the second floor that provided an unobstructed view for miles in all directions. *Courtesy Adams County Historical Society.*

General Oliver Otis Howard, 33, was a classmate of General J.E.B. Stuart, CSA, at the US Military Academy at West Point. A deeply religious man, Howard has been described as an enthusiastic abolitionist. *Courtesy Massachusetts Commandery of the Military Order of the Loyal Legion of the United States and the US Army Military History Institute, Carlisle, Pennsylvania.*

General John Reynolds, 43, was born in nearby Lancaster, Pennsylvania. He graduated Class of '41 from the US Military Academy at West Point. There were reports that he declined an offer to succeed General John Hooker as Commander of the Army of the Potomac because he felt Washington wouldn't give him a free hand. He had not been on McPherson's Farm long until a Confederate sharpshooter on the edge of the woods killed him. *Courtesy Massachusetts Commandery of the Military Order of the Loyal Legion of the United States and the US Army Military History Institute, Carlisle, Pennsylvania.*

10 a.m. On the field: As it reaches the field, the lead division of Major General Abner Doubleday's I Corps spreads out to even the fight. In response, Hill's Confederate divisions begin to widen their flanks, hoping to envelop the Union line. Now freer, Buford moves Devin's brigade further east of the Mummasburg road to hinder two divisions of Lieutenant General Richard S. Ewell's corps, now arriving from Harrisburg, north of Gettysburg. At the same time, Buford keeps sending intelligence to the rear, some of it from local sources. He is seen taking notes from a conversation with Gettysburg resident, David McConaughy, a political firebrand who volunteered his services to U S Intelligence.

DANIEL SKELLY:

"Being anxious to see more of the battle, I concluded I would go up upon the observatory on the store building of the Fahnestock Brothers, situated on the northwest corner of Baltimore and West Middle streets, and just across the street from the court house.[15]

"The observatory was on the back of the building fronting on West Middle Street and, being a three story building, had a good view of the field where the battle was then being fought.

"At about 10 AM, I observed General Howard and his staff coming down Baltimore street from the south of the town. Upon reaching the court house they halted and made an attempt to get up into the belfry to make observations, but they were unable to accomplish this. I went down and told them that if they wished they could go up on the observatory of the store building.

"Upon reaching the housetop, the general, with his field glass, made a careful survey of the field west and northwest of the town; also of the number of roads radiating like the spokes of a wheel from the town."

SALLIE MYERS:[16]

"At 10 o'clock...I saw the first blood. A horse was led past our house covered with blood. The sight sickened me. Then three men came up the street. The middle one could barely walk. His head had been hastily bandaged and blood was visible. I grew faint with horror. I had never been able to stand the sight of blood. But I was destined to become acquainted to it.

"Then, the artillery wagons of the Union army began to come back. At first we could not tell what this meant. Soon came the order: 'Women and children to the cellars – the rebels will shell the town.'"

SARAH BARRETT KING:

"My father proposed that mother, myself and five children go to the toll gate house about a half mile from our home,[17] he would stay in the house and we could return in the evening.

"I put on my best garb, dressed the children in their most substantial clothing, thinking all the time it was serious...perhaps more so than we imagined.

"I filled my pocket with extra stockings and other articles too numerous to mention. I would be a surprising list if I could name the different articles the bosom of my dress contained.

"I filled a large basket with cases and small pieces of bread, two shawls for fear we would have to be out doors in the night."

It was the last time they would see their home until the battle ended.

10:30 a.m.: General John F. Reynolds sends a message to Shurz' division of Howard's XI Corps at Horner's Mills, urging them forward quickly. Reynolds falls soon after dispatching the messenger.

DANIEL SKELLY remained in the upper stories of Fahnestock's store:

"A scout came riding up West Middle street at a full gallop, and halting below us called up, asking if General Howard were there.

"General Howard answering in person, the scout[18] called to him that General Reynolds had been killed and that he should come onto the field immediately. Howard stopped and gave orders to one of his aides to ride back and meet his corps, which was then on the march from Emmitsburg, Maryland, ten miles from Gettysburg, and direct General Steinwehr, upon reaching the field, to occupy Cemetery Hill and fortify it. General Howard had (earlier) noticed the prominence of this hill, and, riding up to the cemetery was impressed with its commanding position. To his other aide, he gave some directions regarding the bringing up of his corps. One thing he said was that the bands should be placed at the head of the columns and play lively airs as they advanced. He then rode out to the front."

Still in her house three miles northwest of Gettysburg, AMELIA HARMON had clear views both west and east:

"Soon, we saw a strong detachment of rebels file out from the fringe of woods, a quarter of a mile distant, to meet a body of Federals advancing rapidly from the direction of the town and, in a few moments, we were witnessing the quick, sharp engagement in which General Reynolds fell.

"Hardly was this ended, when we observed a dark, sinuous line winding around the distant hills beyond the town like a huge serpent. It was Meade's army, advancing on the double to the relief of Reynolds.

"A sudden, violent commotion and uproar below made us fly in quick haste to the lower floor. There was a tumultuous pounding with fists and guns on the kitchen door and loud yells of 'Open, or we'll break down the doors,' which we proceeded to do. We drew the bolt and in poured a stream of maddened, powder-blackened blue coats,

This photograph was taken only days after the battle. It shows where soldiers of Meredith's Brigade fought and attempts to show the spot near where General Reynolds fell. *Courtesy Massachusetts Commandery of the Military Order of the Loyal Legion of the United States and the US Army Military History Institute, Carlisle, Pennsylvania.*

These are the woods in which 18-year old First Sharpshooter Benjamin Thorp (55th North Carolina Infantry, Davis Brigade of A.P. Hill's Corp) confirmed that he was hiding when he killed General John Reynolds. Thorp said he was posted a short distance off the Cashtown Road (Chambersburg Pike) in an old orchard. "There was a stone house nearby on a hill. We could see a mounted officer, believed to be a general, riding back and forth near the edge of the woods to the south of our position. He seemed to be ordering the position of artillery which by this time was coming up from beyond town.

"There was a cherry tree standing on a level piece of land where we were and I remember a log of wood resting against the trunk of the tree. The log had notches cut in it to make steps, as if those who had picked the cherries had used it to climb the tree. When we spotted the mounted officer, I climbed this tree and began interval sharpshooter fire against the artillery crew."

"Captain Henry Webb was standing beneath the cherry tree watching the action through his field glasses. Suddenly he called out to look to your right at the battery on the hill. 'There's a general, try him.' The battery and the general seemed about 400 yards beyond the skirmish firing on our front and I asked Captain Webb to judge this range for me. This was about 10:00 a.m. I guess. The Captain looked closely through the glasses again and told me the range was 1100 yards. I raised my sight to that elevation and fired. I'm too high, I told the Captain, and lowered my sight to 900 and fired again.

"'You are yet too high,' says Captain Webb, 'bring it down a triffle.'

"I then reset the sight at 800 yards, aimed carefully and fired a third time. The Captain shouted: 'Well done Thorp, you got him.' I saw the officer reel and fall from his horse into the arms of a soldier nearby. That evening we had collected a lot of prisoners and they told us that sharpshooters had got General Reynolds." *Courtesy Massachusetts Commandery of the Military Order of the Loyal Legion of the United States and the US Army Military History Institute, Carlisle, Pennsylvania.*

This hand forged iron sharpshooter's rifle, with other relics, was picked up off the field where North Carolinian troops had been fighting. It is similar to the type carried by First Sharpshooter Benjamin Thorp, 55th NC Infantry. These particular items were found near the body of a North Carolina sharpshooter inside John Rupp's Tannery. *Courtesy The J. Howard Wert Gettysburg Collection.*

This is said to be the stone house to which the body of General Reynolds was taken after he was killed. Charles Veil, General Reynolds' Orderly at Gettysburg said the rebels were not more than 60 yards from Reynolds when the General fell from his horse. He never spoke a word or moved a muscle afterwards, said Veil: "I've seen many men killed, but never seen a ball do its work so instantly. His last words had been 'Forward men, forward, for God's sake, and drive those fellows out of those woods!'" *Courtesy Massachusetts Commandery of the Military Order of the Loyal Legion of the United States and the US Army Military History Institute, Carlisle, Pennsylvania.*

who ordered us to the cellar while they dispersed to the various west windows throughout the house. From our cellar prison, we could hear the tumult above, the constant crack of rifles, the hurried orders, and outside, the mingled roar of heavy musketry, galloping horses, yelling troops, and the occasional boom of cannon to the westward.

"The suspense and agony of uncertainty were awful. We could hear the beating of our hearts above all the wild confusion. How long this lasted, I do not know. Of a sudden there came a scurrying of quick feet, a loud clatter on the stairway above, a slamming of the doors and then, for an instant...silence."

HENRY EYSTER JACOBS kept watching from his home on West Middle Street: "The Union forces on the left were weak, and the Confederates had begun to crowd in upon them from Carlisle and Harrisburg ways. Past our house came, running at the double-quick, Howard's[19] 11th Army Corps. They kept the pace without breaking ranks; but they flowed through and out into the battlefield beyond, a human tide, at millrace speed."

St. James Lutheran Church was a block east of the square on the south side of York Street at Stratton. Since early morning the Reverend Abraham Essick had been watching the fighting west and north of the town from the church cupola. *Courtesy Abdel Ross Wertz Library Archives, Lutheran Theological Seminary, Gettysburg, Pennsylvania.*

These men were killed in the fight for McPherson's Woods. From just after sunrise until about an hour before noon, the intensity of the fighting had been on an increase. However, as mid-day approached there was a leveling off – a lull – as both sides attempted to determine each others strength and regroup.

General Oliver Howard took over command of the field with the death of General Reynolds. General Lee had not been pleased with General Heth's premature engagement of the enemy, and he was riding steadily toward the field to determine the situation for himself. *Courtesy Massachusetts Commandery of the Military Order of the Loyal Legion of the United States and the US Army Military History Institute, Carlisle, Pennsylvania.*

The Reverend Abraham Essick stayed at his perch inside the St. James' cupola several hours longer than a church member who climbed up with him. The bullets were dangerously close. Few people realized just how brave, or how fool-hardy, Reverend Essick was until years later. When the old church was being torn down, dozens of bullets were found to be still embedded in the wood of the cupola. *Courtesy Abdel Ross Wertz Library Archives, Lutheran Theological Seminary, Gettysburg, Pennsylvania.*

Peter Thorn had come to America from Germany. Elizabeth and her parents had also come here from Germany. At about the time Peter got the job as care-taker of the Evergreen Cemetery, eight years ago, he and Elizabeth were married. Now, Peter was away with his regiment; and Elizabeth, six months pregnant, was responsible for the care of her elderly parents who spoke little English, and her three small children: Fred, George, and John.

As fast as she could bake bread this morning, soldiers rushing past and through the cemetery into battle, took it out of her hands. She and her parents and her sons also brought all of the tin cups and tumblers outside, sat them near the pump, and kept them filled for the thirsty soldiers.

As the fighting drew closer, she scurried all to the cellar, but she came back upstairs. She overheard an officer telling another that they were killing their own troops because they didn't know the country, and badly needed a guide. After much discussion, the persuasive Mrs. Thorn convinced the officer she could go with him and show him the main roads. Walking on the "safe side of the horse" for protection she gave the officer a quick tour—braving the whizzing bullets and exploding shells.

ELIZABETH THORN: "I told my father and mother what I had done and they were afraid I would get into trouble and I sat with them awhile to quiet them. I could not remain still long as I wanted to know what was going on. So I went upstairs. On the steps I tramped in plaster and looking up I saw where a shell had entered the room. It was one of the few shells fired from Benner's Hill on that day and had bursted outside." *Courtesy Eileen F. Conklin, Women at Gettysburg, Thomas Publications.*

While waiting to move up, some opportunistic Union soldiers stopped at the Globe Inn's bar to fill their canteens with some alcoholic fortification. An officer caught them and ordered the shop closed, leaving JOHN WILLS free to wander.

He first walked up an alley toward the battle, but "whizzing bullets" drove him back to the Washington Hotel at the corner of Carlisle Street and the Railroad:

"While standing there, wounded soldiers were coming in on the railroad track. The first wounded man who came limping on one foot had the whole heel end of one of his shoes shot off and the blood was running out of the shoe. Now there were women at every window of the hotel looking out west in the direction of the fight. When they saw this wounded soldier, they all commenced crying. The second wounded man, a very tall man, came along with his face turned up. He was squirting streams of blood from his throat. The women yet crying when he turned his face toward them, he said: 'Ladies, don't cry. We are doing this to save you people,' when they commenced crying with screams at the height of their voices."

CHARLES TYSON, now reunited with his wife, MARIA, had just reached their home at 216 Chambersburg Street when they were told to turn around and leave:[20]

"The cannonading was then going on in good earnest and the people living on Chambersburg Street were advised to go farther up town. We locked up the house and I put the trunk on a wheelbarrow and started. Going a short distance, I met our neighbor, Mr. Boyer,[21] who had a spring wagon, covered, and in it, his mother-in-law, who sat upon some trunks. He very kindly permitted me to put my trunk on, which I did, and tumbled my barrow over into Mr. Chritzman's yard. We all went up on Baltimore Street and remained there...In the meantime, the churches were being filled with wounded men and the pavements were lined with those slightly wounded. Several blocks of captured Rebels passed out Baltimore Street and I concluded to go down home and bring up a basket of fresh bread to distribute to the soldiers – my wife had baked a large quantity the day before or that morning – but when I got nearly down to the square I met one of our officers riding up the street, warning all women, children and non-combatants to leave the town, as General Lee intended to shell it.

"This caused quite a stir, and the streets were full of people hurrying to and fro preparing to leave. Suffice it to say, I did not go for the bread, but I did go for my wife."[22]

Charles Boyer and his father William had a grocery store on the northeast corner of the square. It was looted, as were most of the stores in town that still had anything of value in them. *Courtesy Adams County Historical Society.*

Catherine Snyder's late husband, Conrad, had owned the Wagon Hotel located south of town at the foot of Cemetery Hill where the Emmitsburg Road joins Baltimore Street. The Snyder home was across Baltimore Street and directly in the path of the Union Army as it continued to rush to battle. By late afternoon wounded began to pour back into town, seeking shelter in the houses. Catherine thought her younger children would be safer further out of town. She sent them out to visit "Aunt Susie Benner" across Rock Creek.

As eighteen year old Mary carefully led the smaller children through a field and across a zig-zag fence, they heard something hissing. At first, little Rosa later recalled, she thought it was a snake until a cannonball whizzed through the foliage and bounced at their feet without exploding. Rosa lost a shoe but was so frightened that she would be left behind that she didn't say anything about it. The children made it safely to the farm of Christian and Susan Benner, but remained there only one day. They moved on from farm to farm trying to stay ahead of the battle.

Meanwhile, back at their home, a shell penetrated the outside wall of the Snyder house. It shattered a stove. A table and chair in the front room were also heavily damaged. Fortunately, Mrs. Snyder and 16-year old Lucinda, who had decided to remain home, were in the cellar. There they remained for the duration of the battle – not really knowing for a week whether the other children were alive or dead. *Courtesy Adams County Historical Society.*

SARAH BROADHEAD, who lived directly opposite the Tysons, was in the same crowd: "As we passed up the street we met wounded men coming in from the field. When we saw them, we, for the first time, began to realize our fearful situation and anxiously to ask, 'Will our army be whipped?' Some said there was no danger of that yet, and pointed to Confederate prisoners who began to be sent through our streets to the rear. Such a dirty, filthy set, no one ever saw. They were dressed in all kinds of clothes, of all kinds and no kind of cuts. Some were barefooted and a few wounded. Though our enemies, I pitied them. I, with others, was sitting at the doorstep bathing the wounds of some of our brave soldiers, and became so much excited as the artillery galloped through the town, and the infantry hurried out to reinforce those fighting, that for a time we forgot our fears and our danger. All was bustle and confusion.

DANIEL SKELLY left the Fahnestock store and set out toward the town square, one block north:
"We went down Carlisle Street to the McCurdy warehouse, just below the railroad, where the wounded were being brought in from the First Corps, then engaged west of the town.

"No provision had yet been made for their care in the town and they were laid on the floor. We remained there quite awhile, giving them water and doing what we could for their relief.

"As the afternoon wore away, the churches and warehouses on Chambersburg, Carlisle and York streets nearest the line of battle were filled with wounded. Then the court house as well as the Catholic, Presbyterian and Reformed churches and the school house in High Street received the injured soldiers, until those places had reached their capacity, when private homes were utilized, citizens volunteering to take them in and care for them.

"In company with a young lady, Miss Julia Culp, a neighbor (she had a brother in the Confederate Army who was killed on Culp's Hill and a brother in the Union Army, who survived the war), I went into the court house with buckets of water and passed from one to another of the wounded, relieving them as best we could under the circumstances. Some of them were so frightfully wounded that a lady could not go near them. These I

Charles McCurdy, whose family lived a few doors west of the square on Chambersburg Street, scurried down Baltimore Street, shown here, en route Grandmother McCurdy's home. She lived a few doors north of the intersection where South Street meets Baltimore Street. *Courtesy Adams County Historical Society.*

gave water to, while she cared for those who were not so severely wounded. Quite a number of our townspeople were there doing everything they could in the relief work as the wounded were carried in."

CHARLES McCURDY's family decided to move from their home west of the square for a safer place further south:
"Our Grandmother McCurdy lived on Baltimore Street, and Mother hastily gathered together the few things she thought might be needed, and after carefully locking up the house the little procession traversed the four blocks that led to Grandmother's house. Soon after we got there, wounded men still able to walk began to go by on their way to Cemetery Hill at the southern end of the town, which had been selected as a rallying point in view of a possible repulse. Soon batches of prisoners appeared on their dreary way to the same goal. These were followed by a larger number in charge of an officer who seemed to be unaware of the selection of Cemetery Hill, and did not know what disposition to make of them. An old gentleman who lived next door suggested that they be put in the jail yard near by. I heard the officer say to him: 'Old man, we don't put prisoners of war in jail.'

"Not long after our arrival we heard from passing soldiers that General Reynolds, who had just reached the field hurrying on in advance of his corps, had instantly been killed and that his body had been brought into town. General Reynolds was related to my grandmother through the marriage of her brother to a sister of Robert Fulton, and on learning of his death, although she was ninety years old, she wanted to be taken where he lay, thinking that in some way she might minister to him. But Father persuaded her that it was not possible and that even if it were, nothing could be done.

"During the cannonading, she was taken to the cellar, a strip of carpet laid on the floor and a rocking chair provided, in which she sat in state until the danger passed."
TILLIE PIERCE:
"Our neighbor, Mrs. Schriver,[23] called at the house and said she would leave the town and go to her father's,[24] who lived on the Taneytown road at the eastern slope of the Round Top.

"Mr. Schriver, her husband, was then serving in the Union army, so that under all the circumstances at this time surrounding her, Mrs. Schriver did not feel safe in the house.

"As the battle had commenced and was still progressing at the west of the town, and was not very far off, she thought it safer for herself and two children to go to her parents, who lived about three miles to the south. She required that I be permitted to accompany her, and as it was regarded a safer place for me than to remain in town, my parents readily consented that I should go.

"The only preparation I made for the departure was to carry my best clothes down to the cellar, so that they might be safe when I returned; never thinking of taking any along, nor how long I would stay."

It was to be a fateful decision.

2 p.m. On the field: One division of the Union XI corps is now on Cemetery Hill. The two other divisions move into the fields north and west of the town where Buford had posted Devin's brigade against the advance of Ewell's corps.

As XI corps relieves the cavalry, Major General Robert Rode's Confederate division emerges from the woods on Oak Ridge, preparing to ram through a gap between the Union I and XI corps. Doubleday shifts three brigades to his right flank, and the Rebels are pushed back with heavy casualties.

General Lee reaches the field at about noon. He sees the Union I corps starting to fall back toward the town. And he sees frenzied activity at the Federal position on Cemetery Hill.

He orders his soldiers forward.

AMELIA HARMON:

"A swish like the mowing of grass on the front lawn, then a dense shadow darkened the low grated cellar windows. It is the sound and shadow of hundreds of marching feet. We

By the time General Robert E. Lee arrived on Seminary Ridge his troops had begun to push the Union backward through Gettysburg. Lee liked this high ground on which the widow Thompson's house stood. Although it was small, and there were wounded all about, he decided to make the Thompson house his headquarters. Lee is said to have wanted the widow Thompson out of there, and offered to rent her a house elsewhere. She refused to leave, saying there was too much work to be done. Mrs. Thompson cooked the General and some of his staff dinner that evening. The General's staff camped in a nearby orchard. Professor Michael Jacobs later wrote that Mrs. Thompson thought General Lee behaved gentlemanly, but complained bitterly of the robbery and general destruction of her goods by some of his attendants. *Courtesy General Lee Headquarters Museum, Gettysburg, Pennsylvania.*

can see them to the knees only, but the uniforms are the Confederate gray. Now we understand the scurrying of feet overhead. Our soldiers have been defeated, have been driven back, have retreated, have left the house, and have left us to our fate.

"We rushed up the cellar steps to the kitchen. The barn was in flames and cast a lurid glare through the window. The house was filled with Rebels and they were deliberately firing it. They had taken down a file of newspapers for kindling, piled on books, rags and furniture, applied matches to ignite the pile and, already a tiny flame was curling upward. We both jumped on the fire in hopes of extinguishing it, and plead with them in pity to spare our home. But there was no pity in those determined faces. They were 'Louisiana Tigers,' they boasted, and tigers indeed they were.

"We fled from our burning house only to encounter worse horrors. The first Rebel line of battle had passed our house and were now engaged in a hot skirmish in the gorge of Willoughby's Run. The second line was being advanced just abreast the barn, and at that moment, was being hotly attacked by the Union troops with shot and shell.

"We were between the lines! To go toward town would be to walk into the jaws of death. Only one way was open...through the ranks of the whole Confederate Army to safety in its rear.

"Bullets whistled past our ears, shells burst and scattered their deadly contents around us. On we hurried...wounded men falling all around us, the line moving forward as they fired, it seemed with deadly precision, past what seemed miles of artillery with horses galloping like mad toward the town. We were objects of wonder and amazement, that was certain, but few took time to listen to our story, and none believed it. All kept hurrying us to the rear. 'Go on, go on,' they shouted, 'out of reach of grape and canister.'"

Starting from her home at 301 Baltimore Street, TILLIE PIERCE headed south, desperate to get herself, Mrs. Schriver and her two children out of the line of fire:

"We started on foot; the battle still going on. We proceeded out Baltimore Street and entered the Evergreen Cemetery. This was our easiest and most direct route, as it would bring us to the Taneytown road a little further on.

"As we were passing along the Cemetery hill, our men were already planting cannon. They told us to hurry as fast as possible, that we were in great danger of being shot by the Rebels, whom they expected would shell toward us at any moment. We fairly ran to get out of this new danger.

"We soon reached the Taneytown road, and while traveling along, were overtaken by an ambulance wagon in which was the body of a dead soldier. Some of the men told us that it was the body of General Reynolds..."

JENNIE S. CROLL:
"We were watching the coming in of Archer's brigade[25] as prisoners when Mrs. C., wife of the cashier of the bank,[26] asked us into her house. We stood for some time at one of her windows watching the battle, and had just withdrawn when a shell came in the window and blew out in the room. Had it exploded, some of us would certainly have been killed. We felt thankful that all 'rebel' shells were not perfect in construction. That same morning we found a number of bullets in the room where the baby was sleeping.

"Word was sent to the citizens to go to their cellars, as the enemy were driving our men and the fighting would probably be house to house on our streets. Mrs. C. proposed that we should go to the vault of the bank,[27] which we did; 19 women and children, two dogs and a cat. While in those close quarters, a message came that Lieutenant Hunt of the 5th Maine Battery, was at the door wounded. He was a brother of Mrs. C, who ordered him to be taken to the cellar, and there, lying on a piano box, Dr. H. extracted the bullet from his leg and cared for his wound."[28]

T. Duncan Carson, 30, was a cashier at the Bank of Gettysburg and had helped take assets out of town. His wife Mary, 30, was caring for their 5 year old son Robert and a baby at the time. *Courtesy Adams County Historical Society.*

Union General Francis Channing Barlow began his Civil War service as a private, but in-the-field promotions came quick. That is Barlow leaning against a tree. Others in the picture are 2nd Corps Commander Winfield Hancock, and his brigade commander General John Gibbon. Also pictured is Major General David Birney, who was with General Daniel Sickles' 3rd Corps at the Battle of Gettysburg. Barlow, the son of a minister and a Harvard graduate, was sometimes referred to as "the boy general" by his troops. *Courtesy Massachusetts Commandery of the Military Order of the Loyal Legion of the United States and the US Army Military History Institute, Carlisle, Pennsylvania.*

General John B. Gordon, CSA, 31, of Georgia, came to the relief of the outnumbered General Doles as Barlow's division pushed Doles' men off a knoll near the Adams County Alms House. Gordon's troops struck hard and when Barlow's division began to collapse, General Schimmelfennig's troops also began to fall back. Soon the entire Union line was running away, toward Gettysburg. *Courtesy Americana Image Gallery, Gettysburg, Pennsylvania.*

2:30 p.m. On the field: Union forces are now under heavy pressure from three directions.

Jubal Early's division has reached high ground near the County Alms House and is attacking from the NE against Howard's right flank, causing it to collapse and throw XI corps into a general retreat through the town. Early pursues in the jammed-up streets, capturing hundreds of Union soldiers.

To the west, A. P. Hill keeps pushing the Federal I corps off Seminary Ridge while Rode's pressure from the north threatens to cut them off.

From a letter written to his mother by the seriously wounded BRIGADIER GENERAL FRANCIS C. BARLOW, USA, describing what happened to his unit at this point:[29]
"A battery of the 4th US Artillery being sent to me, the enemy soon opened on us with his artillery. His number of guns was superior to mine and though another battery was promised me, I never got it. The Captain of my battery[30] had one leg carried away, one gun disabled, and several horses killed, but still kept in position.[31] I had an admirable position. The country was an open one for a long distance around and could be swept by our artillery. We could see their infantry make various attacks upon the other parts of the lines, or rather feel the lines. Finally, the 1st Corps, the 3rd Division of the 11th Corps, and my Division were attacked simultaneously by the enemy's infantry. A force came up against our front in line of battle with supports in the rear. We ought to have held the place easily, for I had my entire force at the very point where the attack was made, but the enemy's skirmishers had hardly attacked us before my men began to run. No fight at all was made.

"Finding that they were going, I started to get ahead of them to try to rally them and form another line in the rear. Before I could turn my horse, I was shot in the left side about half way between the arm pit and the head of the thigh bone. I dismounted and tried to walk off the field. Everybody was then running to the rear and the enemy were approaching rapidly. One man took hold of one shoulder and another on the other side to help me. One of them was soon shot and fell. I then got a spent ball in my back which has made quite a bruise. Soon I got too faint to go any further and lay down. I lay in the midst of the fire some five minutes as the enemy were firing at our running men. I did not expect to get out alive. A ball went through my hat as I lay on the ground and another just grazed the forefinger of my right hand.

"Finally, the enemy came up and were very kind."

Thirty-one year old GENERAL JOHN B. GORDON, C.S.A.:
"I discovered him[32] lying on his back with the July sun pouring its rays into his pale face. He was surrounded by Union dead and his own life seemed to be rapidly ebbing out. I dismounted, gave him water, and asked the nature of his wounds. The bullet had entered his body in front and passed out near the spinal cord, paralyzing him in the legs and arms. Neither of us had the remotest thought that he could possible survive for many hours.

"He asked me to destroy letters from his wife (after reading one for him). He asked that I see Mrs. Barlow after the war and to tell her or our meeting on the field and of his thoughts of her. I learned Mrs. Barlow was with the Union army and near the battlefield. When it is remembered how closely Mrs. Gordon followed me, I will not be difficult to realize that my sympathies were especially stirred by the announcement that his wife was so near. I summoned several soldiers who were looking after the wounded and directed them to put Barlow in the shade."
GENERAL BARLOW:
"Major Pitzera, staff officer of General Early, had me carried by some men into the woods and placed on a bed of leaves. They put some water by me and then went on to the front again.

"During this time, the whole of our line had been driven back, both the 1st Corps and the 11th. The 3rd Division of this corps (Schurz') went at the same time and in

Elias Sheads' oldest daughter, Miss Carrie, ran The Oak Ridge Seminary, a school for young ladies, from her home. When the Union retreat began soldiers fled Seminary Ridge looking for any place to hide and avoid capture. *Courtesy Adams County Historical Society.*

the same way that we did. The 2nd Division (Steinwehr's) was in reserve and I don't know what became of that except that it also was routed.

"I lay in the woods some time until the shells began to come in and then some of my own men who were prisoners carried me in a blanket to a house further off. I was in considerable pain and bleeding a good deal. My trousers and vest and both shirts were saturated with blood."

SARAH BROADHEAD:
"No one can imagine in what extreme fright we were when our men began to retreat. A citizen galloped up to the door in which we were sitting and called out, 'For God's sake go in the house! The Rebels are in the other end of town, and all will be killed!' We quickly ran in, and the cannonading coming nearer and becoming heavier, we went to the cellar, and in a few minutes the town was full of the filthy Rebels."

Townspeople watched the retreating mob from windows and porches. Cannon shot burst, and musket fire rattled behind the fleeing troops. Smoke and dust rising from the streets made a choking, nearly impenetrable screen.
On south Baltimore Street, ANNA GARLACH:
"The street seemed blocked. In front of our house the crowd was so great that I believe I could have walked across the street on the heads of the soldiers.

"The soldiers in retreat called to us, 'Go to the cellar, go to the cellar.'"
ALBERTUS McCREARY did more than watch as the tide of Blue swept past his parent's house on the southwest corner of Baltimore and High streets:
"...Union soldiers running and pushing each other, sweaty and black from powder and dust. They called to us for water. We got great buckets of water and tin dippers and supplied them as fast as we could from the porch at the side of the house off the main street.[33]

"We were so busy, and the noise and confusion were so great that we did not notice how close the fighting was until, about half a block away, we saw hand to hand conflicts. It was a complete rout for the Union soldiers.

"We kept right on distributing water until an officer rode his horse up on the pavement among the soldiers and said, 'All you good people go down in your cellars or you will all be killed.' We obeyed him at once. Several neighboring families had sought our house, for it was large and well built, with strong walls of stone.

"Hardly were we all down in the cellar, when we heard fighting all around the house, over the porch where a few moments before we had been handing out water, and

Col. Charles Wheelock, 97th NY Volunteers, burst through the door of the Sheads' home and headed straight for the basement with a handful of Rebels in hot pursuit. The Rebels stopped just inside to begin arresting other Union soldiers who had sought refuge inside the house. During the commotion Wheelock managed to slip his sword to Miss Carrie so that he would not have to surrender it when taken prisoner. She hid it in the folds of her dress. Later Wheelock escaped and came back for the sword. *Courtesy Massachusetts Commandery of the Military Order of the Loyal Legion of the United States and the US Army Military History Institute, Carlisle, Pennsylvania.*

General Alexander Schimmelfennig, 39, came to the United States from Prussia in 1853. He had been an engineer in the Prussian army. Now, as with many other immigrants from Prussia, he was leading troops in the American Civil War. Schimmelfennig's regiment was in the XI Corps, under General Howard's command. The positions of Schimmelfennig and Brig. Gen. Francis Barlow, just to the north of town near the Alms House, collapsed under a heavy onslaught by the Confederates. *Courtesy Massachusetts Commandery of the Military Order of the Loyal Legion of the United States and the US Army Military History Institute, Carlisle, Pennsylvania.*

over the cellar doors in the pavement. I heard a voice say, 'Shoot that fellow going over the fence.' The order was obeyed and a shot rang out just by the cellar window. There were several small windows in the walls, and their light cast shadows on the opposite wall of men rushing back and forth; those shadows filled all of us with horror. There was more and more shooting, until the sound was one continuous racket. I peeped out of one of the windows just in time to see a cannon unlimbered and fired down the street. What a noise it made, and how the dust did fly!"

ANNA GARLACH's mother, CATHERINE, and a Union General were destined to become legends in those chaotic few hours:[34]

"General Schimmelfennig[35] was mounted and in retreat on Washington Street. At that time, there was an alley running from Washington Street which ended at the barn of my father, Henry Garlach, and connected with another alley north to Breckenridge Street, but had then no outlet south. He turned down this alley and found that his only outlet in either direction was toward the Confederates.

"The Rebels were at his heels and when he reached our barn his horse was shot from under him. He jumped over the alley fence into our yard and ran toward Baltimore Street, but the rebels were in possession of that street and he realized that he must be captured.

"There was an old water course in our yard at the time, and for 12 feet from the street it was covered with a wooden culvert and General Schimmelfennig hurriedly crawled out of sight under this culvert."

Most civilians who had public responsibility got to a safe distance to avoid capture. But a railroad telegrapher, thought to have been 27 year old Samantha French Brenisholtz, is reported to have dismantled her telegraph machine and moved it to Cemetery Hill, where she showed Union soldiers how to "cut it in" to the lines. She is reported to have kept sending messages for Union officers during a large part of the battle in spite of being in such an exposed position.[36]

Back at the corner of West Middle and Washington Streets, prudence dictated that he abandon his upper story view, so HENRY EYSTER JACOBS and his family watched the rest of the day's action through a small cellar window:

"In the rear of the fleeing, routed (Union) troops, the artillery lingered, turning now and then to fire a deterring shot and, as best it might, protect the despairing retreat. But the Confederates kept at their very backs. As I stared from the window, I saw a Union soldier running, his breath coming in gasps, a group of Confederates almost upon him. He was in full flight, not turning or even thinking of resistance. But he was not surrendering, either. 'Shoot him, shoot him,' yelled a pursuer. A rifle cracked and the fugitive fell dead at our door. One after another fell that way in the grim chase from the Carlisle road."

Ten year old CHARLES McCURDY watched the last of the panicky blue-clad soldiers stampede southward past his Grandmother's house on Baltimore Street to take refuge on Cemetery Hill:

"Soon they passed and individual Confederate soldiers appeared, but strange to say there was no organized pursuit. These soldiers began searching the houses for Union soldiers whom they thought might be hiding within. A posse stopped before the gate behind which my mother was standing and inquired: 'Madam, are there any Yankee soldiers in your cellar?'

"'No,' she replied, 'there are no soldiers in my house.' Two were concealed in my grandmother's, and she knew it, but it was not her house."

ALBERTUS McCREARY:

"Our interest in what was going on was so great that we could not resist trying to look out again; but we took the precaution this time to put up a board so that we could look beneath, and were not so much exposed. We could see one house on a side street that seemed to be full of sharpshooters; we saw the flash and puff of smoke every time one fired. They were evidently doing so much harm to the batteries on Cemetery Hill that a gun was trained on this house, and in a very few moments it was filled full of holes, and the occupants were all driven out."

HENRY EYSTER JACOBS:

"There came a lull in the stream of runners and their hunters, then a thunderous pounding fell upon our door of fists and boots. I ran upstairs. One of our own (Pa.) Bucktails named Burlingame,[37] wounded in the leg, was there supported by a group of his comrades who would not desert him, and demanded shelter. We took him in, with two of the others, who said they would stay with him."

SAMUEL BUSHMAN:

"Many Union soldiers took refuge in the houses.[38] They were hidden all over town. They came in completely worn out and left their guns and knapsacks by the dining room fireplace. Mother had just time to throw the knapsacks out of sight back of the fire board, and to lay the guns down and push them under the lounge with her foot when there was a rap at the door. She opened it, and on the steps stood some Rebels who asked, 'Are there any Yankees here?'

"'Do you see any?' she said.

"That didn't satisfy them, and they searched the house, upstairs and down, but they didn't happen to go to the cellar. We gave the fugitives some blankets to sleep on. One of them had been wounded in the face by a piece of shell. He ought to have gone right to the hospital, but he had such a horror of falling into the clutches of the Rebels that he wouldn't leave the house. Mother put hot water and camphor on the wound to relieve the inflammation, and when her supply of camphor ran out, she grated potato and used it with cold water from the well. But the treatment wasn't effective and when the fellow did get to the hospital it was too late, and he died."

GATES FAHNESTOCK:

"Some 12 or 13 came into our house.[39] Mother told them to go wherever they wished in the house. Some went to closets, under beds, in the cellar room, the potato bin – one went and covered himself with potatoes – some went to the attic among boxes with stored winter clothing.

"The Confederates came searching the houses, and mother allowed them to come, but always asked for an officer, which was granted. General Early had come and occupied for awhile part of a house opposite."

The people along Chambersburg Street were learning that their houses were not sanctuary. Desperate men, wounded and dying, overwhelmed them. JENNIE S. CROLL:

"Wounded men were brought into our houses and laid side by side in our halls and first-story rooms until every available place was taken up and almost every house was a hospital. In many cases, carpets were so saturated with blood as to be unfit for further use, walls were blood-stained, as well as books that were used for pillows.

"The first public building that was opened for hospital purposes was the Lutheran Church on Chambersburg Street, generally known as the College Church.

"Forty men were laid in the lecture room and 100 in the church proper, beds being improvised by laying boards on top of the pews. Here they were laid, their army blankets, when they had them, between their racked bodies and the boards, and sometimes knapsacks for pillows."

JENNIE McCREARY was seventeen:[40]

"I went over to the Weaver's to help them roll bandages. The house was soon filled and eventually I overcame my sick, queasy feeling and could look at wounds, bathe them, bind them without feeling sick and nervous. Tears came only once when the first soldier came into the house. He'd walked from the field almost exhausted, threw himself into a chair, looked up at us girls and said, 'Oh, girls. I have as good a home as you. If I were only there.' And then he fainted."

John Scott, 51, his wife Martha McAllister Scott, 43, and their five children lived in these adjacent houses with Martha's 41 year old sister, Mary McAllister, on Chambersburg Street, across the street from the Christ Lutheran Church. John Scott, and the Scott's oldest son Hugh, 17, operated the telegraph, but at the first sign of the Confederates they hid their equipment and left town. Mary and her sister Martha remained in town with the other children. Mary McAllister had a small store where she sold hams, bacon, other meat products and eggs that she purchased from nearby farms. *Courtesy Adams County Historical Society.*

Christ Lutheran Church on Chambersburg Street was sometimes called the "college church" because so many students attended services there. Dr. Henry L. Baugher, President of Pennsylvania College, was also serving as its minister in 1863. *Courtesy Adams County Historical Society.*

Col. Henry A. Morrow was an ex-patriate Virginian who commanded the 24th Michigan Regiment. He and his men inflicted the heaviest casualties of the battle on 20-year old Col. Harry K. Burgwyn's 26th North Carolina Regiment in McPherson's Woods before being forced to retreat into the town. *Courtesy Massachusetts Commandery of the Military Order of the Loyal Legion of the United States and the US Army Military History Institute, Carlisle, Pennsylvania.*

Forty-one year old MARY McALLISTER operated a small store at her home on Chambersburg Street, directly across the street from Christ Lutheran Church:[41]

"Mrs. Weikert[42] lived near us and she said, 'Let's go to the church.[43] We can be of use there.' Martha[44] had torn up sheets for bandages and I gathered up sheets and water and Mrs. Weikert and I went to the church and we went to work.

"They carried the wounded in there as fast as they could. We took the cushions off the seats and some officers came in and said 'Lay them in the aisles.' Then we did all we could for the wounded men.

"After a while they carried in an awfully wounded one. He was a fine officer. They did not know who he was. A doctor said to me 'Go and bring some wine or whiskey or some stimulant!' When I got outside, I thought of Mr. Guyer[45] near the church.

"'Well,' I said, 'Mr. Guyer, can you give me some wine?'

"He said, 'The rebels will be in here if you begin to carry that out.'"

"'I must have it,' I said. 'Give me some.'

"I put it under my apron and went over to the church with it. They poured some of it into the officer's mouth. I never knew who he was, but he died.

"Well, I went to doing what they told me to do, wetting cloths and putting them on the wounds and helping. Every pew was full; some sitting, some lying, some leaning on others. They cut off the legs and arms and threw them out of the windows.

"There was a boy with seven of his fingers near off. He said, 'Lady, would you do something for me?'

"The surgeon came along and he said, 'What is the use doing anything for them?' and he just took his knife and cut off the fingers and they dropped down. Well, I was so sorry.

"A man sat in a pew and he was young and (pale). He said, 'Lady, come here. Do you know if there is a Mason in town?'

"I said, 'Yes, there is one Harper, a printer, but he has left town and I know no other.'[46]

"'Oh,' he said, 'if you could only get to him.' But I was too scared. The church was full and just then there was a shell struck the roof and they got scared, and I was scared. I wanted to go home.

"I looked around for Mrs. Weikert. They said 'They are going to shell the church!' Well, they begged me not to go, but I went out and there the high church steps were full of wounded men and they begged me not to try to cross the street. Our men were retreating up the street. Many wounded ones who could walk carried the worst wounded ones on their backs. I said, 'Oh, I want to go home.' So they let me go at last. I struggled through the wounded and the dead and forgot the horror in the fright.

"I was as high up[47] as Buehler's drug store before I got across the street and got home.

"When I got to the door, it was standing open and the step was covered with blood. 'Oh,' I thought, 'all are dead!' and I ran through. I could hardly get through, for the dining room was full of soldiers, some lying, some standing. Some ran in to get out of the shooting. The Rebels were sending grapeshot down the street and everyone who was on the street had to get into the houses or be killed and that is the way some of these Union men got into our house.

"Colonel Morrow of the 24th Michigan, was in our house. I saw the blood on his face for he had been cut on the head with a sabre, and I said: 'Can I do anything for you?'

"He said, 'Yes, if you would just wash this handkerchief out.'

"I rushed out to get water and I washed it out and laid it on his head.

"There was a young Irishman in there, too. His name was Dennis Burke Dailey, 2nd Wisconsin. He was so mad when he found what a trap they were in. He leaned out of the kitchen window and saw the bayonets of the Rebels bristling in the alley and in the garden. I said, 'There is no escape there.' I opened the kitchen door and they were tearing the fence down with their bayonets. This young Irishman says, 'I am not going to be taken prisoner, Colonel!' And he says to me, 'Where can I hide?'

"I said, 'I don't know, but you can go upstairs.'

"'No,' he said, 'but I will go up the chimney.'

"'You will not,' said the Colonel. 'You must not endanger this family.'

"So he came back. He was so mad he gritted his teeth. Then he says to me, 'Take this sword and keep it at all hazards. This is General Archer's[48] sword. He surrendered it to me. I will come back for it.'

"I ran to the kitchen, got some wood and threw some sticks on top of it. The Iron Brigade was the one that captured General Archer and made him give up his sword. This Dailey was the only officer and General Archer would not give it to a private. So Dailey stepped up and said, 'I am next in command!' and he took the sword.[49]

"Colonel Morrow says to me 'Take my diary. I do not want them to get it.' I did not know where to put it, so I opened my dress and put it in my dress. He said, 'That's the place, they will not get it there.'

"Then all those wounded men crowded around and gave me their addresses. Then this Irishman, he belonged to the 2nd Wisconsin, said, 'Here is my pocketbook, I wish you would keep it.' Afterward, I did not remember what I did with it, but what I did was to pull the little red cupboard away and put it back of that. In the meantime, Martha had gone upstairs and brought a coat of John's. She said, 'Here, Colonel, put this coat on.' But he would not take the coat she brought him. He would not stoop to disguise himself and he gave the others orders that they were to give their right names when they were taken prisoners. So he kept his officer's coat and epaulettes. Then, there came a pounding on the door. Colonel Morrow said, 'You must open the door. They know we are in here and they will break it.' By this time, the Rebels came in and they said, 'Oh, here is a bird!' He was such a fine looking man. But they just demanded his sword. He had a beautiful sword.

"They paroled some. There was a young man there from Michigan, the same as Colonel Morrow. He said, 'Do write to my mother. I am slightly wounded, but I guess they will take me prisoner.'

"That Irishman [Dennis Burke Dailey], he was so stubborn. He was a Major then. He stood back so very solemn. Then they took him prisoner. He asked them to let him come back into the house. Then he said to us, 'Give me a piece of bread.'

"Martha said, 'I have just one piece and that is not good.'

"He said, 'It don't make any difference. I must have it. I have not had anything to eat for 24 hours.' Then the Rebels took him.

"Then the Rebels said, 'Those that are not able to walk, we will not take; we will parole them.' But they said to these wounded men, 'Now if you ever get to fight you know what we will do.' But the wounded ones did not pay much attention to that. Then they took away as prisoners all that could walk. The next thing then was to get these wounded fixed.

"Five surgeons came in and one of them said, 'Now if you had anything like a red flag, it would be a great protection to your house, because it would be considered a hospital, and they would have respect.' Well, Martha thought of a red shawl she had. She got it and I got the broom and we hoisted the front window and were just fixing it on the broom when six or seven Rebels came riding up the street firing and yelling. Well, we did not know what we were doing. They halted at the church to say something to the wounded men on the high church steps who had gathered themselves out of range of the firing, and in a few minutes, a pistol went off and we saw they had shot a man. He was down then and when we looked, he was lying with his head toward us on the pavement. And those men on the steps said, 'Shame! Shame! That was a Chaplain!'[50]

"Those on horseback said, 'He was going to shoot.'

"But the wounded men said, 'He was not armed.'

"They had a good many words and then they rode off again, shooting as they had come."

The McLean's were Gettysburg's most prominent father and son lawyers. Moses McLean had been a long time leader in the Adams County Democratic Party. William, his first born, was educated at Harvard. Afterwards, he returned home to practice law. In 1855 William married Fannie Riggin of Maryland, and started a family. He named his first daughter Hannah Mary, after his mother. Moses and Hannah, along with three daughters and two other sons, lived on Baltimore Street, only a few doors from William and Fannie on East Middle Street. *Courtesy Adams County Historical Society*

From THE DC CHRONICLE

"On the afternoon of the first, as the rebels charged through the town, the pistols carried by them with which they were abundantly supplied, were fired promiscuously at all who might be in the street, looking out of windows or standing in doorways. A squadron of this charging party rode directly up to the front of the hospital[51] and deliberately discharged their pistols at those standing on the steps of the hospital and on the sidewalk in front.

"This firing instantly robbed our army of the most pious, excellent and beloved of Chaplains...the Reverend Doctor Howell of the 19th Pa. The same discharge of firearms put an end to two Privates of NY Militia who were there doing guard duty as well as severely wounded Dr. Parker of the 13th Massachusetts and Dr. Alexander of the 16th Maine. Those committing the downright deliberate murders seemingly exulted over their crimes."

JENNIE McCREARY cut through the Weaver's back yard and crossed the alley to her own home, but there she found even more wounded:

"At home, we found Colonel Leonard shot in the arm and Dr. Parker, shot in the head. Both were from Massachusetts. Parker was wounded while coming down the college church steps; a sharpshooter from Boyer's corner got him with the same ball that struck and killed the Chaplain of that regiment."

While TILLIE PIERCE was on her way south to the Weikert farm, her father, JAMES, left his Baltimore street home on a mercy mission and nearly got himself in trouble:

"My father went down street, he having heard that the wounded were being brought to the warehouses located in the northern part of the town.

"Desiring to assist all he could, he remained there, working for the poor sufferers until pretty late in the afternoon.

"Some of the wounded had been piteously calling and begging for liquor in order to deaden the pain which racked their bodies. Father, knowing that the dealers had removed that article out of town, said he would go to some private parties and try to obtain it. His search, however, was fruitless, as no one seemed to have any.

"It was while thus moving around on this errand that he noticed our men were fast retreating through the street, and hurrying in the direction of the Cemetery.

"Knowing that his family were alone, he concluded it was best to hasten to them.

"On his way home, he stopped for a few minutes at a place just a square west of our house on some business he wished to attend to. When he came out, there was no sign of Union soldiers.

"As he was approaching his home, he noticed a Rebel crossing the street a short distance beyond. He looked at my father, who was entirely alone, stopped, and halloed: 'What are you doing with that gun in your hand?'

"Father, who was in his shirt sleeves, threw up his arms and said: 'I have no gun!', whereupon the Confederate deliberately took aim and fired.

"As soon as father saw him taking aim, he threw himself down and had no sooner done so when he heard the "zip" of the bullet.

"The murderous Rebel passed on, no doubt concluding that he made one Yankee the less.

"As soon as he had passed down Baltimore Street, father got up and had almost reached the house when he was spied and overtaken by a squad of five Confederates coming down an alley, and who greeted him by saying: 'Old man, why ain't you in your house?'

"He replied that he was getting there just as fast as he could. They, however, commanded: 'Fall in!' He certainly did so, and accompanied them until he reached the front porch, when he stepped up and said, 'Now boys, I am home, and I am going to stay here.'"[52]

About 4:30 p.m. On the field: General Lee ordered Ewell to "attack that hill (Cemetery Hill) if practicable." Ewell did not think it "practicable." In Ewell's divisions, Rodes had heavy losses while Early was holding the town with only two of his four brigades and had some 4,000 prisoners. Ewell decided to wait for his third division, Johnson's, to arrive.

Near Taneytown, Meade is finally convinced that Gettysburg will be the site of engagement and orders all corps commanders to march on the town without further delay.

WILLIAM McLEAN:

"We brought out water to relieve the thirst of the dust-covered soldiers in blue, wearied with the strife, occasionally giving a glass of wine to one who was wan and feeble from loss of blood. This was the constant moving panorama.

"Then the ambulances with the most seriously wounded were driven into our street, turned around and went out Baltimore street and the shrieks and groans of the poor sufferers rent the air, as tortured with mangled limbs, they were being carried to the rear. These cries of woe will never pass out of my hearing.

"Then there was a brief, portentous lull of a moment, more terrifying than the sound of battle or the cries of the wounded. The enemy rushed into the street. My wife and little girls and a faithful domestic, Ann Leonard, and myself all crowded into a little narrow platform at the head of the cellar stairs behind the door, as we did not know what was next to happen, when the first words we heard from the outside were, "Don't touch that water, they have poisoned it," referring to the buckets of water that we had taken out for our soldiers, and which remained on the pavement.

"When we found that we were not to be hurt, we came out of our hiding place and the tired Rebels seated themselves all along the curb of the pavement and found recreation and amusement in opening the knapsacks of the soldiers who had retreated and taking out and reading the letters they contained.

"A large, fine looking officer, mounted, turned into our street. When a cheer went up from the men, he stopped and addressed them with jubilation that they had met their foes, driven them back and had taken possession of the town. This officer was General Monaghan of Georgia, I think. The time was between three and four o'clock. My brave, fearless, pretty little oldest daughter, Mary, not then six years old, put her head out of the window and sung in hearing of the Rebel soldiery, 'Hang Jeff Davis on a Sour Apple Tree.'"

When General Winfield Hancock met the retreating Union soldiers on east Cemetery Hill he directed them to take up positions there and on Culp's Hill, to the right. A battle-line was now established along Cemetery Ridge. *Courtesy Massachusetts Commandery of the Military Order of the Loyal Legion of the United States and the US Army Military History Institute, Carlisle, Pennsylvania.*

The Union soldiers who were now rushing to set up a line of defense in the Evergreen Cemetery must have chuckled at the sign greeting them near the Gateway: "All persons found using firearms in these grounds will be prosecuted with the utmost rigor of the law." The cannon points toward the Confederate left flank. *Courtesy Massachusetts Commandery of the Military Order of the Loyal Legion of the United States and the US Army Military History Institute, Carlisle, Pennsylvania.*

THE COLORED SERVANTMAID:

"Some one come and told us we must get out of there and go across the fields to another house. That house was Dave Hankey's. His place was thronged with Rebels and they stopped me and said to Mrs. Hartzell: 'Hey, what you doin' with her? She's got to go along with us.'

"'You don't know what you're talkin' about,' Mrs. Hartzell said, and I was so scairt I hung onto her skirts.

"We got down into the cellar and I crawled way back in the darkest corner and piled everything in front of me. I was the only colored person there and I didn't know what might happen to me."

Having fled their home west of Seminary Ridge, AMELIA HARMON and her aunt were still trying to get behind the Confederate lines:

"After we had walked perhaps two miles, we came upon a group of officers and newspaper men in conference under a tree. We told them our story. The officers looked incredulous, the newspaper men, attentive. One of these, the Confederate correspondent of the 'London Times',[53] seemed greatly interested in our tale and was, I believe, the only one who credited it fully. He courteously offered to conduct us to a place of safety still further to the rear. Dismounting, he walked with us, showing great sympathy, and assuring us that the ruffians who fired our house would meet condign punishment at the hand of General Lee. Also that we would be fully reimbursed by him for our property. (In Confederate money, of course.) He placed us in an empty cottage and went directly to General Lee's headquarters,[54] then quite close by.[55]

The town was now filled with wounded from both sides and occupied by forces of the Confederate Army who established themselves on a line running east to west along Middle Street, neatly placing at least a third of the town in a cross-fire. For miles into the countryside, the troops of both armies encircled the town, bathed their wounded, and made preparations to fight again.

Southeast of the city limits about a mile, and just east of Cemetery Ridge, NATHANIEL LIGHTNER finally made it back to his farm. He found the house turned into a hospital, and the barn being used as headquarters for Major General John Slocum:

"As I came down the pike home, I saw a red flag on the end of the house, and when I got nearer, I saw my yard full of soldiers.

"Under an apple tree I found the surgeons with a man stretched out on our dining room table and cutting and sawing a leg off, and on the grass there lay a pile of limbs.

"I went around to the kitchen door. The floor was covered with wounded men. The stove was red hot and the men were baking and the men were taking and cooking up everything in the house that was edible. They had taken full possession.

"My four barrels of flour and everything in the cellar and spring house were soon used up. My family had taken refuge in the stable where I found them frightened and crying. They had got nothing out of the house, and they did not know what had become of me.

"I went back to the surgeon and asked him what I should do under the circumstances. 'Do you live here?' he asked. 'Is this your place?' he asked. I told him it was. 'Go back, go back; take your family and go to the rear; that is all I can tell you,' said he, and went on with his work.

"'Can't I get some clothing at least out of the house?' I asked.

"'Yes, if you can find any,' said he.

"I went in by his permission, but could not find a thing that had not been torn up and put to use – not even a dress of my wife's.

"We set out with the children, six in number, and made our way back on foot as well as we could, among the oncoming troops and trains, four miles to a relative, where I left them."

ALBERTUS McCREARY and his family remained in the basement of their home at the corner of Baltimore and High Streets:

"We were all waiting to see what would happen next, when suddenly the outer cellar doors were pulled open and five Confederate soldiers jumped down among us. We thought our last day had come. Some of the women cried while others, with hands clasped, stood rooted to the spot with fear. Father stepped forward and asked what they wanted and begged them not to harm his people.

"One fellow – I can see him yet – with a red face covered with freckles, and very red hair, dirty, sweaty, with his gun in his hand, said: "'We are looking for Union soldiers.'

"'There are none here,' Father answered. But the soldier said he would have to search and that we could go upstairs, as the danger was over for a time.

"From that time on we had no fear of harm from individual soldiers.

"We all went upstairs, and the searchers found thirteen of our men hiding in all parts of the house, some under the beds, and one under the piano, others in closets. The prisoners were brought into the dining-room, where the officer in charge took down their names.

"I well remember my father as he said, 'Gentlemen, won't you have something to eat?' The table was just as we had left it such a short time before.

"They were only too glad to accept the invitation. While all were eating, I went around and took down the names of the prisoners, telling them I would write to their friends. Now that they had stopped fighting, both sides seemed to be on the best of terms, and laughed and chatted like old comrades."

LYDIA MEALS and her family had left their home, northwest of the Lutheran Theological Seminary, at the first sign of massive troops movements. They had sought refuge at the home of a nearby relative:

"The place at which we were stopping was surrounded by Rebels who were trying to rob two or three beehives. How I did wish them all to be stung. But on a second, our attention was taken up by the sight of a fire in the direction of our home. When Mother said, 'I believe that is our place, and we will have to go and see,' I said, 'Among all those Rebels?' not knowing we were surrounded by them.

"Someone back of me said, 'Where do you live, Miss?' I told him. 'No, it is not your home, it is further away[56] but I will go with you if you are afraid.'

"So we started. It took us about 15 minutes, when we found our home in the hands of the enemy who left the house when they saw us. Mother went upstairs with a pair of tongs, I picked up the remains of my best hat and parasol. I was very angry.

"Then Mother came to the door with a lot of clothes in her tongs which the Rebels had left in exchange for clean clothing of my brothers who were in the Union Army and we had forgotten in our flight from home.

"'Hush', she said, 'they might kill you.' After awhile a soldier who was in the yard came to the door. We did not go to the door but looked through the window. In a moment, there was not a Rebel to be seen. There was General Lee on horseback with two or three guards."

MARY CUNNINGHAM BIGHAM:[57]

"A sister[58] suffered with rheumatism which caused severe heart trouble. When the first cannonading began, it scared the child so my mother and the children went to Grandfather Cunningham's, two miles south on Marsh Creek, within the Confederate lines. Mother scarcely got the sick child to bed when the Confederates came and declared that they must search the house. Grandfather told them of the sick child and they were very quiet and courteous in her room. But below stairs, they demanded food, and looking through the window at long rows of beehives, they suggested that honey be served. Grandfather said there was no honey in the house, which, of course, they did not believe, so they

Major General Henry Slocum's XII Corps had arrived on Cemetery Hill late on the afternoon of July 1st. His troops now occupy the Federal right from Culp's Hill south along Rock Creek. Slocum took for his head-quarters the barn of Nathaniel Lightner. *Courtesy Massauchusetts Commandery of the Military Order of the Loyal Legion of the United States and the US Army Military History Institute, Carlisle, Pennsylvania.*

threatened that if it wasn't forthcoming they would take it from the bees. Grandfather was old and feeble, but had lost none of his sense of humor. He said that doubtless the bees had gathered a goodly store, and the gentlemen were welcome to all they cared to take.

"These were not the good-natured Italian bees of today. It was a hot day in the middle of July and Grandfather's bees were those bad-tempered snuff colored little fellows that brooked no meddling, so the visitors concluded to eat unsweetened."

HENRY EYSTER JACOBS:

"By 5 o'clock that afternoon, Gettysburg was fully in the enemy's possession. Dole's Brigade of Rodes' division, in Ewell's Corps, quartered itself in our immediate neighborhood.[59] They tore down all our fences to let the troops pass readily; but the harshest critic would find it difficult to find fault with their conduct. They were Georgians, all gentlemanly, courteous and as considerate of the townspeople as it was possible for men in their possession to be. I saw a whole row of them reading from their pocket testaments.

"Of course, they breathed fire and fury at their foes; they were full of what they were going to do to the hated North, but they were kindly, courteous Christian gentlemen, nonetheless."

SUE ELIZABETH STOEVER's father, Dr. Martin Luther Stoever, was a professor at Gettysburg College (Pennsylvania College). He and his family lived on the southwest corner of the Diamond on Baltimore street. A humanitarian, Dr. Stoever could not wait to see what he could do to help outside:[60]

"His first encounter was not reassuring. General Early was dashing along with bluster and self-importance. Stopping, he raised his finger and said: 'I know you. I saw you up at that window last Friday.'[61]

"On that Friday afternoon, Dr. Stoever and his wife had watched the proceeding from a second-story window, and the estimable Doctor, owing to his resemblance to a United States Government official, had been unpleasantly marked in the Rebel General's mind. Early's other duties, however, forbade investigation just then, and the Doctor moved on to meet, a few steps beyond, one of his former pupils, an army surgeon on patrol, who greeted his old professor warmly, and then introduced his companion, Dr. Ward of Wisconsin.

"'Oh, I am so glad to find you just at this moment!', said Dr. Stoever, 'Won't you come with me? There are twenty wounded men on my dining-room floor. During the retreat, forty soldiers crowded into my yard, bringing these poor fellows with them.'[62]

"'I am just as glad to meet you, my dear Professor, especially when you need relief, but we are under Rebel rule and must first ask permission.'

"General Ewell, then in charge of the town, granted leave, but detailed Major Watson (CSA) to accompany the surgeons.

"During the professional visit, Dr. Stout drew aside his old instructor, saying: 'We are very hungry. We have had nothing to eat today. Can you give us something?'

"Dr. Stoever smiled assuringly, and started off to find his kind wife, who, looking 'well to the ways of her household,' had baked bread that morning and tempting cherry pies.

"Of course, it would not do to pass by the attendant, Major Watson, so handing him refreshments, the Doctor, with characteristic sincerity and a touch of humor, said: 'The Good Book commands me to give my enemy food, if he hungers,'

"The Major gracefully received the hospitality, replying: 'We do not have such a luxury as cherry pie in Alabama.'

"Caspar Stoever, just 13, had longed in boyish enthusiasm to serve as a soldier. Now he was moving about offering 'the cup of cold water,' just as worthy of reward, to the thirsty heroes.

"'Your boy is making himself useful,' remarked the Confederate officer.

"'Yes,' replied his uncompromising father, 'and he is a strong Union boy.'

"On parting, the northern scholar and the southern soldier shook hands cor-

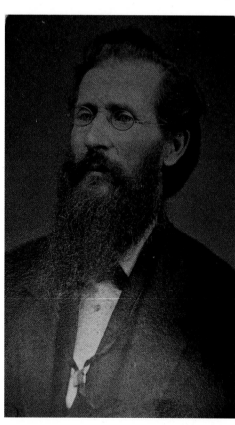

William Meals, 39, owned one of the two marble works in Gettysburg. In 1860 he married Maria Schaeffer, 29, whose father, Dr. D. S. Schaeffer, was a veterinary surgeon who lived out Harrisburg Road just across Rock Creek. When Meals sister Lydia, 20, and mother Nancy, 63, came to his home for protection earlier that day he is believed to have felt all would be safer at the home of his wife's father. It seemed like a good idea that morning when he made the decision, but now there was fighting all around the Alms House and nearby woods. *Courtesy Adams County Historical Society.*

dially, the latter saying: 'We can be friends, although we differ. If you are troubled by any of our men molesting you, just threaten to report them to me.'

"This advice was followed and acted like a charm, when any annoyance from the Louisiana Tigers, who plundered while others fought, threatened the peaceful household."

At this point, the west, north and northeast sectors of Gettysburg were fully occupied by Confederate troops. Dr. J.W.C. O'NEAL was still behind their lines at the Cordori farm, to the west near Cashtown. Returning to Confederate army headquarters to "check in" as he had been told to do, O'Neal felt free to leave when a busy orderly told him to "go to the devil." He decided to go to Gettysburg instead:

"It was between 4 and 5 o'clock in the afternoon when I reached town. Passing the Harry Wantz property, (I saw) two or three cannon pointed up Baltimore street with men behind them seemingly prepared to fire up street.

"I didn't fear these cannon as they were pointed away from me but I thought as they were pointed up street there might be guns up street pointing my way, the balls of which it might not be good for my health to encounter, so I went back to the Wantz property, took an open auxiliary road to Stratton Street and there halted under the wings of a bridge that crossed Stevens' Run.

"I halted there for what seemed a long time. When there was no longer firing, I advanced up Stratton Street to Middle Street and was then within a short distance of my home when I was halted by the line of Ewell's Corps along Middle Street, and the guard said: 'You can't go through there.'

"I replied to the interrupting party, 'I live a short distance from here and want to go to my family.'

He replied, 'I can't let you through.'

I said, 'I'll reward the man who takes me home with a bottle of whiskey.'

"He replied, 'I would do a good deal for a bottle of whiskey and will see whether I can get permission.'

"He left me and in a few minutes came back saying, 'I'll take you home if I am certain you will give me the bottle of whiskey.'

"My reply was, 'When I left home the bottle was there and I suppose it is there yet.'

"I left my horse in the care of Zach Myers, the deputy sheriff, and went with my Confederate guard to my home. When I got home there was joy and confusion in the family for they had had no idea of what had become of me in the two days' absence. I paid my reward of the bottle of whiskey, which was found where I had left it. The confusion in the family induced the guard to leave me at home sometime to get them quieted."

The guard had to take Dr. O'Neal back to his commanding officer, but advised the Doctor to do himself a good turn by inviting the officer to dinner at the O'Neal house. The officer declined with thanks and O'Neal was sent away.

GATES FAHNESTOCK, his sister, and three brothers remained in their home on the Rebel army line along Middle Street:

"The Confederates had possession of the town and were bivouacked or camped on our sidewalks, which were of laid bricks. The Louisiana Tigers of Early's command settled on the sidewalk of our house on Middle Street, went to the barn in the rear and brought out the hay from the haymow and spread it over the sidewalk, making a good carpet softer than bricks. We boys watched them from the second story through the slatted shutters and could hear parts of their talk. They were elated at the result of their first day's fighting and talked confidently of the results of the next day and what they would do to the Yankees then."

In the meantime, some of the more venturesome townspeople were beginning to emerge from shelter. JENNIE S. CROLL:

"What sights met my eyes as I came out of the house! A dead horse just before the door, a soldier breaking open a cellar door with an axe, and in the streets, the direst collection of coffee and groceries of all kinds, boxes and barrels, wagons and guns, dead men and

Martin Luther Stoever, 43, had begun to study for the ministry, but became a teacher instead. He was the first alumnus of Pennsylvania College to occupy a Professorship at the school. His subjects were History and Latin. The Stoever family remained at home during the battle. By the afternoon, their dining room had become a hospital because so many wounded stumbled into their doorway. *Courtesy, Special Collections, Gettysburg College.*

Jacob Weikert had a large family living at home and helping him to work his farm. On this day, it is believed, the Bliss and McMillian families sought sanctuary inside the huge stone house, located at the foot of the Round Tops off Taneytown Road. The more than twenty adults would become so overwhelmed with the wounded and dying they would have little time to think of their own fears. *Courtesy Adams County Historical Society.*

blood everywhere; the rebel soldier and his Yankee prisoner hobnobbing together as if they were old friends met again, and wounded men being carried here and there wherever an open doorway offered a place of rest and security."

GENERAL JOHN B. GORDON, C.S.A.:

"At the close of the day's fighting, I dispatched, under a flag of truce, the promised message to Mrs. Barlow. I assured her that if she wished to come through the lines she should have safe escort to her husband's side. I thought no more about it...thought him dead."

Gordon's message started an unusual train of events, as we shall see later.

With Henrietta Schriver and her children in tow, TILLIE PIERCE finally reached Jacob Weikert's home. The Weikerts lived near the Round Tops, prominent hills south of Gettysburg that were directly along the path of the Union advance:[63]

"It was not long after our arrival until Union artillery came hurrying by. It was indeed a thrilling sight. How the men impelled their horses! How the officers urged the men as they all flew past toward the sound of the battle! Now the road is getting all cut up; they take to the fields, and all is an anxious, eager hurry! Shouting, lashing the horses, cheering the men, they all rush madly on.

"Suddenly we behold an explosion; it is that of a caisson. We see a man thrown high in the air and come down in a wheat field close by. He is picked up and carried into the house. As they pass by, I see his eyes are blown out and his whole person seems to be one black mass. The first words I hear him say is: 'Oh, dear! I forgot to read my Bible today! What will my poor wife and children say?'

"After the artillery had passed, infantry began coming. I soon saw that these men were very thirsty and would go to the spring which is on the north side of the house.

"I was not long in learning what I could do. Obtaining a bucket, I hastened to the spring, and there, with others, carried water to the moving column until the spring was empty. We then went to the pump standing on the south side of the house, and supplied water from it."

At the northern end of the battleground, HARRIET BAYLY was surrounded by hungry Rebels:

"The demand for food was constant; all the chickens were killed by the foragers, and most of them brought to the house to be cooked. Out of a flock of a hundred sheep, nothing remained but a few carcasses left on the hillside fields, where they had been shot and left to die.

We saved a few cows by driving them into shelter, but lost the best of the stock, including several steers just ready for market.

From the time I got home until darkness came we were busy baking and cooking for our uninvited guests, and they literally swarmed over the place.

Being immediately in the rear of the Confederate line of battle north of town, we had hundreds of stragglers...

As a rule, the men, whether stragglers or not, were in good humor, disposed to be jolly and to see only the brightest prospect for victory before them. They were disposed to tease me, saying that they were sure to win the battle, the Yankees were being driven back, and that the seat of war would be transferred from the south to the north.

I said, 'Oh, yes. You boys are well fed, you have been living on the fat of the land for several days, and feel very hopeful, no doubt, but why are you not in line of battle fighting to make your prophecy sure?' Sometimes I got no answer or a laughing reply, 'Oh, there are enough to lick the 'Yanks' without us.'; or, 'We belong to the hospital corps."

SARAH BARRETT KING and her party had gone east of town to the home of John Bender, where they were taken in. Although Bender had fled with his livestock, Mrs. Bender was still there, and was firmly in charge:

"There was a rap at the door and Mrs. Bender asked me to answer. I said, 'they will want food, perhaps.' She said, 'Give them anything.'

"I opened the door. A youth of 17 asked if he could have milk. 'Yes,' I said, 'you will find it in the spring house,' pointing the way, 'help yourself.'

"After while he came back and asked me if I 'would converse with him.' I said, 'Certainly.'

"He was pleased and showed me a small picture and said it was his mother and sister, pretty and refined looking people, I thought. He said he had been a student at Williams' and Marys' College, leaving to go into (the) army as many of the young men had done. He never alluded to the cause, nor did I, except to ask him how he felt in battle. He said, 'At first, the sight of dead and wounded was very sad, but now' he could 'ride or walk over dead bodies and not think of them.'

"By that time, a blustering old fellow dressed in yellow or sun burnt garb from hat to shoes came up and was anxious for fight. He wanted to know where my husband was and why so many men were standing around. I told him my husband was in cavalry service and the men were not needed in the army, as there were plenty in the service to whip them.

"He said, 'Does your husband ride a good horse?'

"I said, 'Yes.'

"He replied then, 'I would like to meet him.'

"I said, 'I know he would like to meet you.'

"The little fellow stood by, never said a word until the old fellow got through. Then he said, 'We are on guard here for the night. You will not be disturbed."

Thirteen year old LEANDER WARREN lived with his parents and six other children near the Rubber Heel Company on Railroad Street. His father, 50 year old David Warren, made no effort to hide his true feelings from the soldiers now camped on his doorstep:

"Father went outside. It was dark. A Rebel officer asked him why he isn't in the Army. Father said, 'I'm too old, but have a son in my place.'

"'What are your sentiments?', the Rebel asked.

"Father replied, 'I'm a Union man.'

"The officer told him, 'You are the kind of man I like to talk to.'

"They argued the question all in good humor for quite a while. Finally, the officer said he'd like something to eat, that he could eat a dog. Father asked Mother to fix him up, but she balked. She said the soldiers had taken almost everything and what was left should be kept for the kids. However, she did admit to having just baked a shortcake and he could have some of it if he wanted.

"'Beats nothing,' he grinned."

JOHN WILLS:[64]

"I could see a dead horse in the gutter directly opposite the Globe Hotel and (one) in front of David Troxel's house. I went up to the square, trying to see what fighting was going on out Carlisle street, and was told to go back.

"Going into the hall, I heard some talking in the cellar. I went down to the cellar. Here I met my sister with a Confederate Lieutenant. She was giving him something to eat and drink. In conversation with him, I asked him why is it that you Confederates all gathered up here at the Globe Hotel? There are other hotels here and none of you go there. He replied that the Confederate Army of Northern Virginia knew of the Globe Hotel long before they came to Pennsylvania."[65]

School teacher, SALLIE MYERS, and her family remained in the basement of their home on West High Street during the day's fight:

"As we were looking out one of the cellar windows we saw some of our men who'd been taken prisoners, and they were standing so near that we spoke to them. They said they expected to be sent off South and wished we would write to their home people. Then, one after the other, they gave us their names and the addresses of the persons to whom we were to write.

"The town was full of Rebels, and we could see a Union soldier lying out in the street with his head cut off. He had probably been overtaken by the enemy's cavalry. We found in our backyard a number of guns loaded and capped that (the retreating troops) had thrown away. They could easily have pillaged the house, but the only thing we missed was a little linen apron I'd been ironing. I think perhaps a soldier took it for a handkerchief.

"They had begun bringing the wounded and injured into town. The Roman Catholic and United Presbyterian churches, a few doors east of my father's home, were taken possession of as hospitals. Dr. James J. Fulton[66] did splendid work getting things in shape. He came and asked my mother for the use of our cook stove. From that time on, we had no rest for weeks. 'Girls,' Dr. Fulton said, 'you must come up to the churches and help us...the boys are suffering terribly!'

"It didn't seem as if I could do such work, but I went. The doctor led the way to the Catholic church. Some of the wounded lay in the pews, and some lay on the floor with knapsacks under their heads, and there were very few persons to do anything for the poor fellows. The groans of the suffering and dying were heartrending. I knelt beside the first man near the door and asked what I could do.

"'Nothing,' he replied. 'I am going to die.'

"That was too much for me, and I went hastily out and sat down on the church steps and cried. But I soon controlled myself and returned to the wounded man. He was wounded in the lungs and spine, and there was not the slightest hope for him. He told me his name was Stewart[67] and that he had an aged father and mother, and a wife. Then he asked me to read the fourteenth chapter of John, which his father had read the last time they had all gathered around the family altar. Later in the day, he and eleven other wounded men were removed to our house."

On Chambersburg Street, MRS. ELIZABETH GILBERT and her husband, JACOB, had taken shelter in the basement of their neighbor, harness maker David Troxell:

In the evening, I returned home[68] with my husband. I remember a Confederate officer who rode down Chambersburg street the same evening and inquired as to the nature of the building in which we lived. He was informed that these were private houses. He assured us we'd be safe in our homes, that our belongings would not be disturbed, while if we left, the houses might be ransacked. He advised us to go into the cellar during fighting. All of the families in our row remained."

St. Francis Xavier Catholic Church was located on West High Street, only a few doors away from where Sallie Myers lived with her family. As the number of wounded being brought to the church increased, army doctors found it overwhelming. At least one of them began knocking on doors to enlist citizen help. The scene was repeated throughout Gettysburg as churches and public buildings soon filled to overflow. All during the day private residences were also invaded. Sometimes by soldiers looking for a place to hide; at other times by the wounded seeking help.

SARAH BROADHEAD was also a refugee at the Troxels:

"'Can we go out?' was asked of the Rebels. 'Certainly,' was the answer; they would not hurt us.

"We started home, and found things all right."

CHARLES McCURDY:

"My father took me with him to see how conditions were at home. We found the door still locked, although a dent apparently made by the butt of a musket was shown, and a bullet had lodged in the door frame. Beside the little front porch that occupied half the sidewalk lay two dead Union soldiers. We went back for the rest of the family. Although nothing had been disturbed in the house, everything in the stable had been taken, including two pigs which belonged to Owen Robinson, the colored sexton of the Presbyterian Church."

Meanwhile, US General Alexander Schimmelfennig was still hiding in a culvert in ANNA GARLACH's back yard on Baltimore Street:

"It was night when my mother[69] went out of the house, following the path to the stable, for the purpose of feeding our hogs. Along the pathway was the woodshed and against the shed and running some distance from it was several ranks of wood and in front of the wood, two swill barrels. We had been using wood from the rank nearest the barrels and there was a space between barrel and the next rank of wood big enough to hold a man. As Mother went up to the barrel, the General said: 'Be quiet and do not say anything.'

"He had taken of the wood and built a shelter overhead to better hide himself.

"It was remarkable that he was not captured. The Rebels had torn down fences from Breckenridge street southward through the yards and there were Rebels on all sides of us and any movement of his in the daytime might have been seen from a number of points."

Far to the south, TILLIE PIERCE was beginning to realize that instead of escaping the fight by fleeing her parent's home in town, she had walked directly into its path:

"Now the wounded began to come in greater numbers. Some limping, some with their heads and arms in bandages, some crawling, others carried on stretchers or brought in

John Lawrence Schick, 41, was the son of a German brewer who sought a better life for his family in America. Young Schick apprenticed as a tailor. As the town grew, so did business, and now Schick was one of the town's leading citizens. Schick lived just north of the square on Carlisle Street. He told friends that he was so nervous, hiding in his cellar during the first day's fighting, that he smoked 21 cigars! *Courtesy Adams County Historical Society.*

The J.L. Schick Dry Goods Shop was located on Baltimore Street just south of the square. Like most Gettysburg merchants, Schick had shipped most of his inventory to Philadelphia, shortly after learning the rebels were moving northward again. Dr. Martin Luther Stoever owned the building in which J.L. Schick's Dry Goods Shop was located. The door just past the Dry Goods Shop is to the foyer of the Stoever residence, located on the second floor. *Courtesy Adams County Historical Society.*

ambulances. Suffering, cast down and dejected, it was a truly pitiable gathering. Before night the bar was filled with the shattered and dying heroes of the day's struggle.

"When night came, I sought rest indoors, but more and more wounded were being brought there. They reported on hard fighting, many were killed or wounded and were afraid of defeat or a rout. Some of the wounded limped, some had bandaged heads, hands, arms or legs, some were crawling and others were carried on stretchers or brought in ambulances. Before night, the barn was filled with shattered and dying soldiers."

The scene was repeated variously all over Gettysburg. Seminary student, MARTIN LUTHER CULLER, had taken sanctuary in the home of a friend on Baltimore street. Late in the evening, they were frightened by a pounding on the door. A corporal's guard of Confederates was demanding admittance:

"When the door was opened, a wounded officer was brought in and laid in the hall. He asked the family that there should not be the least concern about his comfort; that the soldiers on the outside would provide for him."

HORATIO JAMES WATKINS:

"A Reb with his head bandaged and apparently insane from his wound, pounded on the door in the middle of the night at the Minnigh house. Lizzie and I were upstairs. I went to the door and, without a word, the man comes in and goes to the mirror. He raised his hands and 'tore wide open his eyes' and turned toward me. Lizzie screamed and grabbed up the lamp and fled. I seized the poor fellow, rushed him through the door and bolted it quickly."

Several miles northwest, THE COLORED SERVANTMAID and her employer's family found a place to hide at the Hankey farm. But they found no rest:

"Up in the kitchen was a sick officer, and he wanted the women to come up out of the cellar to take care of him and do some cooking and he promised they should be well treated. Mr. Hankey says to him, 'Would you see a colored person protected if she was to help with the work here?' He said he would, and he sent out a written somethin' or 'nother orderin' the men to keep out of the kitchen, and he had the door boarded up half way so they could hand in things to be cooked and we would hand 'em out afterward. No one could go out and no one could come in. We stayed up all night doin' nothin' but cook and bake for the Rebels. Good land! they killed cows and calves and chickens and everything they come across, and brought the things to us to cook. I heard Mr. Hankey pleading with 'em not to kill his calf, but it didn't do no good."

ANNIE YOUNG:

"I shall never forget the sight that greeted us as we came up from the cellar. The moon was shining brightly in the heavens while on the earth, scattered everywhere, were the dead and the wounded, moaning with pain. Our yard and the house were full.

"I actually thought I had been transferred to some strange place, so different did it seem from the home I had seen in the morning. Though the fighting was still going on, it was almost nothing in comparison to a few hours before. The Rebels took their wounded from our house to the rear of their army; so we went to work and took up carpets, brought down beds, and tried to make our wounded as comfortable as possible.

"Our army's center rested on Cemetery Hill, where we had a number of guns and which we could distinctly see from our door. And as the Rebels only held the town, we were in the center and near the front of the Rebel army. Our troops paid respect to the flag[70] that floated over our house, and it was only a stray shell that came near us after the first day's battle.

"The college, which is quite near us, was also taken as a hospital. From the cupola there is a splendid view of the country for miles around and there, under the protection of the hospital flag, stood General Lee, taking note of both armies and sending dispatches all over the field. General Ewell and staff took tea with us Wednesday evening. We, being in their power, kept quiet as to our sentiments until they commenced the subject. We then very warmly expressed our feelings and told them they were unwelcome guests. Many of them were handsome and intelligent, and all polite and accommodating. Seeing there were none but ladies in the house, the General gave us a guard to protect us.[71] General Ewell wanted to make his quarters with us; but, as we could not, rather would not, put ourselves to any trouble to give him two private rooms, he went elsewhere to sleep.[72]

JENNIE S. CROLL:

"I was going up the street to attend to an errand when a Confederate rode up to me and said, 'Can you tell me where I can find Mrs. Barlow?'

"'Who is Mrs. Barlow?', I asked.

"'She's the wife of one of your Yankee generals. He's wounded and wants her.'

"Said I: 'Where does he say his wife is?'

"'He says he left her in a carriage in one of your streets.' I told him I knew nothing of her, but if he would ask at the hotel nearby he might find her.

"'Oh, d__n it,' he said, 'I believe if I'd ask the very man that had her in his house he'd be too scared to tell me anything.'

"I looked up to find about fifty Confederates standing around me. It was almost dark and I found that I was really scared."

At that moment, GENERAL BARLOW was hospitalized in the Josiah Benner farmhouse on Harrisburg road:

"..about dark, three Confederate surgeons came. They gave me chloroform and probed my wound. When I woke up they told me that a minie ball had passed downward from where it entered and through the peritoneum and lodged in the cavity of the pelvis and that there was very little chance for my life. They gave me some morphine and left me. Several Confederate officers passed the night at the house and were very kind and attentive. A brother of Alexander H. Boteler of Virginia bathed my wound several times."

On South Baltimore Street, TILLIE PIERCE's father, JAMES, was out being the 'keen observer':

"...from the window looking out toward the Cemetery Hill, he could distinctly hear our troops chopping, picking and shoveling during the silent hours. Our men were busy forming their line of breastworks, preparatory to meeting the enemy on the morrow.

"At different times...my father, accompanied by some of the soldiers in the house,[73] went to the garret in order to look at the fighting out on the hill.

"...they noticed, on one occasion, a number of Rebel sharpshooters, busy at their work of picking off our men in the direction of Cemetery Hill.

"The south wall of this house had a number of port holes knocked into it, through which the Rebels were firing at our men. All at once, one of these sharpshooters threw up his arms and fell back upon the garret floor. His comrades ran quickly to his assistance and for the time being, they appeared greatly excited and moved rapidly about. A short time afterward, they carried a dead soldier out the back way and through the garden.

Sixty-nine year old John Burns, a veteran of the War of 1812 and a former Gettysburg constable, can be seen on the porch of his house on Chambersburg Street where it branches into the Chambersburg and Hagerstown roads. *Courtesy Massachusetts Commandery of the Military Order of the Loyal Legion of the United States and the US Army Military History Institute, Carlisle, Pennsylvania.*

When John Burns took his rifle and left his home, "Billy" Tipton and his friends were nearby and saw him start out Chambersburg Pike with his flint lock and powder horn.

WILLIAM H. TIPTON: "We were standing opposite his home. John Burns became very abusive to Joseph Broadhead, a one-eyed neighbor of his, insisting on his getting a gun and going along and upon his refusal called him a 'coward – a chicken-hearted squaw', and used language that I will not repeat here.

"Miss Mary Slentz hearing Burns, came out of her home next door and rebuked him for his abuse of Broadhead and advised him to stay home. When he started out he may have worn a blue coat, but we did not see it as he wore a long linen duster. He wore a high crowned felt hat." *Courtesy Adams County Historical Society.*

"On account of this position occupied by Rebel sharpshooters, a continual firing was drawn toward our house...no less than seventeen bullet holes can be seen on the upper balcony. One of the bullets cut a perfectly even hole through a pane of glass. The back porch downstairs and other places were also riddled; showing how promptly and energetically the Union boys replied, when once they detected the whereabouts of the enemy.

"The greatest wonder is that our men did not send a shell into that house after they detected the rebel firing.

"The sharpshooters on this part of the field had their headquarters on the north of our house; it being at the nearest corner to the line of battle, and served as quite a protection to them.

"At night, when all the folks had gone upstairs, these sharpshooters would enter the cellar in search of eatables. They did not call it stealing in war times."

Word began to circulate that at least one resident of Gettysburg had taken up arms in aid of Union troops. A veteran of the war of 1812, 70 year old John Burns donned his swallow-tail uniform coat, did up its old brass buttons and took his ancient musket to the field. Burns told Union officers he was volunteering because the Confederates had driven off his cows and he was determined to get even. And he did, receiving three minor wounds and the threat of a Confederate hanging for his trouble. According to Burns' neighbor, HENRY DUSTMAN, getting the old man off the field was a somewhat less heroic story. Burns fell during the battle near Dustman's home on Oak Ridge, close to the Lutheran Seminary:

"A soldier came to me and said, 'There is an old man laying over there on the cellar door, (pointing across the road to the little brick house), wants to see you.'

"'Who in the world wants to see me now, in all this fighting!' However, I lost no time and went over. There lay John Burns on the cellar door. I said to him, 'Why John, what is the matter?' He said, 'Oh, Henry, I took my gun and went out to fight the rebels, and got wounded,' at the same time, showing me his ankle.

"Doubting his story, I asked where his gun was. He said, 'I took my pocket knife and buried it near that sour apple tree,' at the same time, showing me where he was wounded, 'then crept from there on my hands and knees to this cellar door. Go and tell my wife to get a wagon to take me home in.'

"I said, 'That will be something to do.' However, I went.

"But it seemed to me while walking over that quarter of mile of pike there was a lull in the fighting. I told Mrs. Burns what had happened, that John was wounded and that she should get a wagon and get him home.

William H. Tipton was just over a month away from his thirteenth birthday in July 1863. Apprenticed to the Tyson Brothers Photography Studio "Billy's" thoughts weren't on work this morning. He was running west with a group of curious boys that included Henry Schick, Wesley Kitzmiller, Alex Baugher, George Ziegler and Charles Sheads. *Courtesy Gettysburg National Military Park.*

Major-General Abner Doubleday, whose grandfather was a soldier in the American Revolution, graduated the US Military Academy at West Point in 1842. Two of his classmates, James Longstreet and Lafayette McLaws, were now Confederate Generals and they were making their way to Gettysburg. Meanwhile, Doubleday had his hands full with Henry Heth's troops and with a civilian named John Burns. MAJ. GEN. DOUBLEDAY: "Col. Wister, advised him to fight in the woods, as there was more shelter there; but he preferred to join our line of skirmishers in the open fields. When our troops retired he fought with Meredith's Iron Brigade." *Courtesy Massachusetts Commandery of the Military Order of the Loyal Legion of the United States and the US Army Military History Institute, Carlisle, Pennsylvania.*

"She did not get at all excited, but said, 'Him. I told him to stay at home.' And that was all that she said or did."[74]

Three miles north, at the Bayly farm, most of the Rebels were settling down for the night. But not all of them. WILLIAM HAMILTON BAYLY:
"We are awakened by a knocking at the kitchen door, and mother told me to follow her down stairs. At the door we found a little fellow in a gray uniform, hardly taller than I and only a couple of years older, who said he had been through the battle of the day before, that his company had been cut to pieces, that he was from North Carolina, was tired of fighting and never wanted to see another battle – would not mother conceal him somewhere until the battle was over?

"He was given a suit of clothes and sent to the garret where the feather beds were stored for the summer and several old bedsteads not in use, told to find a bed and in the morning change his gray uniform for the civilian attire.

"The balance of the night passed without incident."

Col. Isaac Wister commanded a brigade of "The Pennsylvania Bucktails," the 150th Pennsylvania Infantry. Burns asked Wister if he could fight with them. *Courtesy Massachusetts Commandery of the Military Order of the Loyal Legion of the United States and the US Army Military History Institute, Carlisle, Pennsylvania.*

Brigadier General Solomon Meredith's 7th Wisconsin Volunteers were part of the famed Iron Brigade. They were positioned this morning on the Union left in and around McPherson's Woods. Burns came huffing and puffing into the woods and staked out a position, from which he is alleged to have felled a Confederate officer on a white horse. Burns is said to have suffered three minor wounds. *Courtesy Massachusetts Commandery of the Military Order of the Loyal Legion of the United States and the US Army Military History Institute, Carlisle, Pennsylvania.*

This is the view looking west out the Chambersburg Pike from the vacinity of John Burns' house. That's Seminary Ridge in the distance. On the right side of Chambersburg Pike, also in the distance, you can see the house and barn of Henry Dustman and the home of Elias Sheads whose daughter Carrie operates the Oak Ridge Seminary for young ladies. *Courtesy Adams County Historical Society.*

On the field: Under cover of the battle's confusion, the two armies continued to build their strength.

By 9 or 10 p.m., there were some 35,000 Confederate troops at Gettysburg, ready to fight. The Federal force was around 10,000 fewer. Soon, however, the advance units of three more Union divisions would arrive. From that point on, Union strength grew more rapidly than Confederate.

Meade did not go to the field immediately on July 1st, sending Major General Winfield Hancock to "size it up." Hancock got things organized, saw that Cemetery Ridge was secured, and sent word to Meade that Gettysburg would be the place to meet Lee once and for all.

Meade came up from Taneytown at about midnight.

When he reached Cemetery Ridge, he found his army in a fishhook-shaped defensive line. He could see that the Confederates were on a line running south on their right along Seminary Ridge, north from their center to the right of way of an unfinished railroad, and turning eastward from there into Gettysburg itself.

At about the same time, an important meeting was taking place in a two story brick house located on the east corner of Carlisle and Water Street. LAURA M. SPANGLER says her parents, Mr. and Mrs. Alexander Spangler, had fled the building with their three children that morning:

"They returned to their home to find all their movable supplies piled in the dining room. In the front room, General Lee sat on a black horsehair sofa in the company of Generals Early, Jenkins[75] and Longstreet. These gentlemen asked for light and, on Mr. Spangler's suggestion, they supplied him with a guard to go to the warehouse and secure candles.[76] Upon his return, the family was advised to go to bed as there was no apparent danger.

"General Jenkins asked Mrs. Spangler if she would mind if a Rebel would kiss her baby, Frank, who was lying in the cradle, and he wept as he did so, saying that he had only recently left his wife and small baby."

SALLIE MYERS:

"That night we were again ordered to the cellar. We closed the windows and shutters. The air was hot and stifling. I fanned my patient. Sitting there, one could hear the shots in the distance."[77]

HENRY EYSTER JACOBS:

"That evening of the battle's first day fell very quiet, very still. The college and the seminary were crowded with the wounded. But it seemed as though a merciful hush had

As the most traumatic day of her life was ending Elizabeth Thorn could look out of the windows of her home in the Evergreen Cemetery Gatehouse across what had become "no man's land." The Confederate line was along Seminary Ridge, right through the middle of town, and out to Culp's Hill. About sundown, upon instructions from a Union staff officer, she cooked dinner for General Howard.

ELIZABETH THORN: "I had put some meat for safe keeping down at the home of Captain Myers[8] and I went down there about dark to get some of it. There was four hams and a shoulder there. The house was filled with wounded soldiers and none of the family was about. I saw a lot of men lying in rows and six of them did not move and that scared me and I took a nervous chill and hurried home without any meat."

It was nearly midnight when Howard showed up with Generals Sickles and Slocum.

ELIZABETH THORN: "The midnight supper of the three generals was made up of two good sized dough cakes I had made, pancakes, three pieces of meat I had, apple butter and coffee."

Howard told her to pack up, but to put things in the cellar for safe keeping. He sent some soldiers to help move things to the cellar, predicting fighting would erupt before dawn. The cannonading began around 3:00 a.m. At 6:00 a.m. an officer burst through the cellar door and ordered that they evacuate the house and move south along the Baltimore pike. With shells bursting around them, Elizabeth grabbed up her three children, and with her parents, made it safely well after sun up on the 2nd to the Mussers' farm[9] near Rock Creek. *Courtesy Massachusetts Commandery of the Military Order of the Loyal Legion of the United States and the US Army Military History Institute, Carlisle, Pennsylvania.*

been laid on the warring passions of mankind. Within the town silence held sway; between the opposed lines beyond, no one seemed to stir. It was a war-torn, bloodied desert there. I lay down to sleep amid that stilled world, when from the brooding silence, out where the battle had raged, I heard a wounded forsaken soldier crying in his soft southern voice, "Water...water." he kept calling, calling; and that solitary cry, its anguish uplifted in the pitiless truce of the night, racked the very heart. But the law of conquerors lay like iron on the town; no one might pass beyond the lines. They themselves made no response to their comrade's call. I fell asleep with his anguish wailing in my ear."

SARAH BROADHEAD:
"As I write all is quiet, but O! how I dread tomorrow."

Casualties for the first day:	
Union:	10,000
Confederates:	7,000.

End July 1.

NOTES

1. This account was written for the Gettysburg Compiler in 1915.
2. Ironically, the house was built early in the 19th century by Reverend C. G. McLean, an uncle-by-marriage to the late Confederate General, Stonewall Jackson. At the time of the battle, it was the property of William Comfort.
3. Union cavalry.
4. From Clifton Johnson's *Battlefield Adventures*, published in 1913. The "servantmaid" worked for a Mrs. Emma Hartzell, a widow with two small children, whose home was just a mile west of town. There is no other identification, but the "maid" was about twenty years old at the time. She claims to have seen Rebels dressed as women scouting the region before the battle. On July 1st, they were all around her in full battle regalia.
5. Six-gun Battery A, 2nd US Artillery, joined the fight.
6. A student at the Lutheran Theological Seminary at the time of the battle, Henry Eyster Jacobs later became its Dean. As an author, he wrote one of the most-often quoted descriptions of the battle. We will pay close attention to it in this book.
7. 301 S. Baltimore Street, where James Pierce had his residence and his butcher shop.
8. Breckenridge Street ran west from Baltimore, connecting to Washington.
9. The handsome brick home still stands at the NW corner of West Middle and South Washington Streets.
10. Robert McCurdy, President of the Gettysburg Railroad.
11. 26 Chambersburg Street, on the east side of town, nearest the fighting of that hour.
12. This is from a letter written to a cousin on July 17th.
13. Charles and Isaac Tyson maintained a photography studio on York Street, directly across from the Globe Inn.
14. Sadie writes that she was in the field hospital during all three days of the battle, 'climbing over heaps of bodies, six and eight deep, and always with the doctor, helping him in his work.' Her father found her at the hospital and took her home where she found a new baby sister, born in the cellar while a battery of forty two cannon roared out 'death and destruction' from her front yard.
15. Skelly was an employee of the Fahnestock's.
16. From an interview published in the Philadelphia North American on July 4, 1909.
17. East of the town.
18. George Guinn, of Cole's Maryland Cavalry.
19. Maj. Gen. Oliver O. Howard, USA
20. South side of Chambersburg Street, three doors west of Franklin Street.
21. 64 year old William Boyer lived at 214 Chambersburg Street. He and his 25 year old son, Charles, ran a grocery store on the Diamond.
22. Tyson reports that he and his party went first to a farm owned by Daniel Benner and then on to Littlestown, ten miles south of Gettysburg, to reach safety.
23. Mrs. Henrietta Schriver, 27, who lived with two small daughters at 309 Baltimore Street.
24. Jacob Weikert.
25. Brigadier General James J. Archer, C.S.A.
26. Mrs. Carson's husband, T. Duncan Carson, was cashier at the Bank of Gettysburg.
27. At the time of the battle, the bank was on the north side of East York Street, about three doors from the Diamond and one door west of the Globe Hotel.
28. A liberty has been taken here: the story about the bank vault is true, but the real voice of the account is uncertain. In archives at Gettysburg, the account is found in a newspaper article, "Days of Dread," written by Jennie S. Croll for the Philadelphia Weekly Press in 1887. But historians say Jennie S. Croll did not move to Gettysburg until 1866, three years after the battle, when she married Luther Henry Croll. Mr. Croll moved to

Gettysburg to become Professor of Mathematics and Astronomy at his alma mater, Gettysburg (Pennsylvania) College. So whose story is she telling? The predominant feeling at the time this book was written was that the voice is that of Mary Horner, wife of Dr. Robert Horner of 51 Chambersburg Street. In turn, Dr. Horner may be the 'Doctor H' mentioned in the account, or it could be Dr. Henry Huber. There is also the possibility that Mrs. Croll was combining the experiences of more than one Gettysburg woman. Whatever the case, it is not known why she chose to tell these stories in the first person, but they are great stories nevertheless, and deserve a place in this book so long as the reader understands the circumstances.

29. Barlow wrote the letter from his hospital bed in a small house on the Baltimore pike on July 7th. His unit had arrived in Gettysburg at about 3 p.m. and was ordered by General Carl Schurz to move through the town to the northwest to shore up the right of the 3rd Division, led by General Alexander Schimmelfennig, already in action. Dole's Rebel skirmishers were outnumbered by Barlow's division, but General Early's forces moved in with a tremendous barrage of cannon fire.

30. Lt. Bayard Wilkeson was from a prominent upstate New York family. His grandfather had been instrumental in the construction of the Erie Canal, and his father, Samuel Wilkeson, was the New York Times Bureau Chief in Washington, D.C.

31. As an inspiration to his men, young Wilkeson chose to remain in saddle and direct them from horseback. General John B. Gordon, C.S.A., finding it impossible to move his division forward in the face of Wilkeson's cannon fire, directed that two batteries (thirty-six Confederate cannon) direct their fire on this Union position. A cannon ball ripped into Wilkeson's leg and killed his horse. Seeing that his leg was nearly severed, the 19 year old soldier made a tourniquet and completely removed the leg with his sword. The knoll was eventually captured by Gordon's forces. Lt. Wilkeson crawled nearly a half-mile to the Alms House where he died that night. Although his father arrived that day at General Meade's headquarters to cover the battle, Samuel Wilkeson didn't learn of his son's death until July 3rd.

32. Barlow.

33. As 10 year old Albertus describes it, the porch would have been located on High St.

34. This account appeared in the Gettysburg Compiler August 9th, 1905.

35. General Alexander Schimmelfennig was in command of the First Brigade of the Third Division of the 11th Corps. He reached Gettysburg on the morning of the first day with his brigade and went into line north of the town. The unit was among the last to retreat through town, hotly pursued by Confederate troops.

36. The incident was reported in "The Veteran" of Worcester, MA on March, 1892. Historians at the Adams County Historical Society pieced together the woman's probable identity.

37. Cpl. H. L. Burlingame, Co. G, 150th Pa.

38. Bushman says two stayed in his family's home until the battle was over.

39. NE corner of Middle and Baltimore Street, directly across Baltimore from the family store.

40. This letter, written to her sister, Julia, of Kittanning, Pennsylvania, was published in 1938 in the Philadelphia Evening Bulletin.

41. From an account collected by historian Robert L. Brake. Mr. Brake's research is a major source for Gettysburg researchers; he reported that this narrative was published in a series of articles that ran in the Philadelphia Inquirer from June 26th through June 29th, 1938.

42. Mrs. Nancy Weikert, a widow, also lived on Chambersburg Street. Her husband, Peter, died in 1861.

43. Christ Lutheran, located on the south side of Chambersburg Street, 5 doors east of Washington Street.

44. Mary's sister, Martha Scott. Mary, a spinster, lived with her brother-in-law and sister in a brick house at 41 Chambersburg Street.

45. George Guyer, a storekeeper, lived at 52 Chambersburg Street.

46. Robert Goodloe Harper, editor of the Adams Sentinel.

47. She means as far up the street toward the Diamond. Crossing there, she would have to double back to her house, which was on the north side of Chambersburg Street.

48. Brigadier General James. J. Archer, CSA.

49. Dennis Burke Dailey was 1st Lieutenant, acting Aide de Camp on General Solomon Meredith's brigade staff.

50. Reverend Horatio S. Howell, 90th Pa. Infantry.

51. Christ Lutheran Church.

52. Pierce was later quizzed by passing Confederates concerning his political stance: "I am an unconditional Union man; and to back it up, I am a whole-souled one", he said. The Rebels told him, "Well, we like you all the better for that; for we hate the milk and water Unionists."

53. Francis Lawley.

54. In a tent across the road from the residence of Mrs. Mary Thompson, on the Chambersburg Pike.

55. Miss Harmon said Lee or his staff assured their safety and promised them rations.

56. Lydia later learned the fire was in a house that was burned by the Confederates to rout some Union sharpshooters.

57. This account is third person. Mrs. Bigham is relating stories told to her by her parents and grandparents.

58. Elizabeth.

59. NW corner of West Middle and South Washington.

60. This account appeared in the Gettysburg Compiler on June 24th, 1903. In it, Ms. Stoever refers to her father as Dr. Godfrey, and to her brother as Caspar Godfrey. We will take it upon ourselves to sweep aside modesty's convention and call them as we see them.

61. The June 26th raid.

62. This somewhat wordy account illustrates that Union doctors were given the liberty to work in Rebel-held streets, and shows the extent to which private homes were used as hospitals.

63. This great, square stone house was a veritable fortress. It was a good thing, too: the "Round Tops," were central to some of the hardest fighting of the battle.

64. The Wills' Globe Inn was on the north side of East York, 5 doors west of the square, or "Diamond."

65. This is one of several occasions in which Wills refers to incidents that convinced him Confederate spies had visited his hotel many times during the months leading up to the battle, and that they had reported favorably to their superiors regarding the Wills family's politics.

66. Assistant Surgeon, 143rd Pa. Volunteers.

67. Sgt. Alexander Stewart, Company D of the 149th Pa. Volunteers.

68. Elizabeth and Jacob Gilbert lived near Sarah Broadhead in what is commonly referred to as the Warren Block of Chambersburg Street.

69. Mrs. Catherine Garlach.

70. "Hospital" flag.

71. Annie and the Crawford family left the house to go to the home of Josiah Benner, leaving Mrs. William Smith and her daughter, Jane, to care for the wounded. Ironically, that same night, the seriously wounded General Barlow was moved from Benner's to the Crawford house.

72. Ewell finally settled his headquarters in the Daniel Lady residence on the north side of the Hanover Road, a better location for field operations to come.

73. The Pierce home, on Baltimore street, became one of many sanctuaries for Union soldiers, either wounded or hiding from the enemy.

74. After being refused a ride by several military ambulance drivers, Dustman did manage to take Burns home in another neighbor's horse and wagon. He was transported at about 6 p.m., July 1st. There is no record of what his wife said when she saw him, but he did live to a riper old age as a local celebrity, so apparently she took him in.

75. Brigadier General Albert Gallatin Jenkins, Cavalry, C.S.A.

76. Mr. Spangler owned a warehouse on the southwest side of the railroad.

77. Sgt. Stewart died of his injuries on Monday, July 6th. If there can be any charm to these stories, perhaps this is one of the places. After the battle, Stewart's widow and brother visited Sallie Myers to thank her for her kindness to the young man. A romance blossomed, and five years later, Miss Myers married the Reverend Henry F. Stewart, the fallen soldier's brother. Reverend Stewart died a year later, but the Stewarts had a son, Harry, for whom she wrote her "recollections of the Battle of Gettysburg," which were based on her diaries. Her Grandson, Henry, saw to the document's preservation.

Caption Notes

1. At the time of the battle the house was owned by Thaddeus Stevens, a Republican Congressman from Pennsylvania who, along with local banker and one-time business partner George Arnold, had extensive holdings in the community.

2. Part of the oral traditions handed down in the Thompson and Foulk families.

3. Tim Smith. *The Story of Lee's Headquarters*. Thomas Publications.

4. From a letter Carrie Sheads wrote May 19, 1866 to Frank Moore. It is housed in the Frank Moore Collection at Duke University.

5. Mrs. Foster lived on Chambersburg Street near Christ Lutheran Church. On the morning of the first she had a narrow escape from death. As she served water to the troops on the steps of her home a shell struck the roof of the porch under which she was standing. The percussion knocked her backward inside just as the entire roof collapsed in a rumble of thunder and cloud of dust and debris. She was spared and her personal account of the battle is contained in The Foster Family History in the GNMP archives.

6. Hannah made sure that her children were safe in the cellar. There was so much water there from the recent rains that she placed her smallest children in wash tubs to keep them dry.

7. Catherine Mary White Foster. *Battle of Gettysburg, A Citizen's Eyewitness Account*. Foster's account was published in The Compiler in 1904.

8. Captain John Myers, 80, veteran of the War of 1812. The 1860 census indicates his daughter Mary, 50, lived with him in a house just at the foot of Evergreen Cemetery Hill on Baltimore Pike.

9. The Musser family were tenant farmers of George Spangler who owned the property.

Thursday
July 2nd, 1863

"July 2nd: There is comparative quiet along both lines this morning."

—Miss Jane Smith's diary.

"At 8:00 a.m., the sky still covered (cumulostratus clouds); at 2:00 p.m., sky 3/10 clear. At 9:00 p.m. there were cirrus clouds.

Thermometer readings:

7:00 a.m.	2:00 p.m.	9:00 p.m.
74	81	76

—Professor Michael Jacobs

NATHANIEL LIGHTNER:
"About daybreak, we slipped out and over through the bushes to Power's Hill, on the corner of my land. There I found the (US) Signal Corps had established headquarters. From that point I could look down on my place and see what was going on.

"My wheat field and orchard were full of wagon trains, and a drove of beef cattle were being herded in the meadow.

"I saw I could save nothing, so went back and moved my family nine miles further away..."

Union General Francis Barlow (Left), severely wounded during the first day's fighting, had been taken to the farm house of Josiah Benner by his Confederate captors. Now, he and several members of the John Crawford household are being moved.

ANNIE YOUNG: (General Ewell) came for breakfast, bringing with him Generals Early and Rhodes. Some of us, myself among the number, having been so frightened by Wednesday's fight, General Ewell gave us two wagons to take us to the rear, where there was less danger, and sent one of his staff with us for protection.

Captain James Powers Smith, of Ewell's staff showed up with an ambulance recently captured from the Union, to remove the Crawford family to safer quarters.[1] Mrs. William Smith and her daughter Jane remained to care for the wounded. Anna and the Crawford family were escorted another two miles or so out the Harrisburg road to the farm house of John Majors. However, it was being used by General Albert G. Jenkins, CSA, as his headquarters, so it was decided the civilians would be safer another half-mile up the road at Josiah Benner's. Ironically, at about that same time the Confederates decided that General Barlow should be moved from Josiah Benner's to the Crawford house.

MISS JANE SMITH:
"Brig. General Barlow was brought in this morning. He was wounded in yesterdays fight, perhaps mortally. I read several chapters of the words of everlasting life to willing ears."

GENERAL FRANCIS C. BARLOW:
On Thursday morning I moved up into another house just inside of the town where an elderly lady and her daughter were very kind to me.[2] I found some books there and passed Thursday and Friday very comfortably under morphia.

The 30th Pennsylvania Infantry, 1st Reserves, were near Fairfax Courthouse, Virginia, a month ago when this photograph was taken. They were part of the V Corps, General Meade's old command, now under General George Sykes. The Corps began arriving on the field early this morning and was posted in reserve behind Cemetery Hill off the Baltimore Pike. General Samuel W. Crawford commanded the Third Division, which included McCandless Bridgade and Company K, the men from Gettysburg. *Courtesy Massauchusetts Commandery of the Military Order of the Loyal Legion of the United States and the US Army Military History Institute, Carlisle, Pennsylvania.*

A COLLEGE STUDENT'S DIARY:
"Thursday, 7 AM: The rebels were reinforced overnight.

"The Federal wounded have but little attention paid to them from the Rebels here in the college hospital."

SARAH BROADHEAD, Chambersburg Street:
"Of course, we had no rest last night. Part of the time we watched the Rebels rob the house opposite. The family had left some time during the day, and the robbers must have gotten all they left in the house. They went from the garret to the cellar, and loading up the plunder in a large four-horse wagon, drove it off. I expected every minute that they would burst in our door, but they did not come near us. It was a beautiful moonlight night, and we could see all they did."

7 a.m. On the field: By daylight of July 2nd, Robert E. Lee has 40,000 to 45,000 men at Gettysburg. Union Commanding General George Gordon Meade has 46,000 in place, but the woods and heights along the Union line's "fishhook" curve keep Lee from seeing them. Meade's view is just as limited as Lee's, so neither man is fully aware of his enemy's strength. Yet.

General Richard Ewell's troops are now stretched through and beyond the town. Ewell's left wing circles east of Culp's Hill, skirts Rock Creek, and plunges south to end near the Baltimore Pike. Lee wants him to strike on the union right, "Baldy" Ewell is still reluctant. Longstreet urges Lee to wait for a Federal attack.

Sticking to his own vision, Lee reworks the scenario, still hoping to threaten both enemy flanks...Ewell from the north, Longstreet from the south. As Lee sees it, Ewell would

Company K, 1st Pennsylvania Reserves (Left), were mostly Gettysburg and Adams County men. During the four years of war Adams County, with a population of only 20,000, sent some 3,000 of its men off into battle. These men may have marched most of the night, but Company K had their spirits raised as they now began to recognize the homes and farms of neighbors.

SERGEANT ISAAC N. DURBORAW: "I was with the company on the march to Gettysburg, and it was amusing as familiar scenes, persons and faces were presented to our view. Some young ladies whom I recognized, as we passed along, not far from my home, and who were waving their handkerchiefs at the soldiers passing by, gazed at me in amazement as I named them, and as they did not recognize me, inquired, one of another, who that could be that knew them. When we arrived at the home of Sergeant Young his own brother Robert came to us, but the Sergeant did not leave the ranks." *Courtesy Commandery of the Military Order of the Loyal Legion of the United States and the US Army Military History Institute, Carlisle, Pennsylvania.*

This is Baltimore Street near the intersection with Emmitsburg Road. The white house on the right belongs to Catherine Snyder whose husband had owned the Wagon Hotel, on the left side of the photograph. Just to the left of the trees lining Baltimore Street is John Rupp's tannery. The trees on the right obscure the house of another tanner, John Winebrenner. Rupp's, Winebrenner's, and Smith McCreary's are among the houses in this area used by Confederate sharpshooters. Union sharpshooters were positioned inside the Wagon Hotel. *Courtesy Massauchusetts Commandery of the Military Ordr of the Loyal Legion of the United States and the US Army Military History Institute, Carlisle, Pennsylvania.*

lunge at Meade's right, ostensibly a feint that would be converted to a real attack if possible, while Longstreet would strike diagonally up the Emmitsburg road, hoping to collapse the Union line. Meanwhile, he would order A.P. Hill to direct his artillery against the Union center.

Lee is anxious for an early morning resumption. But Longstreet continues to argue for a defensive posture, and the morning passes quietly.

DANIEL SKELLY:
"We did not know what to do or expect; whether to remain quietly in our homes, or to go out in the town as usual and mingle with our people. But we were soon assured that if we kept within certain restrictions we could go about the town.

"It was hot and sultry and the lines of battle were quiet..."
But there was some shooting. Sniper's rifles popped and snapped with an irregular cadence that kept everyone hunch-shouldered and jumpy. There was no way to escape it.
School Superintendent AARON SHEELY's farm was near Seminary Ridge, behind Confederate lines:
"My wife was frantic. 'You'll have to go,' I told her, 'but I'll stay.' I hitched two horses, put some provisions into a wagon, and saw her and my little boy drive away."
Tanner, JOHN RUPP lived on Baltimore Street, directly between the two armies:
"Our men occupied my porch and the Rebels the rear of the house and I the cellar, so you can see that I was on neutral ground. Our men knew I was in the cellar, but the Rebs did not. I could hear the Rebs load their guns and fire.

Showers and a few scattered thunderstorms created muddy streets and roads. Drainage was a problem and some cellars were less than dry after showers. This is a view of muddy Stratton Street looking south toward the Dutch Reformed Church which became a hospital. Wounded and dying were laid out on its pews and on the floor. Blood soaked hymnals served as pillows. Surgeons removed some doors and laid them across the backs of pews so that they might serve as amputation tables. *Courtesy Adams County Historical Society.*

"There was one of our men killed under my big oak tree in the lot, and one in Snyder's meadow, close to our house. The Rebs occupied Mr. McCreary's house,[1] from which they could pick off our men as they pleased. Our sharpshooters found it out and kept a lookout and finally shot one in Mr. McCreary's front room, upstairs, and killed him on the spot, and also killed two up in Mr. G. Schriver's house, next to Mr. Pierce's."[2]

Meanwhile, larger plans were unfolding ...
HENRY EYSTER JACOBS. West Middle Street:
"General preparation among the troops stationed into our vicinity, a paralysis of action on the part of the people of the town.

"Rodes' division, posted along Middle street, had set to work upon the stone wall opposite our house[3] as soon as it took its station there the previous afternoon. They turned it right across the street. It served as a breastwork. It lay there, a spectacle of ruin and a promise of destruction, all day."

On south Baltimore street, ANNA GARLACH's mother dug in for a long siege. She and her son arranged a place in the cellar for her family and some of their neighbors, even though there was "a foot or more of water" on the floor:
"In the yard among the lumber were blocks of wood which were to be chopped down for rungs of chairs.[4] Mother and Will[5] rolled into the cellar a lot of those logs and stood them up and then put boards across the logs so as to be out of the water. There were two banks of ground in the cellar, at either end, and these mother fixed by covering with boards and with a board path to various parts of the cellar. Then she put one family on one bank, another family on the other one and a third one on the platform of boards over the water. The baby[6] and I were placed near the cellar steps and Will and Mother sat on the cellar steps. Each party knew the place he or she was to occupy and Mother had an ax behind the cellar door to cut our way out if anything happened.

"We stayed in the kitchen most of the time except when there was firing, then we would go to our places in the cellar."

Looking from her hilltop some three miles north of town, HARRIET BAYLY had an all-encompassing view of the battlefield, including movements of active Confederate troops and the pain of Union wounded still lying in the open among them. All along, Mrs. Bayly had planned to get involved if the war came to Gettysburg, and finally, there it was:

"I packed a market basket full of bread and butter and wine, old linen and bandages and pins, for I belonged to a society which prepared for such things,[7] and mounting a family horse that had been blind for several years, with my niece behind me, I started towards the town and scene of the first day's battle.

"As far as I could see there were men, living and dead, and horses and guns and cannon, and confusion everywhere.

"Getting down into the valley I found our wounded lying in the broiling sun, where they had lain for twenty-four hours with no food and no water. A zigzag fence was standing on the side of the road, and in its angles were many who had taken shelter from the sun, and to avoid being trampled on. The very worst needed a surgeon's care, but while my niece gave food to the hungry and wine to the faint, I looked after their wounds.

"I would cut open a trouser leg or coat sleeve until I found the wound, and then put on fresh bandage. One of the first I touched was a poor fellow badly hurt in the back. I cut open his coat from the waist up and found that the cloth that he had put on the wound had become so dry with clotted blood that I could not loosen it - and had no water. A wounded comrade lying near said, 'Madam, there is a little tea in my canteen that I have been saving; maybe you can loosen it with that.'

"I had been hearing the pitiful cry of 'water, water' all around me, and when I found that these men had none for twenty-four hours, I rose up in my wrath and turning to the Rebels who were walking around men, I said, 'Is it possible that none of you will bring water to these poor fellows?'

"An officer heard me and, finding that what I said was true, he ordered a lot of the men to mount and to bring all that was necessary. They said that the wells at the nearest houses were pumped out, but in strong English with stronger words thrown in, he sent them off with canteens strung over them, and I directed them where to go to find a good spring. Soon we had plenty of water.

"While busy at work, a German surgeon came along, saying that he had been directed to look after the Union wounded. As he could not speak English, nor I German, I was content to hear his expressions of 'goot, goot' when he examined the work I had done. He was as gentle as a woman in his touch, and it did me good to see how tenderly he handled those wounded men."

Back at the Bayly house, WILLIAM HAMILTON BAYLY's father, JOSEPH, returned to find the young Confederate who was given sanctuary the night before:

"Among the first thing insisted upon by my father when he found that a deserter was concealed in the house was to direct him to come out and take his chances with the family, which he did, passing as one of the boys of the household."

Gettysburg's Diamond, or central square, is at the junction of four major streets: Carlisle, York, Chambersburg and Baltimore. Idle Confederate troops found it a good place to gather, since Baltimore street rises for three or four blocks south of the square before descending toward Cemetery Hill. This rise created a protective barrier of hillside and houses between the square and Union snipers at the cemetery. Besides, the Globe Inn was just off the square, and was still open. Business was good for JOHN WILLS:

"Rebs everywhere. They inquired if they could have breakfast and they were told they could. Our tables, the old fashioned long ones, seated comfortably 42, closely fit 46. Those men were principally of Early's division, whose line lay from Baltimore Street down East Middle Street and around south to Cemetery Hill.

"Now, we raised the price of whiskey from 5 cents per drink to 10 cents and the price of meals from 35 cents to 50 cents. While they were eating their first meal, Father and I discussed what we should do if they offered us Confederate money in payment. He said take a stand and go inside of the dining room door and collect the money and if they cannot pay in good money, tell them we will close the dining room.

"When the first man left the table, coming up to me he said, 'Do you collect the money?' I said I did. He asked, 'How much is it?' I replied '50 cents.' To my great surprise he pulled out large rolls of brand new U. S. Government green backs. He said,

This shed, in the backyard of cabinetmaker Henry Garlach, is where Union General Alexander Schimmelfennig hid. After nightfall on the 1st he crawled from the nearby wood covered culvert into the shed, quietly rearranging some of the lumber as a makeshift cover. *Courtesy Adams County Historical Society.*

'Is that money satisfactory?' I replied it was. After he had paid me he said 'If you prefer this kind of money,' pulling out of another pocket a large bag filled with gold, 'I will willingly pay you in this kind.' It was a bag of brown material, buckskin or brown leather, and out of this money they paid us in cash for every meal."[8]

When not tending the battlefield wounded, HARRIETT BAYLY was feeding her share of idle southerners, too:

"The fact that many of the men who were loafing around the house put in regular appearances for meals indicated there were large numbers shirking their duty and keeping well away from danger."

But closer to the lines tensions remained high, aggravated by the insistent pop of rifles, mysterious dust clouds behind the trees, and the sounds of busy industry:

MR. BENNER. A farm southeast of Gettysburg:[9]

"We were all at sea and didn't know what was going to happen. On Culp's Hill we could hear a sound of chopping and guessed that the soldiers were building breastworks.

"Some of the farm fencing had been pulled down the day before, and a neighbor's cows had got into our wheat. Father thought he would drive them out. The wheat was on a hillside, and he walked up the slope to get a good look over the field. On its upper side was a fringe of brush and trees and a stone wall with a couple of rails on top. He was within twenty or thirty feet of this fence when he discovered some men standing behind it. Father would have liked to get away, but he concluded he would be safer to go forward. One of the men was a Rebel general. He had glasses that he was looking through, and he asked Father about the Federals. Father told him he didn't know anything about them, and then he started for home, but the general said: "Oh, no! You can't go back. You'll have to stay inside of our lines."

"So they sent him to the nearest house, which happened to belong to Father's brother, Dan.[10] We didn't know what had become of him, and we didn't dare risk going to look for him."

LEANDER WARREN and his family had spent an anxious night huddled in their home northwest of the square on Railroad Street:

"8AM: A (Confederate) Pioneer Corp. came along and cut down all fences and gates, speaking of (the probability of the) Union shelling the town. Father wanted to leave, but Mother said she had no time, a full oven of bread was being baked for the wounded and she was staying. Some who started to leave were advised by the Rebels not to because their houses would be robbed if they vacated them. Mother and my sisters continued baking."[11]

While building a fort for her family in her basement on Baltimore Street, Mrs. Catherine Garlach also managed to keep an eye on General Alexander Schimmelfennig, still hiding from Rebel troops under lumber piled over a backyard culvert. ANNA GARLACH, reports that, on at least one occasion, her mother tried to feed him:

"Mother made a pretense of going to the swill barrel to empty a bucket. In the bucket, however, was water and a piece of bread and instead of these going into the barrel, they went to the General in hiding. Mother was so afraid that she had been seen and the General would be found that she did not repeat this."

From his father's house at the SW corner of Baltimore and High Streets, fifteen year old ALBERTUS McCREARY could have looked out the south side to see Union troops if he'd wanted to, or he could go to the north side and talk to the Confederates. Since Union sharpshooters were firing toward the unprotected south side, he "went north."

"Along this street[12] from east to west of the town stretched a line of Confederate infantry in reserve. From time to time they were moved away, and others took their place. Most of them were ragged and dirty, and they had very little to eat. I saw one man with a loaf of moldy bread and a canteen of molasses. He would break off a piece of bread, pour molasses over it, and eat it with what seemed great relish. I asked him if that was all he had to eat. He answered, 'Yes, and glad to get it, too.'

"I had many talks with these men as they lay along the pavement and on the cellar doors. They were a sorry lot. I saw one man passing the house on horseback, without shoes and with spurs strapped to his bare heels. The officers seemed to be much better cared for.

"Before the battle I had been wearing my soldier's cap, but an incident occurred that led me to discard it for one of another kind until more peaceful times. I was standing on the pavement in front of our own door, watching a squad of Confederates approaching (we had lost our fear of them by this time). When they came opposite me, the officer in charge called 'Halt!' and pointed at me.

"Two of the men left the ranks, come over to me, and took me by the arms, saying, 'Come on.'

"I was greatly frightened by this and called for my father, who happened to be just inside. He at once came out, and the whole family with him, and asked what they wanted.

"'He is in the army and must come with us,' they said.
Father laughed and said, 'Oh, he is only a school boy,' but they started off with me, and it was only when a number of the neighbors, who had come out of their houses on hearing the commotion, finally persuaded them to believe I was not in the army, that they let me off.

"Oh, how frightened I was. I cannot convey to anyone the feeling."
Ten year old CHARLES McCURDY's family were sticking close to the cellar, for more than one reason:
"A short time before Father had sent in a barrel of flour, another of sugar, a number of hams and a bag of green coffee.

"While it was before the era of canned goods, there were preserved and dried fruits at hand and other dainties, so...the enforced seclusion involved no hardship.

"We had no bread, but resourceful women can do much with flour and biscuits took its place.

"In poking about the cellar, I found some potatoes in a dark corner. They had expended much of their substance in producing long white sprouts, but they proved a welcome addition to ham and biscuit.

"Tallow candles furnished light, for the excitement had proved too strenuous for 'de Gas House,' as the old German in charge of the works called himself when challenged by a Confederate sentry."[13]
In sum, the town, including the wounded, sheltered in its buildings and homes, kept still and waited. This is from a letter written by Major General FRANCIS BARLOW to his mother from a hospital bed in the Crawford house:
"I read and talked a good deal. I eat only some coffee and toast and cherries in those days. The ladies[14] and some of our own wounded in the house did what nursing I required. I saw some of our surgeons and some of the enemies who said there was nothing to be done but to bathe the wound in cold water and wait. Some of the staff officers of Ewell and Early came to see me and I talked very freely with them. They were pleasant fellows. They despised our army and meant to fight to the last. I saw a good many of their men also and was much pleased with them. They are more heroic, more modest and more in earnest than we are. Their whole tone is much finer than ours. Except among those on our side who are fighting this war upon antislavery grounds, there is not much earnestness, nor are there many noble feelings and sentiments involved. I heard the battles close to me. The enemy had no doubt of capturing or utterly destroying our army and I feared it would be so."
SARAH BROADHEAD:
"My husband went to the garden and picked a mess of beans, though stray firing was going on all the time, and bullets from sharpshooters or others whizzed about his head in a way I would not have liked. He persevered until he picked it all, for he declared the Rebels should not have one. I baked a pan of shortcake and boiled a piece of ham, the last we had in the house, and some neighbors coming in, joined us, and we had the first quiet

meal since the contest began. I enjoyed it very much. It seemed so nice after so much confusion to have a little quiet once more. We had not felt like eating before, being worried by danger and excitement."

At that time, TILLIE PIERCE was still working among wounded at the Weickert Farm, south of town near the hills known as the Round Tops:

"About ten o'clock, many pieces of artillery and large ammunition trains came up, filling the open space to the east of us. Regiment after regiment continued to press forward.

"I soon engaged in the occupation of the previous day; that of carrying water to the soldiers as they passed."

LEANDER WARREN:

"Midday: Shells are flying. Some men broke into the hotel[15] cellar and got whiskey, making it real hot for everyone around. A Rebel officer we've gotten to know comes back again, suggests it's best for us to load up a wagon of household goods and get out. He says he'll provide us escort through the lines, so we accept his advice. He instructs a bandsman with a bass horn around his neck to walk us through.

"Down Carlisle street, the dead had their pockets turned out. They'd also turned black from lying in the hot sun."

NELLIE AUGINBAUGH:

"During the first day's battle, a union soldier was shot down right in front of my home. Soon afterward, a confederate came along and he searched the dead man's clothes, but finding nothing of value, he tossed what he did find into the window of my house, saying we might be interested.

"The principal thing was a small picture the dead man carried of apparently his wife and two children. Father went out and rolled the body up in a blanket that belonged to the man and laid it near the house. In a few minutes, another Reb came along, rolled the body out of the blanket, went through the pockets again. This happened repeatedly."

MR. BENNER. Southeast of Gettysburg:

"I was standing in our lane with Mr. Martin, one of the townsmen who was stopping at our house, when here comes a Union soldier. He held his gun all ready to fire, and he was a savage-looking chap, too. 'I had a notion to pull on you fellers,' he said. 'You wear gray clothes and I didn't know but you were Rebels. My Colonel wants to talk with you.'

"We went with him down the lane to where the Colonel was sitting on a rock beside the creek. He questioned us as to the location of the Rebels, but we were just as ignorant about that as a newborn babe. We weren't accustomed to armies, and we didn't understand their movements and hadn't attempted to find out where they were or what they were doing. The soldier went back up the lane with us, and we'd gone about half

Artillery batteries, similar in size and make up to this Pennsylvania battery, are what caused anxiety in Tillie Pierce as she watched them thunder into position east of the Weikert farm house. They were setting up to provide support for the federal left – from the signal corpsmen atop Little Round Top to the III Corps at the rocky hill's western base. *Courtesy Massauchusetts Commandery of the Military Order of the Loyal Legion of the United States and the US Army Military History Institute, Carlisle, Pennsylvania.*

Before the war Sergeant Isaac N. Durboraw, 22, helped his family work their farm out near Two Taverns off the Baltimore Pike. Now, as a member of Company K, 1st Pennsylvania Reserves, he is camped with his unit southeast of Gettysburg. Many of these men have been away from their homes for two years. Now, to come back under the circumstances of waiting to fight and possibly die so close to home without seeing family and friends had to be most difficult.

SERGEANT DURBORAW: "While in bivouac, in J.M. Diehl's field, where we halted just before noon on July 2, to get a little rest, and wait for orders, Robison came to me when cooking my coffee, and told me that Peter Baker, living near by, wished to see me, so I went to his house, and after getting something to eat, returned promptly to the company."

way when Martin's little boy came running toward us waving his hands as if he wanted us to stop. He didn't say anything until he got to where we were. Then he told us some Rebels were at our house. At that, our soldier dropped back, but we went on and found two southern soldiers in our kitchen. They were after food and we let 'em have some."

TILLIE PIERCE:

"During the early part of the forenoon, my attention was called to numerous rough boxes which had been placed along the road just outside the garden fence. Ominous and dismal as was the sight presented, it nevertheless did not prevent some of the soldiers from passing jocular expressions. One of the men nearby, having been addressed with the remark that there was no telling how soon he would be put in one of them, replied: 'I will consider myself very lucky if I get one.'

"While the infantry was passing, I noticed a poor, worn-out soldier crawling along on his hands and knees. An officer yelled at him, with cursing, to get up and march. The poor fellow said he could not, whereupon the officer, raising his sword, struck him down three or four times. The officer passed on, little caring what he had done.

"Some of his comrades at once picked up the prostrate form and carried the unfortunate man into the house. After several hours of hard work the sufferer was brought back to consciousness. He seemed quite a young man, and was suffering from sunstroke received on the forced march.

"As they were carrying him in, some of the men who had witnessed this act of brutality remarked: 'We will mark that officer for this.'"

1 p.m. On the field: Union General Dan Sickles' assignment was on the far left; his own left flank, stretching onto Little Round Top. Personally, Sickles felt he would be better positioned if he were about three quarters of a mile to his front, and asked permission to move his line forward. He was told to stay put. Still, through a mix-up in orders, Sickles had no cavalry support on his left, and he didn't like it. The "better position" to his front nagged at him, and Sickles leaped at the suggestion that he send a strong reconnaissance group to probe Confederate strength in the area where he had proposed his new line. The scouts, members of Berdan's Rifles, found the Rebels and got into a scrap.

Still convinced of a personal strategic genius,[16] and without further consultation, the 38 year old Sickles moved his entire corps forward to a peach orchard along the Emmitsburg Road. That maneuver extended his right north along the road, while his left stretched southeastward nearly to Devil's Den. Sickle's line was stretched dangerously thin, both his and Hancock's left (still on Cemetery Ridge) were exposed, Little Round

The eastern side of Joseph Sherfy's Peach Orchard was on slightly more elevated ground than that which General Daniel Sickles occupied. All morning he had thought about moving his men to this spot, about three-quarters of a mile to the west of the Union flank. He succumbed to that temptation and thereby enticed the Confederates to launch an attack on what they saw as a now highly exposed Union left. *Courtesy Massauchusetts Commandery of the Military Order of the Loyal Legion of the United States and the US Army Military History Institute, Carlisle, Pennsylvania.*

Top was unoccupied by anything more than a signal station, and the outraged General Meade's defensive scheme was unglued.

But the Confederates were slow to do anything about it. Still missing Pickett's division, Longstreet held back, waiting for Law's brigade of Hood's division. After a 24-hour march, Law reached Herr's Ridge, northwest of Gettysburg, about noon and immediately gave his men a 30 minute rest. Then, Longstreet took up another 3 1/2 hours maneuvering west of Seminary Ridge, hoping to give Union pickets the impression of a much larger Rebel force.

In the meantime, Meade rushed to back the now-exposed, protruding Union line with additional troops and artillery.

TILLIE PIERCE was watching from the Weikert farm:

"Several field officers came into the house and asked permission to go up on the roof in order to make observations. As I was not particularly engaged at the time and could be most readily spared, I was told to show them the way up. They opened a trap door and looked through their field glasses at the grand panorama spread out below.

"By and by, they asked me if I would like to look. Having expressed my desire to do so, they gave me the glasses. The sight I then beheld was wonderful and sublime.

"The country for miles around seemed to be filled with troops; artillery moving here and there as fast as they could go, long lines of infantry forming into position, officers on horseback galloping hither and thither. It was a grand and awful spectacle..."

A COLLEGE STUDENT'S DIARY:

"2PM. We're hungry, but the Rebels destroyed our boarding house and eatables are scarce."

4:00 p.m. On the field: As the townspeople hunker down and Longstreet dithers, Major General John Sedgwick's 15,000 Federals complete the march from Manchester, Maryland, bringing Meade's strength to 97,000. On the other side, Major General George E. Pickett's division arrives, and Major General James E. B. Stuart's cavalry finally appears, bringing Lee's total to 75,000, although General Lee gave a cool welcome to General Stuart. In a show of bravado, Stuart had taken the long way to Gettysburg, circling east of the Union army, raiding and harassing it with impunity...some observers pronounced it impudence. Whatever it was, Lee felt his knowledge of the enemy's movements and strength had been severely limited by Stuart's absence; so much so that he had sent scouts in search of the Gallant and his riders. When finally they met at Lee's camp, it was clear that the commanding general was not happy. However, he did not remonstrate other than to say: "Well, General Stuart, you are here at last." In contrast, Lee's chief of staff, Colonel Charles Marshall, recommended that Stuart be court-martialed and shot.

Stuart and his troopers were sent to the Rebel left flank.

DANIEL SKELLY:

"I spent the afternoon in the yard back of the Fahnestock store on West Middle street.[17] There was a high board fence the length of the lot, extending to an alley at the end. There were two large gates opening to the street, along which the Confederate line ran. A Confederate major of one of the regiments was my companion. He told me he was originally from Pittsburgh, having gone south years before the war.

"Our conversation was about the war and the causes leading up to it and the result thus far on both sides.

"About 4 o'clock, our conversation was interrupted by a terrible cannonading off to the southwest of the town[18] and we separated, he joining his regiment in the street and I going to my father's house[19] near the Fahnestock store.

"Our town being in the hands of the Confederates and cut off from all communication with the outside world, we knew nothing about our army and were completely in the dark as to how it was located and how much of it had arrived on the field of battle. The Confederates maintained a clam-like silence on all matters concerning the battle,

General James Ewell Brown Stuart, 30, US Military Academy at West Point Class of 1854, was a Virginian. Before the war he was an aide to General Robert E. Lee in the capture of radical abolitionist John Brown at Harper's Ferry. Now, Lee heavily depended upon Stuart's cavalry for intelligence; however, in the days leading up to Gettysburg and during the first day and a half of fighting Stuart had left Lee blind. The dashing cavalier had led his horse soldiers on raids through the countryside – as far away as Rockville, Maryland, where they captured a Union supply train. *Courtesy Americana Image Gallery, Gettysburg, Pennsylvania.*

This house and barn, and the Peach Orchard on both sides of Emmitsburg Road, belonged to 51 year old fruit dealer Joseph Sherfy and his wife Mary. The Sherfy's and their five children were not home when the firestorm engulfed their orchard. By the time darkness fell on July 2nd one would be able to walk down this road on the bodies of the dead and wounded. "Many of the wounded, friend and foe, had sought refuge in Sherfy's barn, which was riddled with shot and shell like a sieve from its base to the roof." – Lt. Francis E. Moran, 73rd New York Infantry. *Courtesy Massachusetts Commandery of the Military Order of the Loyal Legion of the United States and the US Army Military History Institute, Carlisle, Pennsylvania.*

hence we did not know the significance of this tremendous cannonading. But for the present, it sent everyone to the cellars as a matter of protection."

To the east, SARAH BARRETT KING's hostess had had enough:

"Mrs. Bender said she would not stay although assured as long as she stayed nothing would be disturbed in (the) house. We walked away from a full house. Mrs. Bender never changed her milking suit, left everything behind. I picked up one basket only to find that Mother had taken out the shawls. I started back to find them, thinking they might misunderstand if I left them. Someone had got them. We were sorry to lose them, but more so to leave Benders, as we felt we were going into the enemy's ranks."

So, in spite of the fact that the armies were preparing to resume the active battle, the Kings were on the move again.

Attorney WILLIAM McLEAN, holed up with his family in the basement of their home on Baltimore street, became tired of his dreary situation:

"I ventured upstairs to the second floor and opened slightly the outside shutter of the window to take a little look around. I had a presentiment that it was not a safe place, and had just turned myself away, when a minie ball came crashing through the shuttle and

It was in this part of Sherfy's Peach Orchard that the 2nd New Hampshire and 3rd Maine ran into the swiftly advancing Confederates determined to overrun the entire III Corps. *Courtesy Massachusetts Commandery of the Military Order of the Loyal Legion of the United States and the US Army Military History Institute, Carlisle, Pennsylvania.*

sash of the window in direct line with where my breast had been a few seconds before. It entered the foot board of the bed in which my sick wife had been and passed into the mattress out of which it was picked. Again, I learned that the indulgence of curiosity at such a time was perilous."

4:30 p.m. On the field: The cannon bark as Longstreet orders his attack. In fragments, and without good reconnaissance, his troops move forward, and Longstreet runs straight into one of Sickle's divisions. Recovering their balance, the Confederates attack, and again the Union army flirts with disaster. Fortunately, Union Artillery commander, Major General Henry J. Hunt, saw what Sickles was up to and placed guns to back him up.

On the east side of Emmitsburg Road (Top), near the Sherfy's, is the farm of 42-year old Abraham Trostle and his wife Catherine. It was used as headquarters by General Daniel Sickles on the morning of July 2nd. The Trostle's and their nine children had sought safety elsewhere. As Sickles' men were engaged with Confederate General LaFayette McLaws and four regiments from Mississippi, a shot slammed into the former New York congressman's right leg, leaving it hanging only by flesh. Some of his men helped him from his horse as the III Corps retreated to the Federal line at the base of the Round Tops.

Most of the dead horses in this photograph (Bottom) belonged to the Confederates and were killed by shot, shell and concussion of Bigelow's 9th Massachusetts Battery that saved General Sickles. Bigelow's Battery suffered heavy casualties but it slowed the Confederate advance long enough for Union reinforcements to arrive. It is said that Sickles was carried from the field in a stretcher puffing on a cigar. *Courtesy Massachusetts Commandery of the Military Order of the Loyal Legion of the United States and the US Army Military History Institute, Carlisle, Pennsylvania.*

General Daniel Sickles was eventually taken to a field hospital set up at the Schaffer House, a brick home located across the Baltimore Pike from the farm of Adam and Catherine Wert, parents of school teacher J. Howard Wert. Sickles became a life-long friend of the Wert family, and when J. Howard married Emma Aughinbaugh (Nellie's sister) he gave the bride some momentos of his Gettysburg Campaign: gold tassels from his personal flag, earrings made of buttons off his uniform, and a photograph of himself in uniform. The relics rest on Mrs. Wert's silk black mourning handbag. *Courtesy The J. Howard Wert Gettysburg Collection.*

For a brief time during the late afternoon of July 2, Col. William C. Oates, commander of the 15th Alabama Regiment held the high ground on Big Round Top. From this view he could see the left wing of the Union line, exposed by Sickles' advance into the Peach Orchard. Oates control of the highest ground was short-lived, however, as General Evander Law (replacing the wounded General Hood) ordered Oates to leave Big Round Top and seize Little Round Top. *Courtesy Massachusetts Commandery of the Military Order of the Loyal Legion of the United States and the US Army Military History Institute, Carlisle, Pennsylvania.*

GATES FAHNESTOCK and his family remained in their home on the northeast corner of Baltimore and Middle Streets:

There was[20] "a furious artillery fire, part of which passed directly over the town, making it dangerous to stay upstairs. So we went to the cellar and were there at least a couple of hours. A hole was dug in the cellar floor and a large dry goods box lined with tin was put, and in this box silverware and other valuables were placed; the whole was covered with dirt. This was more a protection against or protection from fire in case the house was burned or destroyed."

SARAH BROADHEAD and her neighbors on Chambersburg Street found themselves just a block north of the central Confederate line which stretched along Seminary Ridge in the west, extending along Middle Street:

"It seemed as though heaven and earth were being rolled together. For better security we went to the house of a neighbor[21] and occupied the cellar, by far the most comfortable part of the house. Whilst there a shell struck the house, but mercifully did not burst, but remained embedded in the wall, one half protruding."

It is likely that the shell came from a Union battery that overshot its mark.

ALBERTUS McCREARY, 201 Baltimore Street:

"The bullets were continually flying across our yard, so that none of us dared to go to the barn. As we had a number of pet rabbits there, we were very much exercised about feeding them. A Confederate soldier offered to feed them for us, and did cross the yard with the bullets shizzing around him. I remember how brave we thought him. There was another Confederate soldier who was so fearless that he climbed a cherry tree in the center of the yard and sat eating cherries in a most unconcerned manner, although the bullets were cutting through the leaves continually. Of course these were stray bullets, for he could not be seen, but his position was just as dangerous. There was a line of

John Bell Hood, 32, was a graduate of the US Military Academy at West Point and a veteran of the Indian wars on the frontier. He was a seasoned cavalry commander who had won promotion to Major General after Antietam. During the 2nd day's fighting at Gettysburg he was aggressively leading his men against the Union left when a minnie ball mangled his left arm, forcing him to turn command over to General Evander Law. *Courtesy Americana Image Gallery, Gettysburg, Pennsylvania.*

As the Alabama troops moved down Big Round Top and up the rugged southeast slope of Little Round Top, they were surprised by heavy fire from the troops of Col. Strong Vincent who had positioned his men on the slopes and rocks of Little Round Top just minutes before. They were there because General Gouveneur Warren, who had earlier been sent to the Round Tops by General Meade, spotted the Confederate advance. Warren dispatched an aide to Meade requesting immediate help because the rebels far outflanked the position of Union forces. *Courtesy Massachusetts Commandery of the Military Order of the Loyal Legion of the United States and the US Army Military History Institute, Carlisle, Pennsylvania.*

sharpshooters just beyond us. The soldier taught us how to distinguish between the sounds of a minie rifle and of a musket ball; also between the different sounds made by the various shells flying over our heads. There were long shells, round shells, and solid shot—each sang its own peculiar song."

Farms in all directions were occupied by one side or the other. The firestorm showed no signs of dying quickly.

MR. BENNER's father's farm was no exception. Christian Benner's farm was south of Benner's Hill, about half-way between the Hanover Road and Rock Creek. His orchard occupied several acres behind the house:

When the brigades of the V Corps scurried up the rocky slopes of the Little Round Top there was but little time to post one's position before the rebels were upon them. *Courtesy Massachusetts Commandery of the Military Order of the Loyal Legion of the United States and the US Army Military History Institute, Carlisle, Pennsylvania.*

The Slaughter Pen, a rocky area at the eastern base of Devil's Den, had to be crossed by the Texans and the Alabamians if they were to take Little Round Top. A rain of minnie balls poured down upon them and shells exploded around them, fragmenting some of the boulders into shrapnel. *Courtesy Massachusetts Commandery of the Military Order of the Loyal Legion of the United States and the US Army Military History Institute, Carlisle, Pennsylvania.*

"I went upstairs and looked out a gable window. Some of our men were in the orchard deployed behind the trees. They'd take and load their guns and fire and then fall back. They were only a skirmish line, and didn't pretend to fight the Rebels, who had cut loose on them at a terrific rate.

"We saw the Rebels driving our men across the open fields to the woods. Every time they got within a couple of rods of a rail fence, they'd lie flat on the ground, except a few who would run forward and jerk the fence down. Then the rest would jump up, and on they'd go. The sound of the volleys they fired was just like you'd take a handful of gravel and throw it on a roof. They yelled like the mischief when they charged. I couldn't distinguish any words, but it was kind of an ugly yell."

On the field: Hunt's barrage quickly stills major portions of Longstreet's artillery. Concurrently, the attack eliminates any chance of Hood moving his Rebel troops south of the Round Tops, putting an end to Lee's hopes of flanking the Union left.

In the fracas, General Meade, who had gone out to see what could be done to improve a bad situation, is nearly carried into the Confederate line when his horse bolts. Meade gets the horse under control, preventing one of the few battlefield captures of an active commanding officer. It does nothing to improve Meade's feelings toward Sickles.

The 1st Pennsylvania Reserves engaged the advancing Rebels in the shadow of the Round Tops and pushed them back into the Wheatfield. SERGEANT ISAAC N. DURBORAW: "Just when I reached the command the orders were given to fall-in double-quick, and hurriedly we advanced to the Round-tops, obliquing into position left in front...fired two rounds, when the order 'Forward!' was given, and every man had to hunt his way as best he could, over, round and through the bushes, rocks, stones and Plum-run swamp in the flat below." If it weren't for the charge of the Pennsylvania Reserves, the Confederates may have captured the Round-tops.

Typical of people fleeing Gettysburg, SARAH BARRETT KING and her children, and Mrs. Bender and two children, passed through lines of soldiers as they looked for sanctuary. They finally reached the Rhinehart farm, well northeast of Gettysburg:

"Mrs. Rhinehart and her four daughters were glad to see us. Their men had taken their stock across the Susquehanna. They were glad to have company.

"I felt indifferent as to fate as we passed through the lines. I imagined they regarded us as fit subjects for an asylum. Someone asked the guard if we dare pass. Certainly, they said. We were safe enough. Rebs all around us."

On the field: Skirting the fight in the peach orchard, some Alabamians swing through the woods to the southeast, trying to get to Little Round Top, where their cannon would have an elevated, profile view of the length of the Union line. While not the enveloping maneuver Hood planned, it would be a damaging blow, if successful.

Reconnoitering, Brigadier General Gouverneur K. Warren gets to the abandoned hill first, spots the Rebel soldiers, and quickly moves troops and cannon to the summit. Thinly stretched, the 358 members of the 20th Maine Regiment spread out on the hill top to become the very bottom left of the Union line. It is left to them to hold off the advancing Confederates.

After a crackling fire fight, the 20th Maine "wheels" from its position, "swinging forward like a gate" in a brash act of heroism, forcing the Confederates into brutal hand-to-hand combat.

HENRY EYSTER JACOBS' home on West Middle Street was at least three miles north of that place, but still in the line of fire:

"The bullets flew everywhere around our house and our family went down to the cellar with only a brief excursion by my father and myself. He proposed that we two go into the yard in the rear of the house to hear the cannonade. We hadn't been there any appreciable time when the bullets that flew around us made us retreat hastily to the refuge of the cellar. There the safety was enough to keep us all unhurt. But one of Rodes' soldiers, seated on our old-fashioned sloping cellar door, suddenly groaned and we heard his body fall over and gently slide downward. He had been killed where he sat."

ALBERTUS McCREARY was a few blocks south:

"The vibrations could be felt, and the atmosphere was so full of smoke that we could taste saltpeter. One of our party was a deaf and dumb man who, though he could not hear the firing, plainly felt the vibrations and could tell when the firing was heaviest as well as we. He would spell out on his finger, 'That was a heavy one.' The whizzing of the shells overhead and the sharp snap of bullets through the trees in the yard kept us well keyed up.

"Our house stood on the corner of Baltimore and High streets, and we did not dare to look out of the windows on the Baltimore street side. Sharpshooters from Cemetery Hill were watching all the houses for Confederate sharpshooters and picking off every person they saw, since from that distance they could not distinguish citizen from soldier. On the High street side, we could stay out on the porch during the heavy artillery firing."

SARAH BROADHEAD:

"About 6 o'clock the cannonading lessened, and we, thinking the fighting for the day was over, came out. Then the noise of the musketry was loud and constant, and made us feel quite as bad as the cannonading, though it seemed to me less terrible. Very soon the artillery joined in the din, and soon became as awful as ever, and we again retreated to our friend's underground apartment..."

Bowdoin College Professor Joshua Chamberlain, who left his rhetoric classes to fight for the ideals in which he believed, had been marching his 20th Maine Regiment all day. The men were dusty and tired, but were immediately sent by Col. Strong Vincent to defend Little Round Top. Vincent was answering General Warren's dispatch for help, but he had only four regiments. Thinly stretched, the 386 men of the 20th Maine, spread out to become the very bottom left of the Union Line. It was left to them to hold off the advancing Confederates. The 34-year old Chamberlain was given orders to "hold this ground at all costs." After a crackling fire fight, the 20th Maine – virtually out of ammunition – wheeled from its position, "swinging forward like a gate" in a brash act of heroism, forcing the surprised Confederates into brutal hand-to-hand combat as the rebels retreated. *Courtesy Massachusetts Commandery of the Military Order of the Loyal Legion of the United States and the US Army Military History Institute, Carlisle, Pennsylvania.*

Col. Strong Vincent, 26, was a graduate of Harvard, and a lawyer before the war. His brigade, part of Sykes V Corps, responded to the call for reinforcements at the Round Tops. Col. Vincent was among those who died defending this high ground. *Courtesy Massachusetts Commandery of the Military Order of the Loyal Legion of the United States and the US Army Military History Institute, Carlisle, Pennsylvania.*

The 20th Maine lost 130 of its 386 men on the wooded slopes of Little Round Top, but they held. *Courtesy Massachusetts Commandery of the Military Order of the Loyal Legion of the United States and the US Army Military History Institute, Carlisle, Pennsylvania.*

CHARLES McCURDY:

"Two doors below our house the College Lutheran Church[22] was filled with wounded , as were all the churches and other public buildings. The auditorium of this church was on the second floor and the wounded had to be carried up a long flight of stairs from the street. Surgeons were at work under very rude conditions.

"The church yard was strewn with arms and legs that had been amputated and thrown out of the windows, and all around were wounded men for whom no place had yet been found."

WILLIAM HAMILTON BAYLY watched from his northside hilltop as the battle slowly ebbed:

"A ceaseless thunder of artillery and the scream peculiar to shot and shell when hurtling through the air, the flashes of fire from bursting shells as darkness came on.

"The movements of the forces fighting there could not be distinguished, partly because of distance, but more particularly perhaps, because of the clouds of smoke that hung over the whole field. A flash of flame and the angry crack of guns a few seconds afterwards indicated where the opposing forces were engaged.

"As darkness gathered the firing ceased and all was quiet, uncanny in its silence as the noise had been satanic in its volume."

On the field: In this battle, forced upon troops of both sides by his arrogance, Dan Sickles' corps was so badly chopped up that it would never function as a unit again. The afternoon's fighting engulfed the Rose buildings, the Wheat field, Devil's Den, the valley of Plum Run, and the slopes of Little Round Top for four hours. Longstreet took the new ground, at great cost to both sides. But Meade played a good tactical game, and the "Fishhook" line stayed in place on Cemetery Hill.

During the battle, Sickles was struck below the right knee by a shell fragment which shattered the leg so badly that it was left hanging by a shred. He was carried to the wheat field in the rear, and the leg was amputated immediately.[23]

In the meantime, General Ewell faced the extreme right flank of the Union line on Culp's Hill. His divisions covered two miles, stretching from the western limits of Gettysburg, through the town itself, and bent southeast, overrunning several farms, including those of both Henry and Jesse Culp, and Daniel and Christian Benner. This curving line ended the Confederate left flank on the east side of Culp's Hill, just a mile behind the widow Lydia Leister's home on Taneytown Pike, which no less a person than Union General George Gordon Meade had commandeered for his headquarters. In spite of all expectations, quiet prevailed along that line during the morning and afternoon. That was fortunate, because, in the course of the day's fighting, Meade had to "borrow" most of Major General Henry W. Slocum's two divisions from Culp's Hill, leaving just one brigade to defend the northern, or right, Union flank. Ewell did not attack in concert with Longstreet as General Lee had planned, believing his artillery inferior to that of Union Brigadier General Henry J. Hunt's, much of it now pointing in his direction.

Ewell held back his infantry until Longstreet's fight was over.

Ten year old **ALBERTUS McCREARY**, at home on Baltimore at High Streets:

"I heard cheering down the street. It seemed to be caused by the passing along High Street, toward our house, of a small body of officers on horseback. As they drew near, the men along our pavement stood and cheered also. One of the men told me it was General Lee and his staff. I had a good look at him as he passed. He looked very much the soldier, sitting very erect in his saddle, with his short-cropped beard and his Confed-

John Winebrenner was one of Gettysburg's more successful tanners. His house and tannery were located on the east side of Baltimore Street, about a half block north of where John Rupp lived and operated his tannery. Samuel McCreary's home and brickyard was down a little side road by the Winebrenner house. All three of those residents' homes and businesses were among buildings caught in the crossfire of the heavy fighting that took place for Cemetery Hill. Confederate snipers particularly favored the upper floors. *Courtesy Adams County Historical Society*

After a fight, blankets and muskets gathered from the dead and the wounded were often rigged as shading to make the fallen as comfortable as possible until they could receive treatment. Whenever there wasn't a barn, a house, or a town where the wounded could be taken, these blanket tents appeared. Even when sheltering buildings existed, they filled quickly after the first few volleys of fire. *Courtesy Massachusetts Commandery of the Military Order of the Loyal Legion of the United States and the US Army Military History Institute, Carlisle, Pennsylvania.*

erate Gray. The whole staff were a fine looking set of men...at least, they seemed so to my youthful eyes; and it is needless to say that I gazed at them with keen curiosity. They rode up as far as a slight elevation in the street, stopped, took their glasses and surveyed Cemetery Hill, where they could see the position of their enemy. This was just before the Louisiana "Tigers" made their famous charge.

"What a racket that did make! It was an infantry charge, and the sound was as if a million boys with sticks were beating on a board fence. It was not in volleys, but continuous.

"When this firing began, we took shelter in the cellar."

7:30 p.m. On the field: Ewell orders brigades from North Carolina and Louisiana to charge East Cemetery Hill itself. Topping the hill, they breach the wall at a point held by Howard's XI Corps. Hancock sends one of his brigades to help, and there begins hand to hand combat with revolvers, bayonets, shovels, hand spikes, pickaxes and stones. Calling the artillery on east Cemetery Hill, "Battery Hell," the furious Rebels turn one of the battery's own cannon on it.

In growing darkness, Hancock's men plug the gap and then counterattack with additional help from units of the I and XI Corps, driving Early's two unsupported brigades back down the hill the way they came.

A UNION SOLDIER'S ACCOUNT:[24]

"Our soldiers were defending their guns with rammers and stones and the Tigers were struggling like their fierce namesakes for possession. It was a grand, though gory example of the heroism of the American soldier.

"After the fight we picked up the wounded. I remember one poor fellow clad in gray who was shot in the head. We carried him to the pump back of the cemetery gate. He was moaning piteously and rubbing his hand over the gaping wound from which his brains were oozing. How we pitied the poor wounded man. Ten minutes ago a foe, now a helpless comrade needing our care."

MR. BENNER:

"They laid them on the floor of our kitchen and up in the barn and out in the yard. Some were groaning and others would swear. The sight of the first wounded man was dreadful, but it is remarkable how quickly one gets hardened to such things. In a little while I could see a man's leg sawed off, or his head sawed off, for that matter, without being disturbed.

Brigadier General Harry T. Hays' 9th Louisiana troopers were mostly French speaking Creoles who were generally considered to be fierce fighters. The Louisiana Tigers – fighting alongside Col. Isaac Avery's North Carolinians – had turned General Barlow's right flank yesterday and were now encamped along the Confederate line down Middle Street. Tonight they planned to drive the Union forces off the cemetery hill and the hill on Henry Culp's farm. *Courtesy Americana Image Gallery, Gettysburg, Pennsylvania and Chicago Historical Society.*

The Union high ground atop Culp's Hill. The steeple on the left is the German Reformed Church on South Stratton Street at High Street. Heavy fighting occurred on these slopes on the night of July 2nd. General Harry Hays' Louisiana Tigers were among the regiments that attempted to take the crest of the hill at Evergreen Cemetery and Culp's Hill. *Courtesy Massachusetts Commandery of the Military Order of the Loyal Legion of the United States and the US Army Military History Institute, Carlisle, Pennsylvania.*

"I talked with a wounded North Carolina man. He spoke sort of regretfully of the war. 'We got nothing against you people,' he said, 'but the war came on and we were forced to go.'

"Beside our kitchen wall was a big half hogshead that water flowed into from a spring, and the Rebels were all the time coming to fill their canteens there. They were seen by the Yankees, who began shelling 'em. The shells would strike in the meadow and throw up the dirt, and one went through the seat of a horse rake in the orchard. Another came into the kitchen. A Rebel was leaning against the door frame, and the shell cut off the jamb opposite and keeled him over into the yard. But he picked himself up and walked in, brushing the dust off his trousers, no more concerned than if the accident was a mere trifle. The shell went into the chimney and exploded and scattered some pretty big stones among the wounded men lying on the floor. But that didn't seem to alarm them. They made no ado whatever.

"After awhile, the firing ceased and three ambulances came to get the wounded at our place. They drove in around our hog pen and the drivers had got out when the shells began to fly again. Immediately, the drivers jumped back in and went off in a great hurry. A little major came into the house and asked for some red cloth to make a hospital flag, and Mother got him a piece. He tied the cloth to a stick and had a soldier climb up a ladder and nail it on the roof so our men would stop their firing in that direction.

"Those Yankees are a lot of brutes or they wouldn't shell ambulances," he said to me.

"Well," I said, "that's no worse than what your fellers did at Chancellorsville when they set the woods on fire and burnt our wounded.

"It was kind of risky for me to talk so, for he could have put me out of the way, and that's all there would have been of it."

This was the ground covered by the Confederates in their assault on Cemetery Hill on the night of July 2nd. Cannon fire from the battery of the 5th Maine artillery regiment and a Union counterattack from the direction of Evergreen Cemetery forced the North Carolina Brigade of Col. Isaac Avery and the Louisiana Tigers to withdraw. *Courtesy Massachusetts Commandery of the Military Order of the Loyal Legion of the United States and the US Army Military History Institute, Carlisle, Pennsylvania.*

JOHN WILLS tried to watch the fight from the roof of the Globe Inn. That led him to a meeting with one of the Confederacy's most interesting men:

"While standing there, I heard a call, saying 'Get off that roof!' I looked out around me, I heard it several times; finally I located it. A Confederate soldier was standing in an open space between the Kendlehart property and Culp's Blacksmith shop on East Middle Street with his gun resting on a paling fence pointed at me."

Finally, Wills was forced off the roof by a Confederate officer with a revolver in his hand. He told John that General Jubal Early wanted to see him. Right away.

"I decided it be best to come down. When I came down to him there were the barkeeper with three men going into the rear door. He said, 'Who are those men?' I told him and he said to bring them along. As we were coming out of the alley and reached the front pavement, Mr. J. Cassat Neely, Esq., an influential citizen and a prominent member of the bar in the Adams County courts, who was a boarder at the hotel, had just come to the front door. (Neely agreed to accompany the party.)

"He (the officer) took us up before General Early, who was sitting on marble slabs at John Cannon Marble Works, at the rear end of the lot at the corner of Baltimore and Middle streets, where the line of General Early's division lay during the battle. General Early asked me what I was doing on the roof. I replied, "I was looking over the battle."

"He asked me what I had seen.

"I told him I was looking at a Confederate battery on Benner's Hill, firing in the direction of Culp's Hill or Cemetery Hill, and also at a Confederate battery north of town on Seminary Ridge between the Mummasburg road and the red barn on the Judge Wills farm, firing in the direction of Culp's Hill or East Cemetery Hill.

"He asked me if I was the proprietor of the hotel? I replied, no, my father was. He asked where is he? I replied he had gone out to his farm on the York Pike to look after his property, as he had been informed that his tenant had left and the Confederates were occupying the house and barn.

"He then told me that I might have been picked off the roof by Union sharpshooters on Cemetery Hill. He said: 'Your people are on the streets; they are at their garret windows and on the roofs. I sent guards from door to door on your streets to tell them to go into their cellars or at least to remain within their houses, the only safe place for them. If you people would but take my advice...I want to save your people!'

The angry General told Wills to go home and, in effect, to mind his own business, which Wills freely admits he was ready to do. At that point, Early and Wills' protector, attorney J. C. Neely, fell into conversation about their respective law practices. Early was a member of the bar at Lynchburg, Virginia.

GATES FAHNESTOCK, NE corner of Baltimore and Middle Streets:

"When what was left of the Louisiana Tigers returned from the battlefield that evening, they were not so jubilant. They were tired, exhausted and discouraged and what they said of the Germans in Howard's command on Cemetery Hill was not complimentary.

"It was an anxious time for us. We had no knowledge of how the battle was going except as we heard the remarks on the sidewalk and some remarks in the court house hospital. We did surmise that the Confederates were not successful that day, but how the Union forces fared, we had nothing. So the night was an anxious one and our earnest position was for tomorrow and that right would prevail.

"Mother, cook and maid were steadily cooking and sending over to the Court House, diagonally across the street, now used as a hospital, bread, cakes and delicacies. She was able to decline to give the same to the Confederate troops, and they did not resent it as they saw the buckets and trays going over to the wounded men, who were Union soldiers.

"The boys helped to carry over to the Court House and we would remain and aid Doctors and Nurses in doing and helping as boys can. There was so much to excite the interest and sympathy of the boys and it was nearly overpowering, but after seeing the first amputations, at which I nearly fainted, there came a remarkable self control. The interest in the wounded and an inspiring desire to do something to help them dominated and held back the extreme sensitiveness."

On the field: Ewell orders Johnson's division up the east side of Culp's Hill to attack the lone brigade still there after Meade's "borrowing." But the remaining Union defenders, well entrenched and behind stone walls, are able to drive most of Johnson's people back. Exhausted, one of Johnson's brigades does manage to reach empty trenches near Spangler's Spring, falling into them for the night, not knowing how close they are to the heart of the Union line.

Meanwhile, others were mopping up after Sickles' and Longstreet's fight. The numbers at the Weickert farm grew even larger. TILLIE PIERCE:
"On this evening, the number of wounded brought to the place was indeed appalling. They were laid in different parts of the house. The orchard and space around the buildings were covered with the shattered and dying, and the barn became more and more crowded. The scene had become terrible beyond description."
MARY CUNNINGHAM BIGHAM's parent's farm home was on the opposite side of the field from Tillie:
"A Confederate officer rode to the door and told Father that the buildings would be required for hospital use. The big red barn was preferred to the house. It was located two miles from the wheat field where they lay in pouring rain."
As on the first day of battle, showers were intermittent, some were locally heavy. Runoff from the fields was mixed with blood and some streams were tinted red.
Back in town, DANIEL SKELLY saw another legend begin:
"Will McCreary[25] and I were sent on some errand down on Chambersburg street, and as we were crossing from Arnold's corner to the Eckert corner,[26] we were halted by two Confederate soldiers who had a lady in their charge. She was on horseback and proved to be the wife of General Barlow,[27] who had come into the Confederate lines under a flag of truce looking for her husband, who had been severely wounded on July 1, and, as she was informed, had been brought into the town. She informed us he was with a family "named McCreary: on Chambersburg street. We directed her to Smith McCreary's residence.[28]
"She did not find the General there, however, for he had been taken from the field to the farmhouse of Josiah Benner on the Harrisburg road,[29] just where the former covered bridge crossed the creek."
Seventeen year old NELLIE AUGHINBAUGH:
"My uncle owned a large store which opened to a large yard adjoining our home.[30] The stores were all closed but the Rebels broke in and helped themselves. Boxes and barrels were dragged into the yard and opened. They knocked the tops off barrels or kegs of salted mackerel, snatched the fish from the brine and ate them, heads, tails and all. It was more than I could stand. Mother was rather the same way. Father was too bitter in his feelings for them to offer help, but mother would sometimes cook the fish for the Rebs, rather than watch them eat them raw.
"They ordered all the townspeople to make coffee and bread for them and to provide their wounded with food in the churches, hospitals and schools and homes where they put them. Father didn't like to, but he would carry provisions to these wounded. However, if he'd known that mother was broiling the fish the men gave to her he would have been angry. She used to have us children watch for his return saying, 'Those poor fellows are somebody's son and I cannot stand to see them eat uncooked fish'. Whenever Father would approach, we'd warn her and she'd take the fish off the stove and quickly give it out. They'd grab it like animals. I have seen them break open packages of baking soda and eat it. They would bring out new clothes from a store, and their own so ragged they'd just give it a little pull here and a pull there and the rags would drop off right on the street and they'd don the new one."

MARY McALLISTER's house and small store on Chambersburg Street was now jammed with wounded Union soldiers while the Rebels occupied the streets. She and her sister did the only logical thing:

"We went to work — for the Rebels, too. Martha cooked and did what she could and I undertook to bake bread.

"I went on the street and the wounded begged so hard for bread and butter that I started to go to Scott's, down the street, to try to find milk or butter.

"Next, then, the wounded officers upstairs were making me go for some liquor some place and I went to Dr. Horner. He said, 'Go to Alex Buehler's drug store.' So I went.

"Alex said he would give me fifty cents worth in their canteen and he filled it. Then there came a shell into their house and knocked a hole in the side of the front door, through the wall.

"'Well!', he said, 'you will be killed if you stay.'

"As I went out, he said, 'Don't let them see it!'

"I think Col. Thompson[31] was upstairs and two others. One, a Captain Gish,[32] was shot through the leg. But they took the whiskey and divided it and you can tell it brought song. So I never went for any more.

"The wounded downstairs was the ones I was most interested in. All this time, one poor man suffered awful. He was struck with a bullet and it came around. You could see it in his back. I went into Mrs. Belle King's where there was a good many surgeons and I begged them to come over and look at this man. I said, 'You can take the bullet out for you can see it.' But they would not come and I threatened to report them and one of them sassed me a little.

"Then I got Dr. Robert Horner.[33]

"We had no light. The gas was out and we had no lamps. So Martha thought of twisting paper and dipping it in lard. I held the lighted paper while the doctor took the bullet out. It was all ragged and the doctor gave it to the man and said, 'There, take that and put it in your knapsack for a keep-sake.'

"The man said, 'I feel better already!' I put wet cloths on the wound."

Fifteen year old ALBERTUS McCREARY:

"Once, hearing laughter outside, I looked out and saw a young boy standing in the middle of the street, throwing stones at the windows on either side and laughing loudly every time he broke a glass. Bullets were flying down the street and every time one whizzed near him he would duck his head, laugh, and immediately renew his efforts to break windows. I saw that he was not one of the town boys, and asked the soldiers who he was. One of them said, 'Oh, that little devil followed the army up from the south.'"

JANE POWERS McCONNELL[34] lived with her husband, Henry, on Seminary Ridge. She and her children had come to town to stay with her family on or before July 1st when the fighting erupted:[35]

"We lived on High Street.[36] There was a neighbor at the other end, ill with small pox. John Burns got it into his head that she was a Rebel sympathizer, which was far from the case.

"John met a group of Rebel officers and soldiers on High street, and a happy thought struck him. He'd play a joke and get even with the woman. He told them this woman had a number of Union men hidden in her house and considerable powder stored out of sight in her cellar. They lost no time reaching the house, and they flew out of it quicker than they entered when she told them she had small pox.

"Just as frightened as they, she followed them out into the street out of fear and ran because she thought the house would be bombarded or burned. She was a sorry looking spectacle without a shoe on, nor any hair on her head. Not a soul took her in until my Father[37] met her down the street. He says, 'Susan, where are you going?' And she told him the story. He brought her home because the fighting was getting fierce. Father put

Captain Jacob V. Gish, Co. B, 10th Regiment Pennsylvania Volunteer Infantry was one of the wounded Union soldiers cared for by Mary McAllister and her sister Martha Scott. *Courtesy Roger D. Hunt Collection at USAMHI.*

Widower Solomon Powers, 60, lived with his daughters on High Street, not too far from his stone yard. Powers was said to be one of the best granite cutters in the east. He had moved his family to Gettysburg when construction on the railroad began. Powers' five daughters, all school teachers, were in their twenties when the battle broke out. Only one, Jane, was married. Her husband was Henry McDonnell, 34, a cabinetmaker. They lived on Seminary Ridge. *Courtesy Adams County Historical Society.*

her in the cellar, but hardly had she been down there long enough to calm down some before all of the people were ordered to the cellars. Fifteen others climbed down there with her, including several of our men who had escaped from the hands of the enemy and several wounded. The thought of contagion never occurred to us, and none contracted the disease."[38]

> **LIZZIE BEARD PLANT:**
> She recalls a Doctor John Bodly of Georgia who worked in her home with the wounded. The doctor, a smaller person who bore many of the characteristics of a woman, was referred to by the family as "the woman doctor." Years later, she wrote that she read a newspaper account of a woman in New England admitting that she had served in a civil war as a doctor and that she'd been in Gettysburg.

JOHN WILLS:
"A Confederate doctor who attended the sick and wounded at the Confederate hospital came to the hotel and engaged a single room. He asked me if I would allow him to take into his room with him a friend, a Confederate Lieutenant. I said, 'Doctor, as you are paying for the room, you can take in with you who you please.'

"Now, we had at the same time boarding with us at the hotel, two Union doctors and I could not understand at the time how and why could those men of the two opposing armies be allowed together, but since have learned from Union soldiers that doctors who were attending the sick and wounded in hospitals in either army could not be taken prisoners of war."

Early in the battle, Confederate units established "sniper's nests" in the upper floors of row houses to give the sharpshooters a clear view of Cemetery Hill. LIEUTENANT COLONEL WILLIAM W. BLACKFORD was an aide to Confederate Cavalry General J. E. B. Stuart. Blackford's brother, Major Eugene Blackford, was among skirmishers from Rode's division who occupied the houses. That night, Colonel Blackford looked up Major Blackford:

"It was the first time I had seen warfare carried on in this way, and wishing to find my brother, I was glad to have the opportunity of examining it. Leaving my horse in charge of the courier who accompanied me, at a place in the street somewhat sheltered from the shells which at times came tearing through the houses, I ascended a handsome stairway to the second floor. This floor along the whole block had been used in each house for parlors, sitting rooms and dining rooms, and the floor above for bedrooms, while the lower floor was occupied mostly by stores. Eugene's men had cut passways through the partition walls so that they could walk through the houses all the way from one cross street to the other. From the windows of the back rooms, against which were piled beds and mattresses, and through holed punched in the outside brick wall, there was kept up a continuous rattle of musketry by men stripped to the waist and blackened with power. It was a strange sight to see these men fighting in these neatly and sometimes elegantly furnished rooms, while those not on duty reclined on elegant sofas, or stretched themself out upon handsome carpets. I was surprised to see in some houses feathers scattered everywhere in every room, upstairs and downstairs, and found it had been done by shells bursting in feather beds on the upper floor. Pools of blood in many places marked the spots where someone had been hit and laid out on the carpets, and here and there a dead body not yet removed, and many great holes in the walls showed where artillery had been brought to bear upon this hornets' nest when their sting became too severe for endurance.

"I inquired for Major Blackford and was directed to a room in the middle of the block where I found him and some of his officers lolling on the sofas in a handsome parlor. On a marble table were set decanters of wine, around which were spread all sorts of delicacies taken from a sideboard in the adjoining dining room, where they had been left, in their hurry, by the inhabitants.

"Outside could be heard the cannonade and the growl of the musketry around Cemetery Ridge, and echoing through the house the reports from the deadly rifles puffing little clouds of light blue smoke from the back windows, while the room was pervaded by the smell of powder."

Seventeen year old JENNIE McCREARY lived on Chambersburg Street:

"I went to bed at 11 p.m. There was a knock on the door and Papa answered. Two Rebels said General Trimble and two aides want supper and lodging. We complied, although the house was full.

"After all were fixed up, the aides say the general decided to stay where he was, but they ate supper and left. Kate and I were in the kitchen when there was another knock on the door. Kate went. Two Union soldiers wanted bread. They'd not gone when there was another knock and it was three Rebels who were asking for bread and a place to sleep as well. We gave them bread but wouldn't let them in. Later, the Rebs tried to break in the house, but a Captain Palmer called out to them that this was a hospital, and they went away."

Day's end: On the field: Meade orders General Henry W. Slocum's two borrowed divisions back to their original position on Culp's Hill, then calls a meeting of his corps commanders. They decide to hold their current position whatever comes next. All commanders but Howard rule out an attack. He wants to wait until 4 p.m. Friday, and then attack the Confederates if they have not resumed the offensive.

Deciding to keep a defensive posture, Meade predicts that if Lee attacks again, it will be on the front of II corps, at the center of the Union line.

DANIEL SKELLY:

"I slept in a room above the Fahnestock store,[39] with a number of other boys. This room fronted on West Middle street and had a window in it opening out to the street, with shutters which were bowed. Not making any light we would remain quietly at the window trying to catch the conversation of the Confederate soldiers who were lying on the pavement below the window. We were eager to catch something that would give us some clue to our army and how they were faring in the battle that had been going on at intervals during the last two days, but did not learn much from them."

MARY McALLISTER:

"Martha and four children lay crossways on a bed in the front room because every other place was full of wounded. I sat on a chair with a skirt folded to lay on the window sill, with the window hoisted. There I slept...with my head on my arms."

SARAH BROADHEAD:

"I have just finished washing a few pieces for my child, for we expect to be compelled to leave town to-morrow, as the Rebels say it will most likely be shelled. I cannot sleep, and as I sit down to write, to while away the time, my husband sleeps as soundly as though nothing was wrong. I wish I could rest so easily, but it is out of the question for me either to eat or sleep under such terrible excitement and such painful suspense. We know not what the morrow will bring forth, and cannot even tell the issue of to-day. We can gain no information from the Rebels, and are shut off from all communications with our soldiers. I think little has been gained by either side so far. 'Has our army been sufficiently reinforced?' is our anxious question. A few minutes since we had a talk with an officer of the staff of General Early, and he admits that our army has the best position, but says we cannot hold it much longer. The Rebels do so much bragging that we do not know how much to believe. At all events, the manner in which this officer spoke indicates that our troops have the advantage so far. Can they keep it? The fear they may not be able causes our anxiety and keeps us in suspense."

MISS JANE SMITH diary:

"Midnight, July 2nd: What pen can tell or thought conceive the awfulness of the strife that has raged from between three and four o'clock of this afternoon until nine tonight! The roar of cannon and rattle of musketry beggar all description. Hundreds of souls have been ushered into the presence of the great 'I Am.' I pray for them.

"There is a silence around us now that is ominous of tomorrow's struggle. Thousands of brave ones lie upon their arms, girded for conflict, snatching a few moments' rest."

End July 2

Elizabeth Thorn, whose fourth child was due in about three months, was restless at the Musser house. Since wounded were being brought this far out the Baltimore Pike she grew most anxious about her home. All of the possessions of this family of German immigrants had been packed in the cellar of the Evergreen Cemetery Gatehouse at General Howard's suggestion. Her father wanted to get back to check on the hogs, so the two tried to slip out of the Musser house around midnight. A wounded soldier raised his body up on one elbow and motioned her to come over.

ELIZABETH THORN: "He showed me a picture with three boys and he told me they were his boys and asked whether I wouldn't allow my boys to sleep in his arms. Father said it would be too sad not to oblige him and I gave him the boys, they lay down beside him, the youngest nearest him and Mother took her place in the corner. Father and I went out to go home. We came to a guard who did not want to let us through but I told him we had left our place and all our things in a hurry and Mother wanted a pillow and he let us go then. As we came to the cemetery we heard the groans of the wounded. Father went down to let out the hogs but he could not find them. The old stable, pig pen and all wood had been used by soldiers to make fires to cook by. Even six scaps of bees were gone.

"Father and I tried to go into the Gateway house but we were stopped. We were told that wounded men were inside and that we should make no light as it might make the wounded soldiers restless. We said we would get what we wanted without a light and we felt around. Father got a shawl and I a quilt."

She and her father returned to the Mussers' farm, deciding to take the family further out of harms way. *Courtesy E. F. Conklin, Women at Gettysburg – 1863.*

NOTES

1. Probably Samuel McCreary, a brick maker whose house had windows that overlooked the cemetery where Union soldiers were dug in.
2. George Schriver, whose house was next door to butcher James Pierce at the SW Corner of Baltimore and Breckenridge, was with his regiment at the time of the battle. On the morning of the first day's fighting, his wife, Henrietta, grabbed up her two children and, with her neighbor, 15 year old Tillie Pierce, set out to the farm of her father, Jacob Weikert, near the Round Tops.
3. NW corner of West Middle Street and South Washington.
4. Anna Garlach's father, Henry, was a cabinetmaker.
5. Anna's 12 year old brother.
6. Six month old Frank Garlach.
7. Probably the Union Aid Society.
8. When Wills quizzed the Confederate officers on the source of their 'northern' money, he was given to understand that it had been funneled to them surreptitiously from prosperous supporters in the northern states.
9. This is another interview in Clifton Johnson's *Battlefield Adventures*. Holding to his policy of not identifying the people he interviewed, Johnson called this person "The Farmer's Son." There is evidence, however, that he is one of the sons of farmer Christian Benner who kept farm holdings about a mile south of Culp's Hill. For lack of any further identification, we will refer to him as "Mr. Benner" throughout the book. He was identified to that extent by Gettysburg historian, Tim Smith.
10. Daniel Benner, Christian's brother, had a neighboring farm.
11. Repeatedly, women tell of baking bread for the soldiers, or handing out bread and butter at their doorsteps. This staple was the commodity they had in greatest abundance. Women baked every day or so in the normal course of events, and it is the snack they would have given their own children. For the soldiers, most of them young men or boys, it would have been the thing that would have filled their stomachs fastest. And, perhaps, it just felt like home.
12. High Street.
13. Gas throughout Gettysburg was turned off as a safety precaution at the first sign of fighting. It remained off during the battle and for several days afterward because of some damage to the gasworks.
14. Mrs. William Smith and her daughter, Jane.
15. John Wills, who operated the Globe Inn, located a block or so east and south on York Street, complained about Confederate soldiers breaking into the whiskey stock in the basement. That may be the hotel young Warren was referring to, although almost directly behind the Warren home on Chambersburg Street at South Washington, stood the Eagle Hotel. All Gettysburg hotels endured occupation, significant damage and some theft during the time of the battle.
16. For no really good reason. A former Tammany Hall politician, Sickles became a Congressman from New York in 1858. He had no particular military background, but that didn't stop him from raising a volunteer brigade and getting himself commissioned as a Brigadier General. All he had was an overwhelming, if misguided self-confidence. And from such raw material is history made.
17. NW corner of West Middle and Baltimore Streets. The building still stands.
18. Sickles and Longstreet engage.
19. Also on West Middle street.
20. Phrase added for clarity.
21. David Troxel's house, the next house west of the Broadheads'.
22. Christ Lutheran Church on Chambersburg street.
23. Sickles donated the leg to the army's medical museum and visited it regularly in later years.
24. From: *Under Both Flags.* Philadelphia, Pennsylvania: People's Publishing Company, 1896.
25. William McCreary, 19, was a brother of Albertus, and son of saddle maker David McCreary, of 201 Baltimore Street.
26. The two young men were at the town square, or Diamond.
27. Arabella Barlow.
28. 57 year old Smith McCreary, a hatter, is Jennie's father. He is active in the local militia and Gettysburg guard. Where Arabella Barlow got the idea that her husband was at Smith McCreary's home is unknown.
29. Contrary to legend, there is an open question as to just when Mrs. Barlow actually found her husband. From the Benner house, he was moved closer to town on the morning of July 2nd to be cared for in the John Crawford house by Mrs. William Smith and her daughter, Jane. By 1:00 p.m. on July 7th, when he wrote a detailed letter to his mother, he had been moved once more...noting that he was "at a small house near Gettysburg, Penn-3 miles out on the turnpike toward Baltimore." He makes no mention of his wife in that letter. It is certain, however, that at some point after the battle, Arabella did find her husband of two years and attended him in the Federal hospital, just as she had done when he was badly wounded at Antietam.
30. Believed to have been at 214 Carlisle Street.

31. Lt. Col. James McLean Thomson, 107th Pa..
32. Captain Jacob V. Gish, Co. B, 107th Pa.
33. Dr. Robert Horner and his wife, Mary, lived at 51 Chambersburg Street, two doors from Mary McAllister's residence. Dr. Horner's brother, Dr. Charles Horner, lived at 47 Chambersburg Street, next door to McAllister.
34. From the Philadelphia North American, June 29, 1913.
35. At this time, Mrs. McConnell had no way of knowing that her husband, a civilian, had been taken prisoner by the Confederates, who may have suspected him of spying.
36. NE corner of West High and South Washington streets.
37. Solomon Powers.
38. The woman, Mrs. Susan McDonald McElroy, reportedly Jane's sister-in-law, was carefully partitioned off from others in the cellar. Her case of smallpox was the only one in town.
The compassion of the father, Solomon Powers, was reflected in his five daughters, Alice, May, Virginia, Lydia and Jane. All worked diligently as nurses throughout the emergency and afterward, and were noted for saving several lives, including one soldier who was being carried out of their house, presumed dead. He was not, and was saved by Virginia Solomon. No fewer than 28 wounded soldiers were in the Powers' home at one time. All five women were, or became, school teachers.
39. Northwest corner of West Middle and Baltimore Streets. Confederate soldiers were encamped the length of Middle Street.

Caption Notes

1. Officer Smith was the son of a Pennsylvania Presbyterian minister. His mother was southern and he had chosen to fight for the Confederacy.
2. Mrs. William Smith and Miss Jane Smith who had elected to remain behind in the John Crawford home. General Barlow, a graduate of Harvard, Class of 1855, had served briefly as a reporter for the New York Tribune before becoming a lawyer. This is from a letter to his mother written just after the battle.

Brigadier General Stephen H. Weed, 32, who rushed his troops and an artillery battery to Little Round Top to help stem the tide of the advancing Texans and Alabamians about to overrun Col. Strong Vincent's men, suffered a severe wound and was taken from the field by stretcher. Weed, who received his appointment to The U.S. Military Academy at West Point in 1850, had served his country against the Seminoles in Florida and was in the expedition to Salt Lake City as the US Government showed its intention to prevent Mormon pologamy. Since the beginning of the Rebellion, Weed had served with distinction, rising to the rank of Brigadier General.

According to Tillie Pierce, Weed was brought to the Weikert farm and placed "in a little room in the southeast corner of the basement." On the night of July 2nd, with only candlelight providing illumination, Tillie talked with the wounded General as he lay on the floor. He made her promise to come see him in the morning. "The poor wounded soldier's eyes followed me, and the last words he said to me were: 'Now don't forget your promise.' I replied: 'No indeed,' and expressing the hope that he would be better in the morning, bade him good night."

When she returned to the damp dark room the next morning Tillie Pierce found that the General had died. Historians believe that if Weed and his troops had not arrived on Little Round Top when they did, that high ground – the key to the entire Union defensive position – would have fallen into the hands of the Confederates within five minutes. *Courtesy Massachusetts Commandery of the Military Order of the Loyal Legion of the United States and the US Army Military History Institute, Carlisle, Pennsylvania.*

Friday
July 3rd, 1863

At 8:00 a.m., sky again completely covered with cumulostratus clouds; at 2:00 p.m., only 4/10 of heavens are covered, but the cumulus or the massive thunder-cloud of summer, at 9:00 p.m., 7/10 cumulus. Wind S.S.W., very gentle. Thunderstorm in the neighborhood of 6:00 p.m. The thunder seemed tame, after the artillery firing of the afternoon. Thermometer readings:

7:00 a.m.	2:00 p.m.	9:00 p.m.
73	87	76

– Professor Michael Jacobs

On the field: Lee wanted to reopen the battle at first light, but when dawn came, there was already heavy fighting on Culp's Hill.

George Meade had weakened himself in that sector, his right, by shifting artillery and hundreds of troops from Culp's Hill to reinforce the left on July 2nd's fight at the Round tops. After that fighting ebbed, Meade began to re-position them, furnishing a rude surprise for the Confederate soldiers who had seized the hill's seemingly abandoned Union trenches hours before. When they literally ran into the Rebels in the dark, the returning Union soldiers thought it was an interesting experience, too.

"A drummer boy with Co. A., 28th Pa. Infantry, WILLIAM T. SIMPSON was among those who were sent to reoccupy the Hill. They reached their positions at about midnight, but for them, the day just would not end:

"The first news that came that the Rebs were near us was when Sgt. Benny Hoff (Co. E, 28th Pa) brought word that the Johnnies were thicker than bees around Spangler's Spring and orders were given for none of our men to go there. It was a flash of lightning that identified the rebels in our entrenchments. Our men were instructed to move on as quietly as possible. Even tin cans and canteens were muffled, and we started to advance about 2 o'clock in the morning. There was no loud talking, and every breaking stick sounded to us like an exploding shell. We moved on stealthily until we could see the hats with the feathers in them, and we knew darn well that they belonged to the Johnnies. I was ordered to find our company commanders and inform them of the presence of the enemy.

"I had a royal time of it. I trod on the hands and feet of the men in my way, and I was called all kinds of names in the most sincere whispers I ever heard. I advanced 100 yards and waited until 4 o'clock (A.M.). The order was given: 'Attention...fix bayonets.' And the circus commenced. A more surprised lot of men were never seen than those Johnnies."

On the field. 4:30 a.m.: Meade said during his meeting on the evening of July 2nd that he believed Lee's main attack would be aimed at the Union center on July 3rd. To augment the center, guns at both ends of the Union line were aimed to provide bands of crossfire over its front. In the process, prominent elevations were also strengthened against another Rebel assault on Culp's Hill. So at 4:30 a.m., artillery along the Baltimore road was already positioned to open on Johnson's Confederate forces on the hill, and did so as Slocum's Federals advanced to recapture their trenches. The entrenched Rebels had no artillery support because of the steep slope and dense woods behind them, so to escape the Union barrage, Johnson's troops had no choice but to move forward. In doing so, they ran straight into Geary's Union division.

The Confederates thrust again and again, and were shoved back each time by the Union brigades. In the shelling and rifle fire, the forest on Culp's Hill was literally blown away. Some of the trees were later found to contain more than 200 bullets.

And that was Gettysburg's wake up call on July 3rd, 1863.

The diary of MISS JANE SMITH:

"May I never again be roused to the consciousness of a newborn day by such fearful sounds. It seemed almost like the crashing of worlds, and I felt that life was rushing by the shores of the time as a mighty flood. That the hardy son of New England was laying him down side by side with his brother of the sunny south. The ragings of passion are stilled by the hand that knows no distinction between those who contend for principle and the deluded followers of the ambitious leaders of this perdition-born rebellion."

SARAH BROADHEAD, Chambersburg Street:

"Shortly after the battle began we were told to leave this end of the town, for likely it would be shelled.[1] My husband declared he would not go while one brick remained upon another, and, as usual, we betook ourselves to the cellar..."

WILLIAM SIMPSON:

"In the fight, brother did fight brother. First Maryland regiment of Steuart's (Confederate) brigade, and the first Maryland regiment of Lockwood's (Union) brigade were directly opposed. There were few men in these regiments who did not know one another.

"Sergeant Douglas McLean (Co. E, 28th Pa.), a tall man, stood up to take one more shot. As he uttered the word, 'shot', he was struck in the mouth. I went over to him and lifted his head to see if he was dead, and he asked me for a drink of water. McLean lived, but had trouble with his throat from then on.

"Two other men were brought up. Sgt. Henry Shadel and Corporal Cyrus Shenkle. Both were badly wounded. Shenkle had been hit in the head and Shadel in the

It was very late in the afternoon of July 2nd when the Confederate push up Culp's Hill began and it continued well into the night. By daybreak the firestorm reduced the once heavily wooded hill to what you see here. *Courtesy Massachusetts Commandery of the Military Order of the Loyal Legion of the United States and the US Army Military History Institute, Carlisle, Pennsylvania.*

Johnston Skelly, 50, was a Master Tailor, who lived with his wife Elizabeth, 54, and seven children on West Middle Street.

The Rebel line ran right down the street in front of Johnston Skelly's house and soldiers were in and out all of the time. He and his wife had their hands full. They tried to keep their three daughters, and thirteen year old George, in the cellar and out of the way. Young Dan, who hadn't made it at West Point, was now back home – bouncing back and forth to the Fahnestock Brothers store down the street, depending upon which location offered the best view of the excitement. *Courtesy Adams County Historical Society.*

Johnston "Jack" Skelly, Jr., 21, and Jennie Wade had been friends since early childhood. One version of the Wade legend says the two wanted to marry, but the war forced a postponement. In 1861 "Jack" and his older brother Charles enlisted and were serving in Company F, 87th Pennsylvania Infantry, along with William Culp, Billy Ziegler, and Billy Holtzworth. During the June 15th fighting at Winchester, Virginia, "Jack" was wounded and captured along with his brother, who refused to leave his side. Corporal Skelly died from those wounds a short time later. As the fighting raged at Gettysburg neither his family nor Jennie Wade knew of his fate; or that Charles was now a Confederate prisoner of war. Legend has it William Culp's brother Wes, serving with the Confederates who captured the Skelly bothers, got to see Jack before he died and was bringing a message back from him to Jennie Wade. However, Wes was killed when his unit attacked Culp's Hill overnight. Jennie became the only civilian fatality of the battle. She was killed on the morning of July 3 in the kitchen of her sister's house. *Courtesy Adams County Historical Society.*

shoulder. As soon as they met, Shadel held out his hand and said to Shenkle, 'Shake. We're good for Philadelphia.'[2]

"I saw Captain A. S. Tourison of Co. E of the 147th following four boys with a man in a blanket who, I thought, was wounded. I went up to him with a laugh and a greeting, but he just looked at me and said, 'My poor boy is dead.' I was thunderstruck. It was Will Tourison. I felt it as though it was a personal loss.

"General Thomas L. Kane was there, too. Wounded, but he always accompanied his regiment in an ambulance. When the fight grew the thickest, he crawled out of his ambulance and urged his men on. He was out of his ambulance the greater part of the third day.

"Dr. William F. Smith told me to take his horse and go to Dr. E. Earnest Goodman at the hospital for more spirits, as the supply was going fast. It was the fastest ride I ever had in my life. While I was going over the Baltimore Pike, I came across an old couple going along the road, and from their dress, I presumed that they were Dunkards.[3] He had on a stiff top hat and his dark blue coat had brass buttons. The old lady wore a blue furbelow and carried an umbrella. Two men who had been killed were brought along right in front of them. The old lady raised both hands and screamed, 'Isn't it awful?' The old man was just as horrified. They looked out of place on that road of death."

Several miles to the east, SARAH BARRET KING:
"We were surprised to see Rebs planting a battery in front of the house, but some distance away. I called Mrs. Rhinehart's attention to it and she went out. A Union shell was dropped in their midst and the battery was removed. They told Mrs. Rhinehart they thought the house was unoccupied and that we had better leave. Minie balls were falling around and against the house and they said the Union men would think sharpshooters were in it and direct their guns on the house.

"We were all in the cellar, Mrs. Bender, her two children and a young girl, Mrs. Warner, a sister of Mr. John Benner, my mother, self and five children with Mrs. Rhinehart and her family. She herself was baking. She came to the door leading to the cellar and called us women, saying 'There were Rebs here and told me we had better leave or we would be killed. What are you going to do about it?'

I said, 'What are you going to do?' She replied, 'I'm going to stay. I told them I would be killed if I left and I might as well be killed in the house.'

"I said, 'I will stay.'"

On the field: Little more than 350 strong, the Second Massachusetts suddenly advanced from the Union lines, moved across an open meadow in full sight of the enemy, and charged the Confederate's strongest position, held by ten times their number. A heavy fire began, and Union troopers fell at every step. In spite of their losses, the regiment moved forward in order.

As they neared the enemy position, a Southern soldier leaped onto a rock and shouted at the top of his lungs: 'Go back! Go back! You can't possibly do it. For God's sake, fellows, go back!' Several of the Union soldiers distinctly heard him offering evidently sincere and well-meant advice. Satisfied that they had felt the enemy's lines as they were told to do, the Union troops turned under fire and retraced their steps. Reaching their original position, they again faced the enemy and returned fire. Over half of the

Correspondents for the New York Herald were not particularly well liked by other reporters because they seemed to be liberally supplied with money and practiced ruthless tactics. They seemed to always have money to entice telegraph repairmen to restore lines, hire couriers to run dispatches, acquire fresh horses, and live comfortably in the field. Most reporters considered themselves lucky to have a blanket to pull around them, but the Herald men had tents with some of the comforts and supplies that went a long way toward making officers welcome and talkative.

However some of their tactics were used against them by Homer Byington the editor of the Norwalk Gazette. Homer, who had never covered a Civil War battle, just happened to be in the right place – Washington, DC – at the right time, as a major battle was shaping up at Gettysburg.

Horace Greeley's Tribune reporters were scattered everywhere, and Greeley was in danger of being scooped if he didn't get someone on the road in a hurry. He paid the Connecticut editor a big bonus to head out to Gettysburg and cover the battle for the Tribune. Byington proved to be one enterprising reporter. Seeing that the telegraph lines to Gettysburg had been cut by Early's Cavalry near Hanover, he rousted telegrapher Dan Trone out of bed, got his battery and key, stole a handcart, and bribed repairmen to come with them. Once the line was repaired, he used most of his bonus to buy silence and exclusive use of the wire.

Homer Byington entered Gettysburg amidst the chaos on the afternoon of July 1st. Early on the morning of the 2nd, he and several veteran reporters got a breakfast briefing from General O.O. Howard on the first days' fighting. Byington then made his way out the federal line to the southern end of Cemetery Ridge where he watched the fight in the Peach Orchard. By dusk, when other reporters sought a comfortable spot near the Leister House Headquarters of General Meade to write their dispatches, Byington slipped away. He was busy telegraphing his story directly to New York before the other reporters had readied their stories for filing in Westminster or Lancaster. Horace Greeley published an EXTRA of the Tribune the night of July 2nd, and by 9:30 p.m. the story of the battles at Gettysburg were available for the whole world to read. *Courtesy Massachusetts Commandery of the Military Order of the Loyal Legion of the United States and the US Army Military History Institute, Carlisle, Pennsylvania.*

Newspaper wagons traveled with the Army of the Potomac and generally the news was several days old. At Gettysburg, however, on the morning of July 3rd when soldiers got copies of the New York Tribune July 2nd EXTRA edition that had been rushed to Pennsylvania, they read of their own exploits! Never before had soldiers anywhere in the world been able to read a newspaper account about the battle in which they were fighting before that battle was over. *Courtesy Massachusetts Commandery of the Military Order of the Loyal Legion of the United States and the US Army Military History Institute, Carlisle, Pennsylvania.*

Second Massachusetts's officers and nearly a third of its men were killed in this maneuver, which turned out to have been undertaken because of a mistaken order.[4]

On the southeastern end of the battlefield, TILLIE PIERCE watched Union soldiers whose attention was divided between the on-going fight at Culp's Hill and a still undefined battle to come:

"Carriages were in waiting out at the barn, to take us off to a place of safety.[5]

"Already, there was occasional musketry and cannonading in the direction of Gettysburg, and we expected greater danger than at any time before.

"Some of the soldiers told us that they had planted cannon on two sides of the house, and that if the Rebels attempted to reach the Taneytown road, as they had the day before, there would likely be hard fighting right around the house; and that if we remained, we would be in the midst of flying bullets and shell. Under these circumstances, we made all possible haste to depart.

"When we reached the carriages, and were about to get in, a shell came screaming through the air directly overhead. I was so frightened that I gave a shriek and sprang into the barn. Even with their suffering the poor fellows could not help laughing at my terror and sudden appearance. One of them near me said: 'My child, if that had hit you, you would not have had time to jump.'"

MARY CUNNINGHAM BIGHAM's farm home near the Emmitsburg Road and south of the Round Tops, had become a hospital for Confederate wounded:

"As soon as it was light, Father took the names and addresses of all those who had survived the night, but many others had died. The pockets of the dead were inside out and, since the Confederates were hard up for clothes, many were in Federal blue and couldn't be identified.

"Union wounded within the Confederate lines were laid down in the orchard, and Father found many lying in pools of water. Later, tents were put over these and, on the whole, they recovered better than those in the barn.

"A small door, cut for everyday use in one of the large ones in the barn, was unhinged and used as an operating table. Father had no way of knowing how things went until an order came to 'use no more chloroform on Union soldiers.' He suspected that things were bad for the Confederates. Soon after, a man came demanding something red to use as a flag; Confederates were retreating and being shelled. The orchard was full of tents and needed a flag to show it was a hospital. Father was not the handyman of the household and so he grabbed the first thing his hand touched from the open drawer. It was white, not red, but there was great haste and, in a few minutes, the white thing was floating from the lightning rod over the barn. When Mother returned from Grandfather's, it was the first spot that caught her eye – a pair of her nether garments gleaming high against the blue."

In the town, DANIEL SKELLY:

"I was down at my father's house[6] and quite a number of Confederate soldiers came into the yard to the old 'draw well.' They were all begrimed with powder and were washing up. Their remarks about a hill they were butting up against were neither moral nor complimentary. Of course, we were in the dark as to the cause of their discomfiture."[7]

On the field: The battle at Culp's Hill and Spangler's Spring lasted 7 hours, ending at **11 a.m.** when the battered Confederates withdrew with heavy casualties.

Slocum's XII Corps was again in its trenches, and the Union right was restored.

The morning's conflict had been the last straw. ELIZABETH THORN was trying to get her family farther away from the embattled town:

"I carried the smallest boy and the (Baltimore) Pike being jammed with soldiers and wagons of all kinds, it was hard to move. We reached the White church and was a lot of town people there. Some of us made up our minds to go over to Henry Beitler's and

Jennie Wade's family had to struggle to make ends meet. The father, James, had several run-ins with the law, and was serving time in a state prison, in 1852, when his wife Mary moved to have him committed on grounds of insanity to the Adams County Alms House. Jennie was twenty years old when a bullet entered her sister's kitchen and slammed into her back, killing her. It is said her apron pocket contained a photograph of "Jack" Skelly. Little information has survived about Jennie's personal character. She was a recently confirmed member of St. James Lutheran Church, but the reputation of her family was less than respected. *Courtesy Adams County Historical Society.*

walked there. When we reached the Henry Beitler place, Father said he was getting weak, we had nothing to eat and drink that day.

"Mrs. McKnight, who lived at the Leister place, was then with us. She and I agreed we would hunt through the house for something to eat like the army men. We went into the cellar and found a barrel. While I held the lie up, Mrs. McKnight ran her arm in almost to the elbow and brought it out covered with soft soap. That was the first laugh we had that day. After washing the arm, we went hunting again and found two crocks of milk, and helping ourselves, we softened the crust of our loaf of bread, and it was soon eaten and we were still hungry.

"There were some soldiers in the front part of the house and Mrs. McKnight and I went around to the front and rapped at the door. An officer came out and asked us what we wanted. He had been in town and said to us, 'Did you know Jennie Wade?' I said I knew her, that she lived near my home. He then told us she got killed."[8]

THE DEATH OF MARY VIRGINIA "JENNIE" WADE[9]

Amazingly, Jennie Wade's was the only battle-related death among the townspeople...and the story is now legend. It seems fitting to tell it here as related by a turn of the century newspaper whose reporter covered a ceremony honoring the fallen heroine.

"When the battle of Gettysburg began, 20 year old Jennie and her mother moved into the home of Jennie's sister, Georgiana (Mrs. John Lewis McClellan) on Baltimore street[10] to care for Georgiana[11] and her infant son.[12] John was serving in the Union army.

"On the morning of July 3rd, 1863, Jennie was instantly killed by a Confederate sharpshooter's bullet which penetrated two wooden doors.

"The house in the immediate vicinity and an orchard on the side of the hill were occupied by Union sharpshooters who had advanced from their line of battle on Cemetery Hill to engage a line of Confederate sharpshooters on the slight rise on the south of the town. The house of Mrs. McClellan was, however, never used as a protection for Union soldiers. The firing between these lines were kept up continuously during the second day of the battle, without any injury to the inhabitants, and Jennie Wade carried water to the wounded Union men around the house and performed many acts of kindness to relieve their suffering.

"On the morning of July 3rd, Jennie was in the kitchen, preparatory to baking, when she was struck in the back by a bullet, killing her instantly. The body was carried to the cellar of the other side of the double house, then occupied by Mrs. Isaac McClean. The house was so closely watched by Confederate sharpshooters that the body could not be carried through the outer cellar door, but was taken through a hole in the wall made by a 10 pound Parrott shell, and by this way through the house of Mrs. McClean.[13]

"Others injured in Gettysburg: John Burns, civilian hero of the battle, was wounded three times on the first day."

ALBERTUS McCREARY:

"I had picked up 8 rifles in the yard on the first day and hid them in a shed under a pile of leaves. A squad of soldiers[14] came in search of guns and ammunition; I think they were getting short of both. I went out as usual and asked them what they wanted. They said they were looking for guns. One fellow took me by the shoulders and said, 'Now Johnny, I know you have a lot of guns hid; show me where they are.' I denied that I had any. He marched me along, and every little while would say, 'Where are they?' And I still denied having any. At last they neared the shed. I stuck out that I hadn't any guns, but when they reached the door I was feeling pretty panicky; I did not know what they might do with me if they found the guns under the leaves. Then the fellow pushed open the door and kicked among the leaves. 'Oh, oh!', he exclaimed, and looked hard at me. My face must have betrayed me fears, for he burst out laughing and patted me on the back, saying in a kind tone, 'Too bad, too bad.' But the guns were gathered up and taken away.

"I saw a great many wounded men making their way to the hospitals which had been hastily established in many places in the town. One poor fellow came limping on one foot, with his hand on his horse for support. He stopped at our steps for a few moments. I ran into the house, got a broom, sawed off the handle, tacked a cross-piece to the end, and soon had a crutch that would enable him to get on more comfortably. He thanked me for it and went on his way more rapidly.

Josephine Miller was a young woman of twenty, living in this small house with 65 year old Susan Rogers and Peter Rogers – a day laborer from Germany. The house was located off Emmitsburg Road and in an area occupied by Union General J. B. Carr of Troy, New York. General Henry W. Slocum says Carr tried to convince the women to leave, but they refused to abandon their bread making. "He informed her that a great battle was inevitable, and advised her to seek a place of safety at once. She said she had a batch of bread baking in the oven, and she would remain until it was baked and then leave. When her bread was baked, it was given to our soldiers, and was devoured so eagerly that she concluded to remain and bake another batch. And so she continued to the end of the battle, baking and giving her bread to all who came. The great artillery duel which shook the earth for miles around did not drive her from her oven. Pickett's men who charged past her house found her quietly baking her bread and distributing it to the hungry." – General Henry W. Slocum. *Courtesy Massachusetts Commandery of the Military Order of the Loyal Legion of the United States and the US Army Military History Institute, Carlisle, Pennsylvania.*

"At another time, two men came along, one helping the other by the arm. The face of one of them was so covered with bandages that we could see only his eyes. The other man said that his lower jaw had been shot away. He was suffering greatly and made a sign for water. I ran quickly and brought it, but he could not drink. He held his head back, and I poured the water on the bandages about his mouth, and it soaked through the bandages into his throat. The unwounded soldier thanked me and gave me a battered quarter which he said he had found in the fire at Fredericksburg.

"Another soldier, who had his wrist wrapped up, stopped at our steps. A surgeon who was in the house came out and asked the soldier what was the matter, and was told that a bullet was in the wrist. The surgeon quickly unwrapped the bandages, and sure enough there was a hole on one side and a big lump on the other. He made a slight cut over the lump, and out dropped the bullet."

In their unrelenting, smaller war, Confederate sharpshooters stayed in many of the attics along Baltimore Street. But ANNA GARLACH's mother was going to have none of that at 323 S. Baltimore:

"A soldier burst in the front door and started upstairs. Mother went up out of the cellar, caught him by the coat as he was going up to the second floor and asked him what he was doing there. She was told that sharpshooters were going to use the house. She held on to him saying, 'You can't go up there. You will draw the fire on this house full of defenseless women and children!'

"He insisted that he must use the house for sharpshooters and Mother insisted that he should leave the house. To this, he answered that it would be instant death for him to leave the house.

"Mother said he could stay but must not fire from the house. After a while he said he would go. He discharged his gun out of the front door and, in the smoke, darted out and got safely across the street into Winebrenner's alley.

"The sharpshooters were in the house...just north of our home. They had taken out a row of brick on the second floor from which they fired towards Cemetery Hill. As every point occupied by sharp shooters became a special target, our house was repeatedly hit.

"Mother and brother Will went to the garret to see what they could from the small window toward the south covered by a board with a handle. They pulled it back far enough to see out. They must have been seen, for shortly after they had replaced the board and were descending the steps, bullets entered the garret."

MARY McALLISTER, Chambersburg Street:

"A couple of men came in and called for something to eat. Martha had baked pie and she brought one into the hall to the table there. She set it down with a knife, and said, 'Now you cut it the best way you can.' He cut it and said, 'You eat a piece.' She said, 'Do you think it is poison? The women here don't poison people.' But he would not eat it; he was afraid it was poisoned. "

This is the Codori Barn just off Emmitsburg Road and west of Cemetery Ridge. Confederates are said to have housed Union prisoners here and sharpshooters were said to have favored its loft because of its proximity to the Union line. On the third day of fighting, as his division marched across these fields, General George Picket watched from here with horror as Union guns decimated his troops as they attempted to overrun the Union center a few hundred yards ahead. *Courtesy Massachusetts Commandery of the Military Order of the Loyal Legion of the United States and the US Army Military History Institute, Carlisle, Pennsylvania.*

On the field: Robert E. Lee was determined either to finish the fight...or to withdraw.

But apparently he was laboring under false assumptions. Historians say that Lee believed the Union army's morale to be down from two nearly-disastrous days at Gettysburg. And he believed that, because of the fight on its left the day before, Meade's right and center were weakened. He was wrong on both counts.

Lee had no way of knowing that the entire Union Army of the Potomac was now in place at Gettysburg, giving Meade a 20,000 man edge, or that some 25,000 of the Union troops had not yet seen battle.

So his plan for July 3rd was to have Longstreet launch a massive assault on the Union center while Ewell continued to hit the right. J.E.B. Stuart's cavalry would cover the Confederate army's left, ready to attack the Union rear if Longstreet broke through the center.

Lee carried his ideas to Longstreet, who again argued for a maneuver around Meade's left flank. Longstreet vowed that a frontal attack would fail in the face of the Union strength that he and his men had observed the day before. But General Lee was adamant.

Lee made one concession, agreeing to add some of A.P. Hill's divisions to Longstreet's attack. With that proviso, the attack would be led by Major General George E. Pickett's division of Longstreet's corps, strengthened by men from all three of Hill's divisions for a combined force of more than 13,000. A massive artillery barrage would destroy or weaken the Union gun positions on Cemetery Hill to pave the way.

Lee pointed to a copse of trees on Cemetery Ridge where Hancock's II corps lay and directed that the marching infantry would center there.

The setup took hours. But finally at **1:07 p.m.,** two Confederate guns near the peach orchard bellowed a call to action.

HENRY EYSTER JACOBS, West Middle Street:
"My father looked at his watch and said: 'We must all go into the cellar.' We complied, and then began the terrific artillery duel of Friday afternoon, unequaled, I believe, for sound and fury in the annals of war."

On the field: One hundred forty Confederate cannon opened the bombardment. Eighty Union guns returned the compliment. And so began a hell fury that drove professional soldiers to the ground, and caused civilians to tremble in fear.[15]

Inspecting the lines, Union Staff Officer HUNTINGTON W. JACKSON suddenly found himself directly in the line of fire:
"The air was filled with fire, smoke and destruction. The noise was terrific. The effect of the firing was instantaneous. Many of our men were moving in the rear of our lines, going for water or hunting for rails with which to build fires to make their coffee; ambulances and wagons were driving from place to place, officers and orderlies were carrying dispatches and orders. In a moment all this ceased – more suddenly than when a violent thunderstorm breaks over a city, the pedestrians seek shelter, and the streets are deserted. Everyone sought his proper post, and not a moving object could be seen except here and there a horseman passing over the field with impetuous speed.

"Thinking that the contest would prove to be nothing more serious than an artillery duel and would end shortly, when I could again resume my ride, I dismounted, threw the reins over my horse's head, lay down, and hugged the earth. No sooner had the enemy's guns opened than ours replied...80 guns planted from Cemetery Hill to Round Top. Never before was such a duel witnessed. The very earth trembled and shook, and the air was alive with death-dealing bolts. The ground was literally plowed with shot and shell, throwing up dirt and stones in every direction. A number of men near me were killed and wounded. The field was again alive with the wounded, crawling to the rear and seeking surgeons, with caissons going for and bringing back ammunition, with fresh batteries rushing to the front to take the place of those disabled, and with the poor dumb

"During the day July 3rd General Lee reconnoitered our position from the College cupola – although, being a hospital, that edifice, by all principles of military honor, should have been free from every hostile use – and had come to the conclusion that our left centre was the weakest part of our lines." – Professor Michael Jacobs, Pennsylvania College. *Courtesy Gettysburg College.*

Lt. Col. Edward Porter Alexander, 28, US Military Academy Class of 1857, was Lee's chief of artillery. At 1:00 p.m. July 3rd 1963, his Confederate cannon on Seminary Ridge began a two-hour bombardment against 90 Union cannon on Cemetery Ridge in what was to become one of the greatest artillery duels in history. Alexander's orders were to soften up the Union position so that an infantry charge by General George Pickett's division of Longstreet's Corps could be successful. *Courtesy Americana Image Gallery, Gettysburg, Pennsylvania.*

Brigadier General Henry Hunt was Meade's chief of artillery. At the time Confederate cannon opened up on the Union position, Hunt had most of his cannon along the crest of Cemetery Ridge, but with a concentration on the center and southern end. Cannon posted on Little Round Top also had range of the Federal center. During the charge by Pickett's division, General Hunt was with Captain Andrew Cowan's battery when Confederate fire felled Hunt's horse. The General was pinned to the ground as the enemy made its rush to overtake the battery. However, all of Cowan's cannon were loaded and fired at point-blank range. The Rebel threat at that point ended in a cloud of mutilation and death. *Courtesy Massachusetts Commandery of the Military Order of the Loyal Legion of the United States and the US Army Military History Institute, Carlisle, Pennsylvania.*

beasts, many in number, some horribly mangled, and others hobbling along upon broken legs."

MR. BENNER was then located on his father's farm, east of the Rebel line which curved south of Gettysburg to the east of Culp's Hill. Less than two miles to his west was Cemetery Ridge:

"I just thought the earth would go down. It didn't sound good to the soldiers either. Lots of them sneaked away from the ranks, and I'll tell you this much – there are skedaddlers out of every fight. Oh, by gosh, yes. I found that out, and there wasn't no distinction in that respect between the two armies. Some of the Rebel officers came and hunted the men up. 'Why ain't you with your regiment?' they said.

"'We don't know where our regiment is,' the men replied.

"'Well, you go find it,' the officers told them. But the fellers would contrive not to get back till the danger was over."

SARAH BROADHEAD remained in the basement of her neighbor, David Troxel of Chambersburg Street:

"The time that we sat in the cellar seemed long, listening to the terrific sound of the strife; more terrible never greeted human ears. We knew that with every explosion and the scream of each shell, human beings were hurried, through excruciating pain, into another world, and that many more were torn, and mangled, and lying in torment worse than death, and no one able to extend relief. The thought made me very sad, and feel that, if it was God's will, I would rather be taken away then remain to see the misery that would follow. Some thought this awful afternoon would never come to a close. We knew that the Rebels were putting forth all their might, and it was a dreadful thought that they might succeed.

HENRY EYSTER JACOBS, West Middle Street:

"With us were two maiden ladies who had come from the country for safety and were now guests at our home. It was possible to distinguish the fire of the opposing sides; and as the cannonade made its thunderous calls and responses, they would exclaim: 'Their side – our side. Their side – our side.' Then, when our side failed to answer, they would cry anxiously: 'Oh, we've stopped.' Our side had not stopped. But on Cemetery Hill, from which we were shelling the Confederate position on Seminary Hill, we had one great gun which seemed to lead our cannon orchestra. The men handling that gun had to cease firing for a while to let it cool off. But the cessation was only momentary. Our maiden ladies always had their chance to call out with joy: 'There it is again. Our side – their side.'

"General Lee that morning had mounted to the college observatory and had studied very closely the disposition of the Union forces. His shrewd eye had discerned the weak point – in Hancock's Corps, disposed to the southwest of the cemetery on Cemetery Ridge. When the terrific duel opened, he had all his artillery concentrated on that point from Seminary Ridge. It was such a duel as forced the sense of hearing, alone and unaided, to grope amid the thundering chaos, and sufficed to leave the mind almost dazed by its concussions. We could distinguish three distinct sounds in the roar of noise: first came the deep-toned growl of the gun, then the shriek of the flying shell, then the sharp crack of its explosion."

On the field: Much of the Rebel cannon overshot the Union line, where soldiers lay on their arms waiting for Lee's infantry. As a result, there was heavy damage among units in the rear, including losses among reserve artillery, ammunition trains, medical units and supply wagons.

Union Staff Officer HUNTINGTON W. JACKSON, on the field:

"The firing from the enemy's batteries continued for nearly two hours. The Union batteries, to prevent the exhaustion of their ammunition and to prepare for the climax of the day, ceased a short time before. It was as evident as if it had been announced by Lee himself where the enemy intended to strike."

On Cemetery Ridge: Anticipating new targets soon, Union artillery commander, Major General Henry J. Hunt, orders his batteries to cease firing to cool the guns, resupply, and to change out some damaged batteries.

On Seminary Ridge: While measuring his own rapidly shrinking supply of ammunition, Confederate Colonel E.P. Alexander sees Hunt withdraw 18 guns, and takes Hunt's action as a strategic opportunity. Alexander sends a message to Pickett: "For God's sake come quick: the 18 guns are gone; unless you advance quick my ammunition won't let me support you properly."

DANIEL SKELLY, West Middle Street:

"And then an ominous calm ensued. What did it mean? We did not know, nor could we surmise. But I ventured out cautiously from our retreat which was our place of safety during the cannonading, and walked up to the Fahnestock corner. However, I could learn nothing about the conflict. The alleys and (Baltimore) street leading up toward the cemetery were barricaded and the Confederate soldiers behind them in line of battle, were preparing to defend any attack from Cemetery Hill."

On the field: Pickett rode to Longstreet, saluted and asked: "General, shall I advance?" Reluctantly, knowing his orders meant the death of far too many good men, Longstreet looked into the distance and nodded his head.

With no hesitation, George Pickett rode out and called: "Forward, guide center, march."

HENRY EYSTER JACOBS, West Middle Street:

"My father, taking the small but powerful telescope, hastened to our garret and trained it on Seminary Ridge. There, as though he were almost upon them, he beheld that sublime heroism of the day forming for its gigantic disaster. He saw Pickett's division swinging into its position – a long line in readiness for the forward movement. He saw it come steadily onward across the intervening plain. The charge was magnificent, heroic."

On the field: A hush fell as three gray lines emerged from the woods on Seminary Ridge into the smoke-veiled farmland between the armies.

George Pickett's soldiers marched toward the Emmitsburg road at route step, battle flags flying in the sulfurous haze. As if in homage to the courage spread before them, Union soldiers raised themselves one by one to watch, saying nothing.

Around noon on July 3rd, Staff Officer Huntington W. Jackson was with General Newton and his staff as they lunched upon the field, between Cemetery Hill and Round Top, with General Hancock. After lunch Newton and Hancock directed Jackson to ride along the front and report the progress which had been made in completing entrenchments of I and II Corps. He found the works nearly finished and capable of affording excellent protection under any attack. It was one o'clock when he had ridden the length of Doubleday's line and was proceeding to Hancock's. Suddenly the air was filled with fire, smoke and destruction. *Courtesy Massachusetts Commandery of the Military Order of the Loyal Legion of the United States and the US Army Military History Institute, Carlisle, Pennsylvania.*

The distance across this field from the woods at the base of the Seminary Ridge to the Clump of Trees on Cemetery Hill is 7/8ths of mile. At 3:00 p.m. July 3rd 1863, 15,000 Confederate infantrymen under Generals George Pickett and James J. Pettigrew stepped forward in a futile charge of the center of the Union position. Two-thirds of them, 10,000 men, were killed, wounded or captured. Pickett lost all three of his brigade commanders and fifteen of his regimental commanders that day. "General Lee, I have no division now," Pickett is said to have told Lee when his commander instructed him to prepare for a possible Union counterattack. *Courtesy Massachusetts Commandery of the Military Order of the Loyal Legion of the United States and the US Army Military History Institute, Carlisle, Pennsylvania.*

Because guns at the Union center were loaded with short-range canister, those batteries held fire momentarily. But the guns on Little Round Top and Cemetery Hill had no such restriction, and made comment immediately.

In the haze of smoke and under fire, a slight misalignment was corrected, and the Confederate troops marched on. JAMES H. WALKER, was a member of Company K, 9th Virginia Regiment., C.S.A.

"That soldiers could be halted and dressed under such fire is remarkable, and must prove that they were under no dread of failure. When this was done, at least a fourth of the division had fallen, but they did not seem to be aware of it. They still kept their eyes to the front and on the enemy, marching forward with the gait and air of soldiers on parade."

On the field: At the Emmitsburg road, skirmishers labored to clear farm fences lining both sides of the highway. As the marching troops stepped onto the road, all Union guns came into play. The fusillade was unanswered by Confederate artillerymen on Seminary Ridge, who were forced to hold fire to keep from hitting their own line.

HENRY EYSTER JACOBS, West Middle Street:
"'Quick!' my father called to me. 'Come! Come! You can see now what in all your life you will never see again.'"

Staff Officer HUNTINGTON W. JACKSON, on the field:
"Presenting a front of about half a mile in length, on they came, line upon line. Crossing the Emmitsburg road, all but Wilcox's brigade, which was the support on the right, turned slightly to the left, then forward, to the front, continuing to march directly toward the front of Gibbon's and Hayes' divisions of Hancock's troops. The supreme moment of the battle had arrived, and the Union batteries, some double-shotted from the Cemetery to the Round Top, poured round after round of solid shot, shell and canister into the compact ranks at the rate of four discharges a minute. The slaughter was fearful. Great gaps were torn through the columns, speedily to be closed up, and still they pressed on. Hancock's men stood ready to receive them."

JAMES H. WALKER, on the field:
"The flag of the 9th Virginia went down repeatedly, the last time, when about 50 yards from the Stone Wall, when it was picked up and carried forward by a member of Company K."

When the cannonading began on July 3rd, General George Meade and his staff abandoned the home of Lydia Leister that they had been using as headquarters. The 52-year old widow Leister had rounded up those children still living with her and left her farm on July 1st. During the bombardment a few newspaper reporters, intent upon covering the action, took refuge in the cellar behind the house, coming out now and then to see what was going on. Taken a few days after the battle, this photograph shows the effects of the Confederate artillery fire. *Courtesy Library of Congress.*

Only Brigadier General Lewis A. Armistead, 46, and 150 Confederates pierced the Union line in what has become known as Pickett's Charge. Armistead and most of the other Confederates who pierced the Union line at The Angle were killed, a few were captured. *Courtesy Americana Image Gallery, Gettysburg, Pennsylvania.*

Lt. General James Longstreet, a Georgian, had not been in favor of the invasion. He thought it too risky. Apparently conversations with General Lee caused him to believe the General would go along with his proposal to engage in defensive tactics – in other words, make the Union attack them after the Confederates chose the ground. Longstreet agreed to command one of the three southern corps. He felt betrayed by Lee at Gettysburg. *Courtesy Americana Image Gallery, Gettysburg, Pennsylvania.*

ALBERTUS MCCREARY, Baltimore Street:

"One of my brothers and I went to the garret, where a trapdoor in the roof gave us a good view of Cemetery Hill and of the fields near the Emmitsburg Road. Standing on a ladder, with our heads above the door, we could plainly see a man drop by the cannon. Once the flag staff was broken and the flag fell, but it was quickly put up again.

"A wonderful thing it was to see that long line of Confederates charge across the fields in good order until they struck the masked batteries. When the batteries opened on them, everything fell into the greatest confusion, and soon clouds of smoke hid them from our sight."

MARY McALLISTER, Chambersburg Street:

"The wounded men in our house told us...'We know our cannons. We know our men, and those cannons, and we are getting the better of them. Don't be scared, for we believe they are whipped.'"

Union Staff Officer HUNTINGTON W. JACKSON:

"Hundreds were mowed down. In a space but a few feet square, ten of the enemy's dead were seen lying one upon another. The Vermont brigade of Doubleday's division, made famous by their fine conduct in this, their first battle, formed a line at right angles to the established line of the army and opened a destructive raking fire upon the enemy's right flank. Shrinking from this unexpected attack, many threw themselves upon the ground, surrendering as prisoners; others fell to the rear.

"After a desperate fight of a few moments in front of Hayes' division, the whole command broke and rushed back, leaving the field covered with the dead, dying and wounded. Once, as they reached our lines, the Southern and Union flags could be seen a short distance apart, flying over the same works, and being waved to and fro by their color bearers as if imploring assistance.

"Starting from the summit of Round Top and continuing along to Cemetery Ridge and Culp's Hill, there went up cheer upon cheer from the men who were relieved from the terrible strain, anxiety and anticipation of death. The wave of sound rolled from

Brigadier General George Pickett, 38, was a graduate of the US Military Academy at West Point, and like Lee, Longstreet, and Stuart, was a veteran of the Mexican War. A native of Richmond, a romantic, and an able commander, he was one of "old Pete" Longstreet's favorites. That may be why Longstreet was unable to look at Pickett when the time came to order the advance. *Courtesy Americana Image Gallery, Gettysburg, Pennsylvania.*

General Winfield Hancock had no way of knowing that when he was promoted to Commander of II Corps following the battle of Chancellorsville that he would face the brigade of his old friend Lewis Armistead at Gettysburg. During Pickett's Charge Hancock was wounded while riding the line shouting words of encouragement to his troops. *Courtesy Massachusetts Commandery of the Military Order of the Loyal Legion of the United States and the US Army Military History Institute, Carlisle, Pennsylvania.*

one end of the field to the other and back again for many minutes. A division of Union soldiers made a charge in front of Round Top, capturing a number of prisoners, flags and cannon."

CHARLES McCURDY and his father heard the same cheer...from the third floor of their home on Chambersburg Street:
"A dense volume of smoke hid everything from view, but we could plainly hear through this screen, the Rebel yell and the answering Union cheer. Weird and inspiring sounds.
"Soon everything became still."

On the field: Only a few hundred Rebel soldiers reached Cemetery Hill. Those few who went over the stone walls fronting Union positions gained nothing for it but death or capture. More than 7,000 men lay dead or wounded on the smoking fields behind them. Survivors trudged back to their leaders.

Those who returned had been fifteen minutes out, fifteen minutes there, fifteen minutes back.

Standing at the verge of Seminary Ridge, General Lee met them, encouraged them, expressed his sympathy, urged them to soldier on. As Major General Cadmus M.

New Hampshire born Charles Carleton Coffin, 39, was a rarity among newspaper reporters of the day: an abstainer from liquor and tobacco; he was also known to be absolutely trustworthy. Ten years before the war began, Coffin and his brother-in-law Moses G. Farmer had installed the first electric fire alarm system in Boston. When war erupted Coffin became a correspondent for the Boston Journal. He was at Bull Run, with General U.S. Grant in the West, and just prior to Gettysburg had covered the Navy Ironclads off Charleston. Coffin and journalist Whitelaw Reid had shared the cellar steps behind the widow Leister's house during the bombardment and watched Pickett's charge together. Coffin filed his dispatch from Westminister, Maryland, some 30 miles south of Gettysburg. This is what he wrote of the final moments of the charge:
"Lines waiver. The soldiers of the front rank look around for their supports. They are gone, fleeing over the field, broken, shattered, thrown into confusion by the remorseless fire...The lines have disappeared like straw in a candle's flame. The ground is thick with dead and the wounded are like the withered leaves of autumn. Thousands of Rebels throw down their arms and give themselves up as prisoners. How inspiring the moment! How thrilling the hour! It is the high-water mark of the Rebellion – a turning point of history and of human destiny. CCC." *Courtesy Massachusetts Commandery of the Military Order of the Loyal Legion of the United States and the US Army Military History Institute, Carlisle, Pennsylvania.*

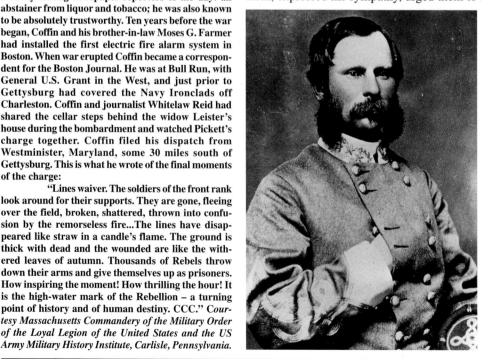

General Cadmus Marcellus Wilcox.

Wilcox approached him, nearly in tears, to report the condition of his brigade, Lee said, "Never mind General, all this has been my fault. It is I that have lost this fight, and you must help me out of it in the best way you can."[16]

On the Confederate left flank, Stuart's cavalry never reached the Union right, turned back by Brigadier General David M. Gregg's countercharging Union horsemen. Led by a young rising star, Brigadier General George Armstrong Custer, the final charge ended in a virtual head-on collision that tumbled horses and riders head over heels. In riotous hand-to-hand fighting that followed, some 500 were killed, wounded or later listed missing.

And the battle of Gettysburg ground to silence.
Not even a bird sang.

Ears ringing, TILLIE PIERCE and her friends returned to the Weikert farm:
"Fences were thrown down near and far; knapsacks, blankets and many other articles lay scattered here and there. The whole country seemed filled with desolation.

"Upon reaching the place, I fairly shrank back, aghast at the awful sight presented.

"The approaches were crowded with wounded, dying and dead. The air was filled with moanings and groanings. As we passed on toward the house, we were compelled to pick our steps in order that we might not tread on the prostrate bodies.

"When we entered the house, we found it also completely filled with the wounded. We hardly knew what to do or where to go. They, however, removed most of the wounded, and thus after a while, made room for the family.

"As soon as possible, we endeavored to make ourselves useful by rendering assistance in this heartrending state of affairs. I remember that Mrs. Weikert went through the house and after searching awhile, brought all the muslin and linen she could spare. This we tore into bandages and gave them to the surgeons to bind up the poor soldier's wounds.

"By this time, amputating benches had been placed about the house. I must have become inured to seeing the terrors of battle, else I could hardly have gazed upon the scenes now presented. I was looking out one of the windows facing the front yard. Near the basement door, and directly underneath the window I was at, stood one of these benches. I saw them lifting the poor men upon it, then the surgeons sawing and cutting off arms and legs, then again probing and picking bullets from the flesh.

"Some of the soldiers fairly begged to be taken next, so great was their suffering, and so anxious were they to obtain relief.

"I saw the surgeons hastily put a cattle horn over the mouths of the wounded ones, after they were placed upon the bench. At first I did not understand the meaning of this but upon inquiry, soon learned that that was their mode of administering chloroform,

At noon on July 3rd General George A. Custer's cavalry brigade was under orders to move from the Hanover Road, east of Gettysburg, to the Union left at Big Round Top. However, he was hastily recalled to aid in repelling Major General J.E.B. Stuart's attack on General David Gregg's cavalry, composed of some 4,500 soldiers. Galloping into the fray yelling "Come on, you Wolverines!" Custer led the 1st Michigan into a collision with the Confederate horsemen that was so violent that many horses tumbled end over end crushing their riders beneath them. The fight lasted some three hours with Custer's troopers playing a major role in barring Stuart's force of 6,000 from reaching the Union rear at the same time of Pickett's Charge. This allowed the Federals to concentrate on the main fight along Cemetery Ridge. *Courtesy Massachusetts Commandery of the Military Order of the Loyal Legion of the United States and the US Army Military History Institute, Carlisle, Pennsylvania.*

These temporary hospital tents house some of the wounded men of Hancock's 2nd Corps who defended the Union Center against Pickett's Charge. *Courtesy Massachusetts Commandery of the Military Order of the Loyal Legion of the United States and the US Army Military History Institute, Carlisle, Pennsylvania.*

Abram Bryan, 53, was a successful farmer. A free-Black, he had lived in town before buying a farm off the Baltimore Road. Adams County Tax Records indicate his property was valued at $1,400.00. That, plus his personal worth measured his success by community, not racial, standards. Bryan, his wife Elizabeth, and two teenaged sons left the area days prior to the battle. Unfortunately, the Bryan farm was in the thick of the fighting for Cemetery Hill. Exploding shells and whizzing bullets damaged the house and barn, but not so much that they couldn't be used to shelter dying and wounded. The Bryan barn served as a hospital for weeks. *Courtesy Massauchusetts Commandery of the Military Order of the Loyal Legion of the United States and the US Army Military History Institute, Carlisle, Pennsylvania.*

in order to produce unconsciousness. But the effect in some instances was not produced, for I saw the wounded throwing themselves wildly about, and shrieking with pain while the operation was going on.

"To the south of the house and just outside of the yard, I noticed a pile of limbs higher than the fence. It was a ghastly sight! Gazing upon these, too often the trophies of the amputating bench, I could have no other feeling than that the whole scene was one of cruel butchery.

"Twilight had now fallen; another day had closed, with the soldiers saying that they believed this day the Rebels were whipped, but at an awful sacrifice."

NELLIE AUGINBAUGH and her family had stayed at their home on Carlisle street throughout the fighting. Now, there was a sea-change:

"Rebel officers warned the residents to leave their homes because they had guns on the town and were going to shell it. We left town and walked past the Cemetery where the tombstones were chipped from having been used as shields. Hundreds of wounded and dead lay on every side and we often had to pick our steps over them. All called for water and many times Father took a canteen from a dying man and went the long way back to the pump we had passed, filling it and giving him water. We passed many killed in the act of getting over a fence. A few had no heads. Sometimes a head would be sticking between the rails of a fence with no body. After going a distance of some 8 miles, we came to a home of friends and Father asked if we might come in. We were welcomed but told there's no food and nowhere to sleep except the kitchen floor."

SARAH BROADHEAD:

"Who is victorious, or with whom the advantage rests, no one here can tell. It would ease the horror if we knew our arms were successful. Some think the Rebels were defeated, as there has been no boasting as on yesterday, and they look uneasy and by no means exultant. I hope they are correct, but I fear we are too hopeful. We shall see to-morrow. It will be the 4th of July, and the Rebels have promised us a glorious day. If it only ends the battle and drives them off it will be glorious, and I will rejoice."

That evening on the field: Lee began quietly to fold his wings, pulling in Ewell's divisions from Gettysburg and Longstreet's divisions from the far right flank. On one hand, he was concentrating his forces against the possibility of a Union attack on the following morning (July 4th). On the other hand, he had decided to leave the field if possible and return his battered army to Virginia. At that moment, logistics were of paramount concern.

Although severely wounded, the Confederate army remained a mighty force in number. Lee had lost a third of his estimated 75,000 men, leaving some 50,000; many of them "walking wounded." To withdraw, he would need foragers to feed the main body, cavalry to protect its flanks. Those men who could not walk would have to be transported on roads left rutted and muddy from the army's passage north.

In truth, their fate was being decided in a debate then taking place at George Meade's headquarters on Cemetery Ridge.

Three of Meade's generals, Howard, Hancock, and Pleasonton, called for an immediate counterattack. But others, notably Hunt, believed that was exactly what Lee expected and desired.

Meade decided to rest his army.

And the door swung wide for Lee.

Attorney WILLIAM McCLEAN, East Middle Street:
"The battle of Gettysburg had been decided, and the enemy was sullen and gloomy. The streets were barricaded, as an attempt to dislodge the rebels was apprehended, and we had the distressing prospect of fighting going on around our houses.

"I ventured to speak to a North Carolina officer on the street, a Captain Smith, and asked him into the house to seek his interposition to prevent harm being done to us or our home. We invited him to share in what little food we had for the evening meal. He was a perfect gentleman and we gained the assurance of protection, so far as was in his power to afford it. We laid ourselves down, not knowing what awaited us."

From the house on the Rhinehart farm, SARAH BARRETT KING could see that the fields to the west now had many riderless horses, wounded and in agony, and that injured soldiers were wandering away:

"I was sitting in the window that opened on the lawn. I think it was 9 o'clock or near that time. A soldier on horseback brushed by the window, coming around the north side of the house. Others followed until it seemed a regiment had gathered there.

"Mrs. Rhinehart, with her little short pipe in her mouth, went forward. They said, 'Mother, can't you give us something to eat?'

"'Well,' she answered, 'I just put my bread in the oven. You fellows kept fighting all day, I could not get my bread baked.'

"They went to the oven and brought loaf after loaf out tearing it open. The dough was not baked inside and fell to the floor. They said, 'Can't you bake it?' She replied, 'There is the stove, put it on and bake it.'

"They wanted butter and she said, 'Why, you drove off my cows. How could I have butter? I have apple butter.' She gave them that. They were fond of it and some of them wanted to take some of this apple jack to camp.

"While they were feasting, two young men in gray uniforms with black stripes came to me and said, 'Madam, we will sit on your stoop tonight and guard your house. Of course, we can't take care of barn and garden,' and added, 'That is, if General Lee does not attempt to take Culp's Hill tonight.' We felt perfectly safe then.

"Not five minutes after there was a whisper in the room and one after the other stepped out quietly and quickly, going away in a southerly course. One more mystery was added to the day."[17]

ANNA GARLACH, Baltimore Street:
"We were aroused by some soldiers who asked to be allowed to go in the shop where Father made coffins. They said General Barksdale[18] had been killed and they wanted to make a coffin for him. Mother told them that if they went into the shop and made a light the house would be a target. She told them there was plenty of wood outside in the yard and they could help themselves to as much of it as they wanted, and then they should go to a shop down in the town. They agreed to do this and, helping themselves to some wood, went to the shop of Daniel Culp near the Court House. They began the coffin that night, but the retreat was ordered before it was finished. This coffin was finished later and Jennie Wade was buried in it when first interred."

Brigadier General William Barksdale, a former U.S. Congressman from Mississippi who led the Confederate attack on Sickles' Third Corps in the Peach Orchard, overran the position of Brigadier General Charles K. Graham's troops in less than five minutes. Barksdale was moving his men eastward to Plum Run and Cemetery Ridge when he was riddled with bullets and knocked from the saddle by Union marksmen trying to stop the advancing Rebels by killing their inspirational leader. He died that night. *Courtesy Massachusetts Commandery of the Military Order of the Loyal Legion of the United States and the US Army Military History Institute, Carlisle, Pennsylvania.*

GENERAL BARLOW remained hospitalized at the Crawford house:

"The after dark fighting of the previous night was not repeated and, except for the rattling of the moving caissons and wagons, all was quiet. During the evening, a Rebel soldier who had been slightly wounded came limping into the room where I lay and, squatting on the floor beside me, began conversation. He belonged to Stonewall Jackson's old Corps and it so happened that we had shared, on opposite sides, in most of the battles in which his command had been engaged.

"'I'm tired of the war', he said. 'We-uns may be wrong, but I hope we are not. Anyhow, I wish the fighting was over.' Then he had much to say as to the manner and means by which he had been constrained to enter Confederate service and concluded by remarking, 'Well, I suppose we shall have another hard battle tomorrow, and I must go to my regiment. It won't take more than another day to decide this fight.' So saying, he rose, and bidding me goodbye, limped away."

Gettysburg native, CAPTAIN HENRY N. MINNIGH, Company K, 30th Pa. Infantry, had led his unit in action at the Wheat Field on July 2nd. They were now stationed near the Round Tops, and with the battlefield quiet, their thoughts turned naturally in another direction:

"Many of the company whose homes were in Gettysburg or the immediate vicinity, quietly slipped away, and believing that our work, for a while at least, was ended, I also went, saying to the boys when I started, 'Boys, if you go home, don't fail to get back tomorrow morning.'[19]

Mindful of his own instructions, Minnigh walked northward through the citizen's cemetery, taking Baltimore Street to the courthouse at the corner of Middle Street. Parts of the route were still covered by Confederate sharpshooters, forcing him to cross streets and alleys at a bound. Surveying Middle Street from the corner at Baltimore, it appeared that his father's residence at 69 West Middle street was so completely covered by the marksmen that it would be impossible for him to cross the distance. Then he spotted a less cautious traveler:

"I observed things closely, and saw a certain officer who was apparently not acquainted with the dangerous surroundings, turn the corner where I was standing, and walk deliberately down the middle of the street without being molested. But, Alas! the poor fellow, when he got below Washington street, was taken prisoner. So I took advantage of what I had seen and walked down the street, with misgivings, I confess, for doubtless many rifles were aimed at me, with a Rebel finger on each trigger ready to send as many messengers of death if I should turn either to the right or to the left. It was an awful moment, but I determined to carry out my plan, which was to spring into a flower garden on the east side of the house when I would reach that point, for I would then be in a safe place.

"On! On, to hesitate would be fatal; and how terrible it would be to die so near to the loved ones; still on I went, not hurriedly, for the enemy must not even think that I have a purpose in view. Oh! If only the yard gate were open! Ah, it is open! A spring, and I am through it, and behind the cover of the house; I am safe, but what a shower of minie balls strike the pavement over which I came, and how they tear through the palings of the fence on both sides of the gate, terrible messengers they are, but harmless now as far they concerned me.

"None of the family were visible, so I entered the unlocked door of a back kitchen, which was empty, then into the main building I went and all through it from main floor to attic, and found no one. Disappointed, I turned to the cellar and was met on the stairway by a sister, who failed to recognize me in the semi-darkness, who said, 'Here! what do you want?'[20]

"On the spur of the moment, I said, 'Can you supply me with just a bite to eat?'

"With this, she retired below and I followed to the foot of the stairs and took a seat near the lower step, and this is what I then saw: Father and Mother,[21] four sisters and a brother, two or three improvised beds, an almost consumed tallow dip on the end of a barrel in a far off corner, and each person being a perfect image of dejection and despondency.

"Sister Lucy whispered something to Mother, who then entered an adjoining pantry, doubtless to get the 'bite to eat,' while a younger sister approached me inquiring, 'I wonder how much longer we will have to remain in this cellar?'

"I merely answered, 'Not long,' but I discovered that they were entirely ignorant of the state (of) affairs without. She looked at me closely, and then followed Mother into the pantry.

"Presently, Mother approached me, bearing a huge piece of bread in her hand, and peering very closely into my face, then, as if in glad surprise, she ejaculated, 'Oh, you bad fellow, I know you now! Here's your supper.'

"I will not attempt a portrayal of the scene that followed, but in a few words I revealed the state of affairs without, and brought them from that lower world, in which they had dwelt several days, into the light and comfort of the upper world once more.

"Soon, an ample supper spread the board, and then all retired to the comfortable beds, of which they had been deprived for two nights, and I had not enjoyed for two years."

Seminary student, MARTIN LUTHER CULLER, had sheltered in a house on Baltimore street during the worst of the fighting; Union troops to the south, Rebels in the back yard. As at the Minnigh household, no one was sure what would happen next:
"Suddenly, there was a knock upon the side door. Opening it, we saw several Confederates, standing, bowing and saluting. We were amazed at their proposal. They said, 'We

Sergeant Isaac Durboraw, Company K (Left photo, center), like most of the members of Company K, was thankful for a lull in the fighting. His unit was now back in reserve behind Cemetery Hill along Rock Creek. Only a few of the men in the Company had been wounded in the previous afternoon's fighting. Now, those who were able were restless to slip away and see their families. "I now told Capt. Minnigh I was going home, and that he should neither say Yes or No!", Durboraw recalled. Captain Henry Minnigh figured there was little he could do to stop them, "Boys if you go home, don't fail to get back tomorrow morning."

SGT. DURBORAW: "I went back to the place where we had piled our knapsacks, the day before, but could find neither knapsack nor Creamer the guard, but looking round I eventually found it in a quarry on the banks of Rock Creek. I had only three miles home and soon reached it, only to find it filled with wounded soldiers, General Meredith being one of the number. I slept on the floor that night, and the next morning with a knapsack well filled, I returned to the company. I did not find many of the people in the neighborhood at their homes, and their houses were occupied by skulkers and shuysters absent from their commands. When I got back to the company I shared out the contents of my haversack." *Courtesy Massachusetts Commandery of the Military Order of the Loyal Legion of the United States and the US Army Military History Institute, Carlisle, Pennsylvania.*

Captain Henry M. Minnigh (Right photo, in front of rank), with most of his men slipping quietly off to visit their families, did the same. He didn't have as far to travel as Sgt. Durboraw, but his journey was far more perilous. The Rebels still occupied town. Minnigh, 23, had been a student at Pennsylvania College but dropped out to teach. He had grown up on the family farm northwest of Herr Ridge, but four years ago his parents moved into a house on the northeast corner of West Middle at South Washington Street. *Courtesy Massachusetts Commandery of the Military Order of the Loyal Legion of the United States and the US Army Military History Institute, Carlisle, Pennsylvania.*

beg the extreme pleasure of having the ladies and gentlemen of this house come to the out-kitchen and take supper.' We accepted their invitation.

"These weather beaten men and soldiers of many battles stood, and asked the ladies and gentlemen to be seated that they might serve us with the excellent supper which they had prepared. They had chicken, biscuits, tea, coffee, butter, honey, milk and all the delicacies of the season.

"Of course we ate and thanked them. But they knew no more of the outcome of the three day's battle than we did."

On the field: Robert E. Lee knew.
His course now clear, he began to put out the word, pull his troops in, organize them...and point them south.

HENRY EYSTER JACOBS:
"About midnight Friday the streets began to fill with men – again a human tide, flowing, flowing, but now like some great current that had passed through innumerable scenes of wreck, bearing its jetsam with it."
CHARLES McCURDY:
"Campfires twinkled along Seminary Ridge, marking the Confederate line of battle. But only to deceive."
JOHN WILLS:
"My wife, who was then single,[22] living opposite General Early's headquarters, saw the commanding officer riding along the line with horse's feet muffled by some means (so you) could not hear the horse's hoofs on the street, and in a low voice, urging his men to their feet, saying 'We must get out. We are losing entirely too many men.'

"She said, 'It was a sight to see those men, in ranks abreast, from curb to curb, with their bayonets glistening in the moonlight, marching out West Middle Street and out of town.'"
MR. BENNER:
"I heard their wagons going all night."
MARY McALLISTER:
"I felt like saying goodbye to them, but it would have seemed like mockery."

Figures vary from source to source, but the final toll of the Battle of Gettysburg seems roughly this:
Union dead: 3,155
Confederate dead: 3,903
Union wounded: 14,529
Confederate wounded: 18,735
Union missing in action: 5,365
Confederate missing in action: 5,425
Out of the 33,264 wounded, Robert E. Lee carried over 12,700 south in his 17-mile long wagon train, leaving behind some 6,035 Confederate wounded among the 21,000 men then in hospital tents, homes, churches and barns at tiny Gettysburg.

End 3rd Day

NOTES

1. Sarah and Joseph Broadhead lived on the western edge of the town, with a view of Seminary Ridge to the west and of the fields to the south.

2. Hospitalization in Philadelphia.

3. A religious sect.

4. The Southern soldier who shouted to the advancing troops met one of the Union troopers at a reunion years later. He asked, "Can you tell me what you fellows were trying to do when I hollered for you to go back? " "Are you that fellow?" replied the Yank. "Well, I want to tell you it made a tremendous impression on the few of us who heard you."

"It was the finest sight I ever saw, the way your men came forward," exclaimed the Southerner.

"No, answered the Yankee, " it was not so fine as the chivalrous interest in the lives of brave men which prompted you to advise us to retreat!" And they clasped hands.

– Reported in an account of the Gettysburg encampment.

5. The Federal Army removed civilians from the Weikerts and other nearby homes to a safer location several miles south and east of Two Taverns, along the Baltimore Pike.

6. On west Middle street.

7. These were troops taken to assist in Johnson's assault on Culp's Hill.

8. "Mrs. Peter Thorn Tells of Battle Days." *The Gettysburg Compiler* (July 26, 1905).

9. *Philadelphia Public Ledger and Daily Transcript* (September 16, 1901).

10. On South Baltimore street, on the hill rising to the Cemetery.

11. Georgiana was among the delegation who traveled to Gettysburg in 1901 to honor her sister.

12. There is always proof that life goes on in spite of historic events. The Gettysburg Compiler reported:

> "L. K. McCLELLAN was born in the McClellan residence on Baltimore Street on June 26th, lying with his mother during the ensuing three days of battle in what is known today as the Jennie Wade house. On the day she was killed, Jennie was there, baking bread for her sister, Georgia Wade McClellan. The child's father, John Lewis McLellan, was enlisted in the Union forces, then serving his last of four tours of duty with the 21st Pa. Cavalry.

13. Jennie Wade had a picture of her fiancé, 'Corporal Johnson Skelly,' in her pocket when she was shot, according to an affidavit in the Adams County Historical Society.

14. Confederate soldiers.

15. Military historians believe that, over the course of the three days at Gettysburg, Confederate artillery fired 20,000 rounds. Union guns fired 32,000. The guns reportedly were heard by people living 175 miles to the west.

16. Reported by Colonel Sir Arthur J. L. Fremantle in his book, *Three Months in the Southern States*. Fremantle, a member of the Coldstream Guards, came to America as a British observer of the war and traveled 14 weeks with the Confederate army. Another writer, Lt. Colonel W. W. Blackford, of J.E.B. Stuart's cavalry, believed that any bad judgment on Lee's part was due to ill health. Lee, and many of his soldiers, was suffering from a severe case of diarrhea. Blackford tells of seeing Lee, obviously unwell, excuse himself and leave his head-quarters tent repeatedly.

Poor diet, living off the land, and, perhaps, raiding abundant fruit orchards as they marched may have taken their toll on Lee's army. The theory may carry some weight. But in his book, *War Years with Jeb Stuart*, Blackford does not comment upon the slowness to action on the part of Longstreet and Ewell, foot-dragging compounded by Ewell's own ill health and by Longstreet's reticence about taking offensive action against what he saw as a too-powerful opposing force. Both argued, but neither man...loyal to Lee...ever refused to obey him.

17. Without understanding its significance, Mrs. King was probably witnessing the first stages of Lee's withdrawal from her area.

18. Brigadier General William Barksdale, C.S.A.

19. The story raises the question of duty: could these soldiers be accused of deserting their posts? It is passed over rather lightly. Minnigh writes of his pride in the fact that although "these brave fellows could easily imagine the dangerous surroundings of loved ones during the terrible conflict, in their homes within the bounds of the battlefield, yet, not a man left the ranks or fled from duty and", he continues, "while most of them got home after the battle, by a peculiar device, only one failed to return."

20. The 25 year old Minnigh had been in the army since 1861, so his sister may be excused for not recognizing him instantly.

21. Henry and Elizabeth Minnigh.

22. Martha Martin lived with her parents, Mr. and Mrs. Ephrain Martin, on West Middle Street. Mrs. Martin taught millinery classes. Her brother Robert, who lived just off the square, was town Burgess.

Saturday
July 4th, 1863

"Ye gods! What a welcome sight..."

– Daniel Skelly

Retreat

Rain showers at 6:00 A.M.; from 2:15 P.M. to 4:00 P.M.; and at 4:00 A.M. on the 5th. Thermometer readings:

7:00 A.M.	2:00 P.M.	9:00 P.M.
69	72	70

– Professor Michael Jacobs

On the field: In torrential rain and sullen gloom, Robert E. Lee's army set out for Virginia.

Stretched over seventeen miles, a wagon train creaked and lumbered down the Chambersburg Road. It was laden with the wounded and heavy supplies, its drivers struggling in the muddy track. Foot soldiers and some 4,000 prisoners began their trek on the Fairfield Road. Both columns would join at the Potomac near Williamsport, Maryland.

Cavalry flanked the columns to ward off a Union attack. None came, and civilians looked on in wonder as the columns trudged past, days long.

In the town: As an employee of the Fahnestock store, DANIEL SKELLY had arranged a sleeping room on the store's third floor for himself and some friends because they wanted to be where they could see everything that happened. They got their wish; the Fourth of July started with a real bang:

"About 4 A.M., there was another commotion in the street, this time on Baltimore, the Fahnestock building being at the corner of West Middle and Baltimore streets. It seemed to be a noisy demonstration. Going hurriedly to the window, I looked out. Ye gods! What a welcome sight for the imprisoned people of Gettysburg! The boys in blue, marching down the street, fife and drum corps playing, the glorious Stars and Stripes fluttering at the head of the lines."

As word spread, the celebration widened; a great victory cheer began to swell from battle stations to farm fields, to forest encampments. TILLIE PIERCE heard it from the Weikert farm on the southeastern side of the battlefield:

"On the summits, in the valleys, everywhere we heard the soldiers hurrahing for the victory that had been won. The troops on our right, at Culp's Hill, caught up the joyous sound as it came rolling on from the Round Tops on our left, and soon the whole line of blue rejoiced in the results achieved. Many a dying hero's last breath carried a thanksgiving and praise to Him, who had watched over and directed the thoughts and movements of the last three days."

Union soldiers sheltering in buildings along the foot of Cemetery Hill were quickly called out to find Confederate stragglers. Sgt. HENRY MONATH was a member of Co. I, 74th Pa. volunteers:

"In looking up Main street¹ we could see the citizens on the street waving their handkerchiefs for us to come, that the Rebels left during the night. We few men held a council on the street, and decided that we would move forward in the city.

"Into every house we went were Rebel soldiers sleeping. We had at least 100 or more Rebels on the square and placed a guard over them."

Civilian or not, TILLIE PIERCE's father got involved in the mop-up, too. Baltimore Street:

"There was a ring of the front door bell. It was the first time the bell had rung since the conflict commenced. No one ventured out on the street during those three days, fearing that they might be picked off by sharp-shooters.

"Hearing the ringing, Mother said: 'Oh, must we go and open the front door?' For she thought the battle would again be renewed. They, however, opened the door, and to their surprise, the Methodist minister stood before them. He exclaimed: 'Don't you think the rascals have gone?'

"Father was so overjoyed, that not taking time to consider, ran out just as he was, intending to go to the Cemetery Hill and inform our men of the good news.

"He had gone about half a square from the house, when, on looking down, saw that he was in his stocking feet. He thought to himself: 'No shoes! No hat! No coat! Why if I go out looking this way, they will certainly think that I am demented!'

"He turned to go back, and while doing so, saw a musket lying on the pavement. He picked it up, and just then spied a Rebel running toward the alley back of Mrs. Schriver's lot. Father ran after him as fast as he could and called: 'Halt!'

"The fellow then threw out his arms, and said: 'I am a deserter! I am a deserter!'

"To which Father replied: 'Yes, a fine deserter you are! You have been the cause of many a poor Union soldier deserting this world; fall in here.'

"He obeyed; and as Father was marching him toward the house, he spied two more Confederates coming out of an adjoining building, and compelled them to 'fall in.'

"These also, claimed to be deserters; but the truth is, they were left behind when Lee's army retreated. He marched the three men out to the front street, and as there were some Union soldiers just passing, handed his prisoners over for safe keeping.

"He then went into the house, put on his shoes and hat, took his gun and went up to the alley back of our lot. There he saw a Rebel with a gun in hand, also trying to escape. Father called on him to halt. The fellow faced about, put his gun on the ground, rested his arms akimbo on it, and stood looking at him. Father raised his musket and commanded: 'Come forward, or I'll fire.'

"The Confederate immediately came forward and handed over his gun. On his way to the front street with this prisoner he captured two more and soon turned these over to our men.

"Father then examined his gun for the first time; and behold! it was empty."

West, on Chambersburg street, SARAH BROADHEAD watched the last of the Rebels troop out of Gettysburg, looking over their shoulders as the victory celebration grew more boisterous:

"I heard a great noise in the street and going to the door I saw a Rebel officer on horseback hallooing to some soldiers on foot to 'Hurry up, the Yankees have possession of the town and all would be captured.' I looked up street and saw our men in the public square and it was a joyful sight, for I knew we were now safe. Soon after, the Rebels sent in a flag of truce, but what was communicated we did not know, and, in consequence, the people were more scared than ever, the report spreading that it was to give notice to remove the women and children before shelling the town. As soon as the flag of truce had gone, our sharpshooters were pushed out to this side of town, and were all around us."

Actually, the flag may have been sent because of aggressive gestures made by some of the townspeople. JOHN WILLS:

"Some of our very patriotic citizens who, in their excitement or want of good judgment, proceeded to barricade the streets by filling hogsheads and barrels with ground taken from their lots and placing them across the streets of West Middle Street, West Chambersburg Street. They took our farm wagon, turned up on edge, across Chambersburg Street. They placed railroad ties across Carlisle and they placed lumber across York Street. Now some of our citizens, in their excitement, attempted to fire on them. The Confederates at once sent word that if any of the citizens fired on them again. they would shell the town."

Wills reports that some of the town's older, cooler heads – including his father, Charles Wills – convinced the amateurs to back off and let the professionals cover the retreat.

On the field: Flags of truce can be carried in either direction. In the diaries of his observation tour with the southern army, Colonel Sir Arthur J. L. Fremantle of the British Coldstream Guards wrote:

"Lawley, the Austrian[2] and I walked up to the front about 8 o'clock, and on our way we met General Longstreet, who was in a high state of amusement and good-humour.

"A flag of truce had just come over from the enemy, and its bearer announced among other things that 'General Longstreet was wounded, and a prisoner, but would be taken care of.'

"General Longstreet sent back word that he was extremely grateful, but that, being neither wounded nor a prisoner, he was quite able to take care of himself."

Other reports circulated among the Union army that both Longstreet and A. P. Hill had been killed. Both were well and busy that morning, rounding up their soldiers.

Regarding Longstreet specifically, Fremantle added the observation that:

"The iron endurance of General Longstreet is most extraordinary: he seems to require neither food nor sleep. Most of his Staff now fall fast asleep directly they get off their horses, they are so exhausted from the last three days' work."

Miles to the east, skirting the field where the climactic Cavalry charge had taken place, SARAH BARRETT KING and her children had departed the Rhinehart farm, and were on their way home:

"We came to the woods the Rebs camped in. It was deserted, not a soul, but everything used in camp left behind. We felt happy. We passed two Rebs on guard. Soon they passed us with this information, 'Your men are after us.'

"We went on to Dr. Schaffer's, dining with them, nerving up for the trip to town, as we saw fires somewhere west. We journeyed on, found the street barricaded,[3] but soon the Stars and Stripes in the square met our gaze and we felt the Fourth was ours."

Left behind and now surrounded, Rebel stragglers kept turning up in the town. Sgt. HENRY MONATH, US Army. Baltimore Street:

"A lady came to me while guarding and asked me to come to her house and take out two men. I followed the woman to her house, but did not enter her front door as she did. I went to the rear of her house. The lot was surrounded with a very high, rough board fence. I had to stand on something about two feet high in order to look over the fence.

"As I looked over, I saw two large Rebel soldiers. 'You're prisoners,' I said, and the answer was, 'Come, Sergeant, there stand our guns against the tree; take and do with them what you please.'

"I had my musket cocked, got over the fence, came to a shoulder arms, and marched toward them. The woman came to the rear and asked me if I could not let the men eat breakfast before I would take them away, as she had already prepared it. I told her yes, and would feel happy to take breakfast with them. I sat down and ate my breakfast, and then marched them to the square.

"In the meantime, all prisoners on the square were marched to the rear, so I marched my two men back to the hotel.[4]

"In this lot where I took the two men, from 1,000 to 2,000 muskets of different kinds were stored."

About that time, Catherine Garlach's "backyard guest," General Schimmelfennig, joined the celebration on Baltimore street. ANNA GARLACH:

"Mother hurried down and out, anxious to know what had become of the man.

"He was already out of his hiding place before she reached him. When I first saw him he was moving across our yard toward the Benner property. He was walking stiff and cramped-like. At the fence was a number of Union men and they proved to be some of his own men. They thought he had been killed and when they saw him, they went wild with delight. I saw them crowd around him and some kissed his hand and they seemed beside themselves with joy.

"That was the last we saw of General Schimmelfennig at that time.

"The two days he was there were hot days and his thirst must have been something awful for in the two days and three nights he did not have anything to drink or eat that we knew of, except what Mother gave him on that one occasion."

But battles are not done until the last bullet is fired, and the retreating Confederate's fear of counterattack kept the town ducking for the rest of that day. GATES FAHNESTOCK, corner of east Middle and Baltimore streets:

"We went out to clean off the sidewalk. A bullet grazed the side of the house above our heads. We went inside and kept off that sidewalk. The sharpshooters, Confederates, stationed on Seminary Ridge, were, we found, shooting at any uniform crossing the street and covering the retreat of the Confederate forces."

Closer to the snipers than the Fahnestocks, HENRY EYSTER JACOBS of West Middle Street knew exactly where they were:

"To the west of the town, there was a little run of water at the Hagerstown Road. At that run, the Confederates had left a line of pickets whose rifles covered the street intersection at our door. As the Union men rode down Washington Street and crossed Middle Street, the watching pickets fired on them. One cavalryman was shot through the arm in front of our eyes. It was the Confederate's way of covering their retreat, and no doubt it was war. But it looked like murder to an eye witness.

"My sister, Julia[5] was only 16 years old then. She stood the situation as long as she could. Then she went to the front door of our house, from which approaching Union soldiers could see her, and began to call to them as they approached the corner: 'Look out! Pickets below! They'll fire on you!' She became a living danger signal, and a most effective one. The men, as they caught her words, halted, watched their opportunity, and made their passage of the death spot in flying dashes. She saved many lives.

"After some time the riflemen at the Hagerstown Road, only three squares away, realized how she was foiling their best marksmanship. They turned their guns on her. They could not hear her cries of warning, but they had seen her standing there, and the actions of their foes..perhaps, too, some warning gestures of hers made evident she was the danger signal. Girl or no girl, she must be silenced. But Julia was not silenced. When the bullets began to frame her where she stood at the threshold of the door, she retreated a few steps into the hall and called her warning still. We could see the leaves and twigs of our linden trees fly as they were snipped by the bullets, but none of them reached her. For half an hour she warned the Union soldiers, and then the need for her steady cry passed. Our own pickets came up, flung themselves upon the ruined stone wall which had served Rodes' men as a breastwork and reformed it across Middle Street. After that it was a duel between the two bodies of riflemen...and the Confederates were good shots.

"Our men amused themselves by raising old hats on points of sticks above the level of their breastwork, and we could see those hats fly off as the bullets of sharpshoot-

Amos Whetstone, 25, a senior at Lutheran Theological Seminary, did not enlist in the emergency company of students because he had accepted a pastorate. He was watching the action from the porch of the Weikert boarding house on Chambersburg Street when a shot from the nearby Eagle hotel, where Confederate officers were quartered, struck him in the calf of the leg. *Courtesy Abdel Ross Wertz Library Archives, Lutheran Theological Seminary, Gettysburg, Pennsylvania.*

ers lifted them. All this time, from noon on, it had been raining heavily. The two forces of duelists, soaked in the downpour, lay in their positions until dark, banging away at each other. And we in the house, after we had a chance to speak to the new arrivals, felt the first sense of security we had known for days in the retreat of the Confederate forces, mingled with a rising sense of awe as we learned what a momentous battle had been fought around us."

MARY McALLISTER. Chambersburg Street:

"I went over to old Mrs. Weikert's, and on her back porch was a man. He said, 'Take care, you will be shot. OH! I believe I am shot!' He looked down and a bullet had just gone through the fleshy part of his leg. Mrs. Weikert had student boarders and this was one of those students.[6] I started out to hunt for something good for a wounded man that was in our house. He wanted bread and butter, so I thought I'd go to see if Mrs. Abram Scott had any. A man came to me and said, 'Do get in off the street. You will be shot because of the sharpshooters.'"

UNIDENTIFIED HOSPITALIZED UNION SOLDIER:

"We were taken to a large barn.

"In and around that barn were gathered about 15-hundred wounded soldiers, Union and Confederate. They were begrimed, swollen and bloody as brought in from the field and, for the most part, had received as yet but little surgical treatment. Some were barely alive, others had just died and many were in a state of indescribable misery. In the center of the barn stood an amputating table, around which two or three surgeons were busily performing their dreadful offices. A handsome young German captain, whose leg had been shattered by a musket ball, was placed upon the table and chloroformed. After the operation of removing his injured limb was complete, he was brought to where I lay and placed beside me. The pallor of his face betokened great loss of blood and extreme weakness. After some minutes, he opened his eyes and turning languidly toward me, inquired, "Is my leg off?" Being told that it was, he gazed intently at his hand and, observing that a ring had been removed from his finger, remarked, 'I would not care for this, were it not for a little friend I have down there at Philadelphia.' In a few hours, he was gone."

Near Seminary Ridge, MARY CUNNINGHAM BIGHAM's family watched the last of the Rebel forces vacate her family's land:

"After they were gone, Father noted a mere stripling with his head down on the meadow gate, crying as if his heart would break. When Father asked the cause of his grief, he sobbed out that 'Our men are gone and now the Yankees will kill me.' Father was a comforting person. He assured the boy that he wouldn't be killed, that there was food in Pennsylvania and it wasn't at all a bad place to be."[7]

In spite of the celebration, some of JOHN WILLS' political problems nearly caught up with him that morning:

"Mother was coming from her bedroom saying she had been awakened by the Rebel Doctor, Captain Simpson, before daylight and told he was leaving with the troops and to 'tell your son to take good care of my horse.' I immediately ran to the barn to congratulate myself on my new horse, but spirits fell when I discovered that not only his horse but our two farm horses were gone as well as the bridles and harnesses.

"While sweeping off the pavement a little later, I did not see that a citizen had arrested Captain Dr. Simpson and brought him back into town and down the alley. A corporal guard of Union soldiers came to the hotel. They asked me if there were any Confederates in the house. I told them of the Confederates who were boarding with us and of their leaving that morning, when a boy who was sitting in front of the hotel jumped up and said, 'Yes! A citizen and Confederate officer just now went into the alley.'

"They at once arrested me for harboring Confederates. I said to them this is all a mistake and if you will allow me to see your superior officer, I will explain the matter satisfactorily to him."

"They said 'As you are a citizen and if you can do that we will grant you the privilege.'

"They took me up to the Diamond and left me in (the) charge of a German Lieutenant who was in charge of a company of German soldiers. They were wild with excitement. When I tried to explain the matter to him he said to me, 'Keep quiet and stay here. I can't control my men.'

"A heavy shower of rain commenced when this German company all ran over to the McLellan House and got under the trees. The whole space of that corner was crowded with Union soldiers and people from the country.

So John "lit out."

"I went to my room and changed my clothes from a suit of linen to a suit of black cloth, went to the barber shop, had my mustache and goatee cut off. I went out, and on the crossing between the Weaver store corner and the Judge Wills building, I met this same Corporal's Guard and they did not recognize me."

Reality

JENNY S. CROLL, Chambersburg Street:
"Our houses were filled for the most part with the wounded; provisions were well nigh exhausted; bridges in all the country round about were burned; all the fences for twenty miles around were gone; our railroad was destroyed; the country people, having suffered in many ways, were unable to bring in any supplies, and 35,000 wounded soldiers were left here to be fed and cared for besides the surgeons, nurses and numerous attendants on such an army of invalids. With it all was the prostrating heat of July weather and a mighty multitude of flies."

ALBERTUS McCREARY, Baltimore Street:
"In going over the field that first day after the fight, the many strange and terrible sights made a strong and lasting impression on my mind. In one place there were as many as forty dead horses where a battery had been planked; the bodies were much swollen, the feet standing up in the air. Broken wagons and guns, belts, cartridge-boxes and canteens, blankets and all sorts of soldier equipment were lying around everywhere. The fences were all down; only a few posts, here and there, were left, like sentinels on guard.

"Dead soldiers were everywhere. Near a small house lay the bodies of two Confederate soldiers, and on looking into the house, I saw two others, one on a bed and the other on the floor. I went in to see if the one on the bed might not be alive. He was dead. He was a young man, and on his breast was a medal of some order. I was tempted to take it off, but I did not because I thought it might lead to his identification.

"The stench from the battlefield after the fight was so bad that everyone went about with a bottle of pennyroyal or peppermint oil.

"The burial of the dead commenced at once, and many were buried along the line where they fought and fell, and, in many cases, so near the surface that their clothing came through the earth."

MR. BENNER. Near Culp's Hill:
"We had found two dead Rebels lying back of our barn and no one came to bury them till late the next day. They'd been left with a blanket spread over them. One had his thumb and every finger on his right hand shot off.

"At the house next to ours on the road to town a Rebel sharpshooter had climbed up in a tree in the yard and buckled himself fast to a limb with his belt. He was picking off our men and of course it wasn't easy for them to make out where he was because the thick leaves hid him. But at last they noticed a puff of smoke when he'd sent a bullet in among them and, don't you forget it...that was the last shot he fired. They aimed at the place the smoke came from and killed him. After the battle, I'll be doggoned if he wasn't still in the tree hanging by his belt."

ALBERTUS McCREARY. In the center of town:

"There were some sorry-looking homes in our neighborhood. The Confederate soldiers had entered them during their occupation of the town and tried to see how much damage they could do. I went home with a young friend of mine whose family had been in a neighboring cellar during the three days of the battle, and found that almost everything had either been cut to pieces or destroyed in some way. Pieces of furniture were burned and broken, a desk had been destroyed, bookcases knocked down, and the books torn and shattered. To add more to the disorder and destruction, the soldiers had taken a half-barrel of flour, mixed it with water to make a thin paste, put into this the feathers from feather-beds and thrown it over everything – walls, furniture and down the stairways. Of course, the owners were indignant and angry, for it meant great loss to them; but there was nothing to be done about it.

"A Union soldier came to the house for something to eat on the morning of the fourth day, and says that he had been hid in the belfry of the school house from the morning of the first day until then. He had run in during the retreat, and there was no way of getting out without being captured. He was almost starved, for he had had only a few drops of water in his canteen and a little hard tack. We soon fixed him up, and, refreshed with food and water, he started out to find his regiment."

HARRY ERNEST TROXEL. Center of town:

"I was a little boy with pockets in my pants, and I went along the street and filled those pockets with bullets that lay scattered about.

"Several Rebel sharpshooters had stationed themselves in our shop,[8] and the Union cannon made it a target to drive 'em out. I think eleven shells went into the place. It was full of finished buggies and carriages, and vehicles that were being repaired. The shells knocked some of 'em into kindling wood."

SARAH BARRETT KING. On the east side:

"Our house had been occupied by Rebs who took good care of Father and he was sorry they were captured there.

"My room seemed to be as I left it with the exception of a little pile of gray rags. I didn't pay much attention to it at first, it was so small. My curiosity was at length aroused. I could not imagine what I had left lying on the floor. I discovered it was the remnant of pants and a hat. Then I looked in a trunk where my husband kept his clothing, and a fine blue suit, a Christmas gift, was missing, and I suppose these gray rags were left in exchange. I gathered them up on a stick and threw them out in the street."

The mop up begins

MR. BENNER. South of Benner's Hill:

"We went back home and found two Rebels in our shed, eating chicken. They seemed to think it was time for them to get out of there, and they slipped away down the lane.

"Pretty soon, our soldiers began to arrive on the farm, and Mother went to baking pancakes to give them. She made the pancakes out of flour and salt. The Rebels had taken everything else in the food line. Oh, bless you, yes. They just took all that they could make use of. The whole house was mussed up and turned upside down. It looked like they'd gone to the bureau drawers and pulled them out and dumped what was in them on the floor. They took only a part of our flour, but they got all our meat and all our chickens and our five horses. Our field of wheat was trodden down, and so was our grass and oats. The soldiers had dropped their guns here and there and we often mowed into those guns with our scythes afterward. At first, we thought we'd lost our cattle. They strayed away during the battle, and there seemed small chance of our seeing them again, but we got them together in a few days. The thing that troubled us most was being left without horses. They were a dead loss to us, and besides, it was a great handicap not to have them for working the farm. Father was a man who didn't often say anything, but when we came home after the battle and looked around, he said, 'I feel just like starting off and never looking back.'"

Perhaps he should have looked for new horses on Chambersburg Street. JENNIE S. CROLL:

"Some poor starved army horses that had been turned loose to pick up a living strayed up this street, walking, not in the middle, but in solemn procession, along the pavement. When they reached the breastworks,[9] finding they could neither climb over nor go around, they turned aside into the hall of a dwelling whose door stood open. In single file, they proceeded through this hall, the rooms on either side filled with wounded, to the back porch which ran along the back building. This porch was slightly inclined, and in their weak condition, several slipped and fell. The lady of the house, greatly unstrung by the terrible experiences of the preceding days, threw up her hands, exclaiming: 'Oh, Lord, what will come next?'"

Meanwhile, back at the Globe. JOHN WILLS:

"It became known to the Union soldiers by some means that the proprietor of the Globe Hotel had liquors buried in his garden. A German Lieutenant came to the hotel and was going to confiscate the liquors. I remonstrated with him, when father went up to the Provost Marshal's office and told him, 'Captain, if you need any liquors for your sick and wounded, you are welcome to it free of charge, but I don't want your men to steal it from me.'

The Captain, thanking father for his kind offer, said it shall not occur again.

"Those liquors, when taken up which were buried, were ruined by being water soaked. We disposed of it by selling some off cheap, and giving it away and throwing some out."

CHARLES McCURDY also knew people who hid things:

"There was a farmer named Pitzer living near Round Top, his farm being the scene of some of the fiercest fighting. Mr. Pitzer had no faith in paper money and had accumulated a store of gold and silver coin amounting, it was said, to some thousands of dollars. He kept this money at home, apparently having as little confidence in banks as he had in greenbacks. Whether in a moment of panic, when he found himself about to be surrounded by fighting, he hid his money in a bake oven in his yard, or whether he had adopted it before as his strong box, I do not know. At all events he hid his wealth there and it was found and taken."

Jumping briefly to 1884, this article concerning Jim Parr, a veteran of the 3rd Georgia regiment, appeared in the Athens, Georgia Sunday Banner-Watchman. Parr, it reports, found the bake oven while looking for a stone to use as a grave marker:

"While Parr was rummaging through the flat rocks of the floor of this oven, he heard a jingling sound, and striking a light, discovered a pile of gold and silver and a number of paper bills on the bank of Gettysburg. He secured about $1200 of this money, as much as he could conveniently carry off, intending to return for the remainder. But when he got back it was gone, someone else also discovering the mine."

Now, back to CHARLES McCURDY:

"In the evening of the second day's battle, a Confederate cavalryman rode up to the residence of Mr. Alexander Buehler in Gettysburg. Mr. Buehler had a drug and book store in the front of his dwelling,[10] which of course was closed. He was a man of the very highest character, universally esteemed and trusted. The soldier who carried a valise on the pummel of his saddle inquired for him and when he appeared told him that he had been sent by General Mahone, a brigade commander of the third corps, to ask him to take charge of the valise he carried until called for. Mr. Buehler consented and carried the bag, whose contents were very heavy, to his bedroom and put it under his bed. The next evening the same soldier appeared, reclaimed the bag and rode off."

According to McCurdy, Buehler later realized that he had been General Mahone's personal banker. It isn't known what the general did with the money.

According to the Athens Sunday Banner Watchman, Jim Parr took his share home to Georgia, paid a substitute to finish the rest of his hitch in the army, and started a business after the war.[11]

Lt. Frank Aretas Haskell, an aide to General Gibbon, Hancock's II Corps, took time to look around town when his duties allowed it. "I saw John Burns, the only citizen of Gettysburg who fought in the battle, and I asked him what troops he fought with. He said; 'I pitched in with them Wisconsin fellers.' I asked what sort of men they were, and he answered: 'They fit terribly. The Rebs couldn't make anything of them fellers.'

"And so the brave compliment the brave. This man was touched by three bullets from the enemy, but not seriously wounded."

– Lt. Frank A. Haskell
Courtesy Massachusetts Commandery of the Military Order of the Loyal Legion of the United States and the US Army Military History Institute, Carlisle, Pennsylvania.

These are the five daughters of Solomon Powers in a photograph taken many years after the battle. They were all in their twenties in 1863. Lydia, Jane Powers McDonnell, and Alice are in the back. Up front are Mary and Virginia. Independence Day 1863 took on a special meaning for Jane. Her husband, Henry, was released by the Confederates after having been held a prisoner for three days. Neighboring farmers on Seminary Ridge vouched for him and finally convinced his captors that he wasn't a spy. McDonnell quickly made his way to Solomon Powers' house on High Street. There he found Jane, the children, her sisters, and his father-in-law living in the cellar and caring for some twenty-eight wounded and dying soldiers. *Courtesy H.L. Grimm, Human Interest Stories of Gettysburg, 1927.*

Nightfall

SARAH BROADHEAD. By lamplight:
"It has been a dreadfully long day. We know, however, that the Rebels are retreating, and that our army has been victorious. I was anxious to help care for the wounded, but the day is ended and all is quiet, and for the first time in a week I shall go to bed, feeling safe."

End July 4th.

NOTES

1. Monath had spent the night in the cellar of a building at the foot of Cemetery Hill. He is probably referring here to Baltimore street.
2. Francis Lawley, correspondent for the Times of London, and FitzGerald Ross, Captain of Hussars in the Imperial Austrian Service.
3. York Street. Mrs. King lived at the corner of Liberty and York.
4. Probably the Wagon Hotel, at the foot of Cemetery Hill.
5. Later Mrs. John H. Harpster, wife of a staff officer in the Second Army Corps who survived to become a missionary.
6. Amos Moser Whetstone, student at Gettysburg Theological Seminary.
7. The boy wrote to Mr. Bigham some months later, telling the elder man that he had been right about Pennsylvania, and that he, the boy, had joined the Union Army.
8. Troxel's father was a carriage maker .
9. On Middle or Chambersburg street.
10. On Chambersburg Street, near the Diamond.
11. This is a great story, and is worth the telling. But, in this case, the reader may want to sprinkle a grain or two of salt. Reader's choice.

Aftermath

Part One

The Days Immediately Following the Battle

"I am becoming more used to sights of misery. We do not know until tried what we are capable of."
– Sarah Broadhead, July 7th, 1863.

"The armies just about ruined the country here.

"Lots of farmers who were well to do before the battle were poor afterward. Their hay and feed was gone, their growing crops ruined, their cattle stolen, and on some places all the boards had been ripped off the barns for firewood. A good many who had lost their horses went to the condemned sales of army horses and mules and stocked up with those old cripples, all lame, or collar sore, or used up in some way."[1]
– The Colored Farm Hand

On the field: George Meade waited until Sunday, July 5th, to send troops after Lee. A cavalry brigade went out the Chambersburg Road and Sedgwick's Corps was detailed to follow the troops on the Fairfield Road. Meade left Gettysburg on the 7th.

Subsequently, Union forces found Lee waiting for the flooded Potomac to ebb near Williamsport, Maryland. The Federal soldiers did not attack, and Lee finally crossed into Virginia on July 13th.

By that time, Gettysburg had other things to think about.

ADAMS COUNTY SENTINEL:
"Our town is one vast hospital filled with the wounded in the recent battles. The churches, the courthouse, warehouses, colleges, seminary and many of the private homes are filled. Many of the barns and houses for miles around town are filled with thousands of the wounded, mostly wounded Rebels. The Rebel army, in its hasty retreat, left thousands behind. Every attention in the power of the people is being bestowed on these unfortunate sufferers.

"The Rebel sharpshooters were in a tight position while in the occupancy of our town. One of them, when ordered across the street, was afraid to venture, but finally

"There were parties engaged in burying the dead in the fields where they fell. A dead soldier in blue was lying along the side of the turnpike, black and swollen from the heat and rain, disfigured beyond recognition." – Attorney William McLean. *Courtesy Massachusetts Commandery of the Military Order of the Loyal Legion of the United States and the U.S. Army Military History Institute, Carlisle, Pennsylvania.*

concluded to get down on his hands and feet, remarking that our men would take him for a hog. We would have taken him for that whether on his hands and feet or not.

"The people of Adams County have more or less suffered from both armies, but those in the vicinity of the battlefield have suffered and lost the heaviest. We regret to learn that the house and barn of William Bliss, with all their contents, were totally destroyed. The house and barn occupied by Mr. William Comfort were also destroyed. The house and barn of Mr. Alex Currens were both burned. The barns of Messrs John Herbst and Alex Cobean were both destroyed."

As the Smoke Clears

WILLIAM McLEAN. Baltimore Street:
"On Sunday morning, I inquired where there was probably the most need for food. I was informed that men were suffering in the McPherson barn on the Chambersburg pike. My good wife went to work, baked biscuit, prepared gruel and we gathered fresh Antwerp raspberries in our garden and loaded up with as much as I could carry. I started on foot, of course, to the barn. As a civilian, I must confess to a little trepidation in going to what was so recently the front and, hearing the firing of artillery, as the retreat was being followed up.

"There were parties engaged in burying the dead in the fields where they fell. A dead soldier in blue was lying along the side of the turnpike, black and swollen from the heat and rain, disfigured beyond recognition. When I entered the barn, it was crowded with the wounded of both armies, some of them having fallen four days before and without having any food except in some cases the little hardtack in their haversacks, and without any surgical attention. There was so many of these wounded and so closely packed together that I was obliged to tramp on some of them in distributing my supplies. You may imagine how pleased and grateful they were for this fresh food.

"One of them told me that, as he was lying on the field, General Lee had given him a drink out of his canteen. Lee's headquarters were in this locality. Many of these poor fellows must have died afterwards from gangrene."

School Superintendent, AARON SHEELY ventured into the fields near his farmhouse on the Chambersburg Road:
"I went out on the battlefield...the poor wretched still lying there cried for water. It was not long before my arms were full of canteens of both the Union and Confederate injured. An officer came up and told me to let the Confederates alone, that it was enough to help our own people.

These soldiers were killed during the first day of fighting near McPherson's Woods. It was weeks before all of the dead soldiers were buried and months before all of the dead animals had dirt thrown over them. *Courtesy Massachusetts Commandery of the Military Order of the Loyal Legion of the United States and the U.S. Army Military History Institute, Carlisle, Pennsylvania.*

Mother Ann Simeon Norris, who had approved of the Sisters of Charity escorting the young women of St. Joseph's Academy to the roadside on July 1st to pray for Reynolds' First Corps as they rode northward into battle, received news on July 5th of just how bad the fighting had been from a detachment of the Confederate Army as it moved south. They suggested that she might want to send help to the soldiers that were wounded and dying. *Courtesy St. Joseph's Provincial House Archives.*

Dispatched by Mother Ann Simeon, Father James Francis Burlando escorted to Gettysburg a dozen Sisters of Charity of St. Vincent de Paul. Although the distance was less than 12 miles, the heavy rains had turned the road to mud and travel was slow. Even the retreating Confederate army had difficulty because of the thick mud, but the Sisters of Charity arrived late that same afternoon with food, bandages, sponges and some clothing. *Courtesy St. Joseph's Provincial House Archives*

"I drove back to the farm, loaded up with water and returned. What little water there was on the battlefield was filled with blood."

NUNS ST. JOSEPH'S ACADEMY AT EMMITSBURG were among the first outsiders to bring help for the wounded. Mother Ann Simeon writes that she dispatched "Father Burlando and Sister Camilla O'Keefe with 15 other nuns of the sisters of St. Josephs" after Rebels retreating through Emmitsburg passed the word on the morning of Sunday, July 5th.

"The Confederates suggested the order may want to send help to the soldiers that were wounded and dying."

As they arrived, Sister Camilla wrote of: "Hundreds of both armies lying dead almost on the track over which we were to pass. On both sides were men digging pits and putting bodies down by the dozen. One nearby made a pit containing 50 bodies of Rebels.

"We didn't see a woman that evening. They either escaped to the country or hid in their cellars. The following day they appeared in their homes looking like ghosts, so terrified were these poor creatures during the frightful battle."

She added: "No wonder."

Apparently the sisters missed SARAH BROADHEAD:
"Early this morning I went out to the Seminary, just outside of town, and which, until the retreat, was in the hands of the enemy. What horrible sights present themselves on every side, the roads being strewn with dead horses and the bodies of some men, though the dead have nearly all been buried, and every step of the way giving evidence of the dreadful contest. Shall we – for I was not alone – enter the building or return home? Can we endure the spectacle of hundreds of men wounded in every conceivable manner, some in the head and limbs, here an arm off and there a leg, and just inside a poor fellow with both legs shot away? It is dreadful to behold, and, to add to the misery, no food has been served for several days. The little we have will not go far with so many. 'What can we do?' is the only question, and the little we brought was distributed. It is heart-sickening to think of these noble fellows sacrificing everything for us, and saving us, and it out of our power to render any assistance of consequence. I turned away and cried. We returned

As the convoy of nuns approached Gettysburg Sister Camilla O'Keefe noted: "hundreds of both armies were lying dead almost on the track over which we were to pass. On both sides were men digging pits and putting bodies down by the dozen." *Courtesy St. Joseph's Provincial House Archives.*

These Confederate dead are being laid to rest on the Rose farm. The mass grave is just off the Emmitsburg Road over which the wagons carrying the Emmitsburg nuns and their supplies passed. Scenes like this were repeated on almost every farm and inside the town, too. Approximately 51,000 men of both armies were killed, wounded, captured or listed as missing in the bloodiest three days of the American Civil War. *Courtesy Massachusetts Commandery of the Military Order of the Loyal Legion of the United States and the U.S. Army Military History Institute, Carlisle, Pennsylvania.*

to town to gather up more food if possible, and to get soft material to place under their wounded limbs, to help make them more comfortable. As we returned, our cavalry was moving out to follow the Rebels, and the street was in an uproar. When I reached home, I found my husband's brother, who had passed through the battle unhurt, and had come to see us. I rejoiced at seeing him, for we feared he had fallen, and at once set to work to prepare a meal to appease his hunger. As I was baking cakes for him, a poor prisoner came to the door and asked me to give him some, for he had nothing to eat for the past two or three days. Afterward, more joined him, and made the same statement and request. I was kept baking cakes until nearly noon, and, in consequence, did not return to the Seminary. The poor fellows in my house were so hungry that they could hardly wait until the cakes were baked."

Every large building in town, and there were more than one-hundred, was converted into a hospital. Most private homes had become hospitals, too, as wounded sought refuge and help wherever they could find it. While the Sisters distributed their supplies and did all they could to comfort the wounded, the McClellan House Hotel, Carlisle Road at the Railroad, made space for them to sleep on the parlor floor. *Courtesy Adams County Historical Society.*

Thirteen year old LYDIA ZIEGLER was just returning home:

"A friend had given us six large loaves of bread. All along the road we found wounded men who had not eaten for three days, begging for bread and water. Father took his pocketknife and cut off bread and gave it to the wounded. Mother would have to put it into the mouths of some who were too weak to lift even bread to their lips or take water which we kids carried from little streams or springs nearby. We made cups from leaves which we fastened together.

"When we got home we found almost everything gone. There were no beds, no clothes. It had been converted to a hospital. We found the feet of our four fat hogs lying in the pen. Two white cows survived, however. The soldiers apparently needed them for milk rather than beef."

TILLIE PIERCE, the Weikert Farm:

"Tuesday July 7th, in company with Mrs. Schriver and her two children, I started off on foot to reach my home.

"As it was impossible to travel the roads on account of the mud, we took to the fields. While passing along, the stench arising from the fields of carnage was most sickening. Dead horses, swollen to almost twice their natural size, lay in all directions. Stains of blood frequently met our gaze and all kinds of army accouterments covered the ground. Fences had disappeared, some buildings were gone, others ruined.

"The whole landscape had been changed and I felt as though we were in a strange and blighted land. Our killed and wounded had by this time been nearly all carried from the field."

DANIEL SKELLY, West Middle Street:

"Wherever there was a bit of woods which had been in direct line of artillery fire of both sides, good-sized trees were knocked off, splintered and branches thrown in every direction.

"Emergency hospitals were set up on the field. Surgeons were busily at work with the restricted equipment at their command, performing the necessary amputations among the severely wounded men remaining in the hospitals. The desperately wounded were being cared for, many of them dying and being carried away for burial or friends taking charge of their bodies.

"Fences were all destroyed and the country all open so that we could drive or walk across the country instead of having to take the Emmitsburg or Taneytown roads. The whole countryside was covered with the ruins of the battle. Shot and shell, guns,

John H. McClellan, 55, and his brother George, 57, ran the McClellan House Hotel located on the northwest corner of the square. It is said that some of the townsfolk referred to the McClellan House as the "temperance hotel" because the local temperance society held meetings there. John Burns, a "teetotaler," developed a habit (when he was constable) of dropping by, as he made his rounds, to see who might be available for conversation. *Courtesy Adams County Historical Society.*

These three Confederate Prisoners were being held along Seminary Ridge. Rebel prisoners were put to work on the burial details. One of them, whose name is not preserved, observed: "The sights and smells that assailed us were simply indescribable. Corpses swollen to twice their original size, some of them actually burst asunder with the pressure of foul gases and vapors...the odors were nauseating and so deadly that in a short time we all sickened and were lying with our mouths close to the ground...most of us were vomiting profusely." *Courtesy Massachusetts Commandery of the Military Order of the Loyal Legion of the United States and the U.S. Army Military History Institute, Carlisle, Pennsylvania.*

Tuesday, July 7, Elizabeth Thorn, her three small sons, and her elderly mother and father were greeted with this view of their home (Right). Earlier, as they walked home along Baltimore Pike, Mrs. Thorn recalled "We saw some of our furniture going by on some wagons and my boys wanted me to go out and stop it." She never learned who stole the furniture or trunk of fine linen the family had brought from Germany. Now, they were facing their home that had no glass in the windows.

"Everything in the house was gone except three feather beds and a couple of pillows. The beds and a dozen pillows we had brought from the old country were not fit to use again. The legs of six soldiers had been amputated on the beds in our house and they were ruined with blood and we had to make way with them.

"It was a busy time for father and me when we got back. We would get orders to dig graves and father and I dug 105 graves for soldiers in the next three weeks. When I left home the first time I had put on a heavier dress than usual and when we got back there wasn't a single piece of our clothing left. I lived in that dress for six weeks.

"Sixteen soldiers and one colored man had been buried in the garden near the pump house. In one field lay fifteen dead horses and in the other field nineteen dead horses. They were right beside the cemetery and were not buried and the stench was awful. For days I could hardly eat because of the disagreeable odor.

"For all the extra work of burying the soldiers we never received any extra pay from the cemetery or from any other source, only the monthly salary of $13.00." *Courtesy Massachusetts Commandery of the Military Order of the Loyal Legion of the United States and the U.S. Army Military History Institute, Carlisle, Pennsylvania.*

These are Union dead near the Peach Orchard. There were graves to be dug for some 6,000 soldiers, and some wearily estimated that at least half that many extra-large graves would be needed for horses and mules. "I assisted in gathering some of the dead and the wounded, and it was anything but pleasant. The dead horses were burned and the odor from the burning horseflesh made our departure smell like an escape from a hateful charnel house." – Drummerboy William T. "Billy" Simpson. *Courtesy Massachusetts Commandery of the Military Order of the Loyal Legion of the United States and the U.S. Army Military History Institute, Carlisle, Pennsylvania.*

pieces of shells and bullets were strewn about the fields in every direction and everything that the carnage of battle could produce was evident.

"Ziegler's Grove showed the effects of the Confederate artillery fire. Good-sized trees were knocked off and splintered in every imaginable way. The bodies of horses that had been killed were lying about.

"The sight around Meade's headquarters along the Taneytown road was terrible, indicating the exposed position it occupied, subject to every shot and shell that came over the ridge above it. Around the house and yard and below it lay at least 12 or 15 dead horses, shot down no doubt while aides and orderlies were delivering orders and messages to headquarters.

"A short distance below the house there was a stone fence dividing a field. Across this was hanging a horse which had been killed evidently just as he was jumping the fence, for its front legs were on one side and the hind legs on the other. In the road a short distance away was another horse which had been shot down while drawing an ambulance.

It was up to the farmer or resident to bury horses or mules that died on their property, if they wanted it done quickly. Sometimes, those caught looting the battle field or stealing guns were sentenced to the animal burial detail. *Courtesy Massachusetts Commandery of the Military Order of the Loyal Legion of the United States and the U.S. Army Military History Institute, Carlisle, Pennsylvania.*

"In the front room of the house was a bed, the covers of it thrown back; and its condition indicated that a wounded soldier had occupied it. I was told that General Butterfield, Meade's chief of staff, who had been wounded, had been placed upon it before being taken to a hospital.

"The Trostle house was entirely deserted. In their kitchen, the dinner table was still set with all the dishes from the meal, and fragments of food remained, indicating that the family had gotten up from their meal and made a hurried getaway."

The Dead

MR. BENNER, south of Benner's Hill and east of Rock Creek:
"I went over to Culp's Hill. They were burying the dead there in long narrow ditches about two feet deep. They'd lay in a man at the end of the trench and put in the next man with the upper half of his body on the first man's legs, and so on. They got them in as thick as they could and only covered them enough to prevent their breeding disease.

"All the pockets of the dead men were turned out. Probably that was done by the soldiers who did the burying. They thought they might find a ring or money or something else of value."

DANIEL SKELLY, on the field:
"On the Codori farm, there were still some dead Confederates who had not been buried. They were lying on their backs, their faces toward the heavens, and burned as black as coal from exposure to the hot sun.

"One of the saddest sights of the day's visit on the field I witnessed near the Devil's Den, on the low ground in that vicinity. There were twenty-six Confederate officers, ranking from a colonel to lieutenants, laid side by side in a row for burial. At the head of each was a board giving their names, ranks and commands to which they belonged. A short distance away was another group of thirteen arranged in the same way.

"They had evidently been prepared for burial by their Confederate companions before they had fallen back, so that their identity would be preserved and they would receive a respectable burial."

THE COLORED FARM HAND, on the field:
"It made me sick, the bodies were so numerous and so swelled up, and some so shot to pieces – a foot here, an arm there, and a head in another place. They lay so thick in the Valley of Death that you couldn't walk on the ground. Their flesh was black as your hat – yes, black as the blackest colored person. I been told that come from drinkin' whiskey with gunpowder in it to make 'em brave. A man would face anything then.

"There were thousands of the very prettiest kinds of muskets layin' around, and any amount of blankets and lots of other stuff. Clearing up was a hard job, and any one who wanted to work could make big money. A man wouldn't turn around unless you gave him half a dollar. As quick as they could, they throwed a little dirt over the horses, and they dug long, shallow trenches and buried the men in them. The work was done in a hurry, and in some places you'd see feet or arms sticking out."

WILLIAM SIMPSON, DRUMMERBOY, on the field:
"I assisted in gathering some of the dead and the wounded, and it was anything but pleasant. The dead horses were burned and the odor from the burning horseflesh made our departure smell like an escape from a hateful charnel house."

REBEL PRISONERS were put to work on the burial details. This person is not identified:[2]
"The sights and smells that assailed us were simply indescribable. Corpses swollen to twice their original size, some of them actually burst asunder with the pressure of foul gases and vapors...the odors were nauseating and so deadly that in a short time we all sickened and were lying with our mouths close to the ground...most of us were vomiting profusely."

In the days immediately following the battle, Union soldiers were charged with the task of locating where their dead had fallen, identifying them if possible, and reclaiming weapons and supplies. They had to contend with hundreds of souvenir hunters. Several months after the battle the Gettysburg Star-Sentinel published the following article: "Twenty-eight thousand muskets have been gathered upon the field of Gettysburg. Twenty-four thousand were found loaded, twelve-thousand containing two loads, and six-thousand from three to ten loads each. In some cases, half-a-dozen balls were driven in on a single charge. In some other cases, the former owner had reversed the order, placing the ball at the bottom of the barrel and the powder at the top." *Courtesy Massachusetts Commandery of the Military Order of the Loyal Legion of the United States and the U.S. Army Military History Institute, Carlisle, Pennsylvania.*

UNIDENTIFIED UNION SOLDIER on the field:

"Six men came upon a soldier, dead, seated with his back against a tree. His eyes were riveted on some object held tightly in his hands. As we drew nearer we saw that it was an ambrotype of two small children. Man though I was, hardened through those long years to carnage and bloodshed, the sight of that man who looked on his children for the last time in this world, who, away off in a secluded spot, had rested himself against a tree that he might feast his eyes on his little loves, brought tears to my eyes.

"We stood looking at him for some time. I was thinking of the wife and baby I had left at home and wondering how soon, in the mercy of God, she would be left a widow and my baby boy, fatherless.

"Not a word was spoken, but we dug a grave and laid the poor fellow to rest with his children's picture clasped over his heart. Over his grave, on the tree against which he was sitting, I inscribed the words:

"Somebody's Father.

July 3, 1863"[3]

UNIDENTIFIED:

"On my uncle's farm, just below Big Round Top, eighteen-hundred of the dead were buried in a single trench. They were covered very shallow, and at night you could see phosphorescent light coming out of the earth where they were buried

"Such of the wounded as were able to crawl dragged themselves to the streams and to the shade of bushes, and they often got to spots so secluded that they were not easily discovered. Moving them sometimes opened their wounds afresh and they bled to death. We found two on Tuesday afternoon. One of them, with a compound fracture of his leg, lay in a swamp where he had sucked water from the mud."

MR. BENNER, south of Benner's Hill and east of Rock Creek:

"A neighbor of ours, old Mr. Taney, came to get some flour on Tuesday and he said, 'Over here in the woods I found a dead man.'

Lee's Army left behind an interrupted rail service. Telegraph lines were cut and railroad tracks were twisted, most often by the cavalry who galloped ahead of the rest of the army. These twisted rails are a result of burning wooden cross-ties, which heated the iron rails, and made them easy to bend out of shape. *Courtesy Massachusetts Commandery of the Military Order of the Loyal Legion of the United States and the U.S. Army Military History Institute, Carlisle, Pennsylvania.*

Dr. Jonathan Letterman, Army Chief of Surgeons since November 1862, is seen here with his staff. Courtesy Massachusetts Commandery of the Military Order of the Loyal Legion of the United States and the U.S. Army Military History Institute, Carlisle, Pennsylvania.

"So Father and I took a mattock and a shovel and went along with Mr. Taney to the spot where he'd come across the body. There it was, all bloated up, seated leaning against a tree. We had to make the grave a rod or so away on account of the tree roots. It was impossible to handle the man to get him there, he was so decayed like, and we hitched his belt to his legs and dragged him along and no sooner did we start with him than his scalp slipped right off. We just turned him in on his side and covered him with earth."

LEANDER WARREN, Railroad Street:

"There was a 'Captain Blood' who came around collecting all blankets and tents. The women not only freely gave, but some even washing them first, expecting them to be used for the wounded, but we found out the man and his crew took them to New York and sold them there.

"Basil Riggs had a contract to raise the dead and put them in coffins. I had a one-horse team and he had a two-horse team. He could haul nine at a time, me...six."

JOHN WILLS, Globe Inn, York Street:

"There were two embalming rooms in town. One was in a room on York street adjoining the Judge Wills building. The other was in a brick school house on Mummasburg road. A number of citizens made quite a good thing out of this gruesome business, taking up the dead for those people and assisting in preparing them for shipment home. Men engaged in this work drank a lot of whiskey, buying it in large quantities. I also discovered they were buying up all the pint and quart flasks and having them filled with whiskey and taking them out and selling them to the soldiers in hospitals and elsewhere at very, very high prices. I put a stop to that trick."

For the Survivors

DANIEL SKELLY:

"The Sanitary Commission took possession of the Fahnestock store, as the goods of that firm had been sent away for safety.

"The room was 100 feet long and right in the center of the town. The commission filled it up with everything that could be of use to the wounded, both in provisions and clothing.

"The firm of Fahnestock Brothers received numerous inquiries about wounded soldiers who were scattered over the field in the hospitals hastily set up at points most conveniently located to take care of the casualties. With Mrs. E. G. Fahnestock, I frequently rode back and forth among these stations, either in buggy or on horseback, look-

These medicines, the knife, and sharpening stone, were staples of army surgeons. During the battle they were in short supply. It wasn't until the trains began running again that doctors and nurses had enough to treat the tens of thousands of wounded and dying of both sides that were left in Gettysburg. *Courtesy The J. Howard Wert Gettysburg Collection*

ing for wounded men about whom information was sought. Sometimes it was difficult to locate them. We made other trips to the hospitals in the college and seminary buildings also. Frequently on these trips were included supplies of delicacies for the men."

SARAH BROADHEAD:

"July 7 – This morning we started out to see the wounded, with as much food as we could scrape together, and some old quilts and pillows. It was very little, but yet better than nothing. We found on reaching the hospital[4] that a wagon-load of bread and fifty pounds of butter had arrived, having been sent in from the country, and a supply of what the soldiers call "hard tack," had been distributed. All got some to eat, but not as much as they desired. Government meat is promised for to-morrow, and a full supply of provisions. I assisted in feeding some of the severely wounded, when I perceived that they were suffering on account of not having their wounds dressed. I did not know whether I could render any assistance in that way, but I thought I would try. I procured a basin and water, and went to a room where there were seven or eight, some shot in the arms, others in the legs, and one in his back, and another in the shoulder. I asked if any one would like to have his wounds dressed? Some one replied, "There is a man on the floor who cannot help himself, you had better see to him." Stooping over him, I asked for his wound, and he pointed to his leg. Such a horrible sight I had never seen and hope never to see again. His leg was all covered with worms. I inquired, 'Was there no doctor in the building? If there was, I must see him.' One was brought, and I asked how the men ever came to be in such a condition. He said, 'Enough men had not been detailed to care for the wounded, and that that man had been wounded in the first day's fight, and held by the Rebels until the day previous, and that they (the surgeons) had not yet had time to attend to all, and, at any rate, there were not enough surgeons, and what few there were could do but little, for the Rebels had stolen their instruments.' He declared further, that many would die from sheer lack of timely attendance. We fixed the man as comfortably as we could, and when the doctor told me he could not live, I asked him for his home, and if he had a family. He said I should send for his wife, and when I came home I wrote to her, as he told me, but I fear she may never see him alive, as he is very weak, and sinking rapidly. I did not return to the hospital to-day, being very much fatigued and worn out, and having done what I never expected to do, or thought I could. I am being more used to sights of misery. We do not know until tried what we are capable of."

Amputations were still being performed weeks after the battle because of the spread of infection. This tent was located at the newly established General Hospital, Camp Letterman, as it was called, was some two miles out the York Pike on George Wolf's farm. School teacher Sallie Myers noted in her diary July 24th: "They have moved all from the churches and private houses to a General Hospital near where the Porter Guards were encamped two years ago." By the end of July, more than 10,000 of the wounded that could withstand travel were moved by newly restored rail service to permanent hospitals. That still left some 15,000 wounded to be cared for in this town of less than 2,500 residents. Church congregations and school authorities had to clean from their buildings the blood and destruction caused by both armies before they could convert them to their former uses. *Courtesy Massachusetts Commandery of the Military Order of the Loyal Legion of the United States and the U.S. Army Military History Institute, Carlisle, Pennsylvania.*

The U.S. Sanitary Commission, a civilian agency dedicated to caring for the wounded, established a tent at Camp Letterman. The Rev. Dr. Gordon Winslow, 60, Sanitary Inspector of the Army of the Potomac, and his wife are seated. They are flanked by several surgeons. *Courtesy Massachusetts Commandery of the Military Order of the Loyal Legion of the United States and the U.S. Army Military History Institute, Carlisle, Pennsylvania.*

These items belonged to Catherine "Aunt Katie" Wert. There is an "invalid" cup made especially to administer fluids to anyone, in this case a soldier, unable to sit up and drink. The scissors were used to cut rags and bandages. Ms. Wert had a tent of wounded assigned to her care. *Courtesy The J. Howard Wert Gettysburg Collection.*

TILLIE PIERCE, on Baltimore Street:

"..my thoughts and attention were directed to the General Hospital, located about one mile east of the town. This was a large collection of tents, regularly laid out in camp style.

"As we passed along the camp streets we could look into the open tents and behold the row of cots on either side. Upon these couches lay the sufferers who, a short while before, had endured the terrors of battle, and were now hovering on the verge of Eternity.

"Here also were established the Christian and Sanitary Commissions, ever exerting their moral and human influences. In their large tents was contained almost every-

This tent at Camp Letterman was assigned to the care of Anna M. Holstein who also nursed at Antietam. *Courtesy Massachusetts Commandery of the Military Order of the Loyal Legion of the United States and the U.S. Army Military History Institute, Carlisle, Pennsylvania.*

The Camp Letterman Kitchen. *Courtesy Massachusetts Commandery of the Military Order of the Loyal Legion of the United States and the U.S. Army Military History Institute, Carlisle, Pennsylvania.*

thing that Christian civilization could suggest to meet the necessities of those who had suffered in the conflict.

"The province of the Sanitary Commission was to provide more especially for the bodily wants; whilst that of the Christian Commission, besides supplying necessaries for the body, took an earnest interest in the welfare of the souls of the wounded and dying."

SARAH BROADHEAD:

"July 8 – Again at the hospital early this morning. Several physicians and lady nurses had come on from Washington the previous evening, and under their care things already began to look better. The work of extracting the balls, and of amputating shattered limbs, had begun, and an effort at regular cooking. I aided a lady to dress wounds, until soup was made, and then I went to distribute it. I found that I had only seen the lighter cases, and worse horrors met my eyes on descending to the basement of the building. Men, wounded in three and four places, not able to help themselves the least bit, lay almost swimming in water. I hunted up the lady whom I had been helping, and told her to come and see how they were situated. When we came down she reverently exclaimed, 'My God! they must be gotten out of this or they will drown.' I gladly, in answer to her request, consented to assist her. She called some nurses to help, and getting some stretchers the work was begun. There were somewhere near one hundred to be removed to the fourth story of the building. The way they happened to be in such a miserable place was this. On the first day, during the battle, they had been taken into the building for shelter. On Thursday and Friday the Rebels planted a battery just behind this hospital, which annoyed our troops not a little, who, in endeavoring to silence it, could not avoid throwing some shells into the building. Some entered several of the rooms, and injured one of the end walls, and the basement became the only safe place to which the wounded could betake themselves, and the heavy, rains, following the engagement, flooded the floor. I did not think all could be removed to-day, but the lady said it must be done, and by hard work she had it accomplished. We had the satisfaction of seeing them more comfortably fixed, though they lay on the bare floor with only their gum blankets under them, but dry and very thankful for so little. I fed one poor fellow who had had both legs and one arm taken off, and though he is very weak and surely cannot live, he seems in right good spirits. Some weeks since I would have fainted had I seen as much blood as I have to-day, but I am proof now, only caring to relieve suffering. I now begin to feel fatigued, but I hope rest may restore me."

Ten year old SADIE BUSHMAN, who had been pressed into service as a nurse during the battle, insisted on picking up where she left off:

"I was only home a day or two when the United States Christian Sanitary Commission started a hospital at the scene of the battle, and I ran away and worked as a nurse there. At night, when I would come home, I would get a whipping for going, but I would be away and among the sick men next day.

These are some of the more fortunate wounded soldiers counting the days before they are discharged or given permission to re-join the ranks of their units. During the Civil War 15% of the soldiers wounded in battle died from their wounds, compared with less than 1% during the Vietnam War. *Courtesy Massachusetts Commandery of the Military Order of the Loyal Legion of the United States and the U.S. Army Military History Institute, Carlisle, Pennsylvania.*

"I was placed in charge of one of the wards and I was so small I had to climb up on the beds to attend to the sick and wounded men."[5]

Seventeen year old NELLIE AUGHINBAUGH:

"The young ones were assigned to the cooking, etc. We could wash their faces and hands, comb their hair and feed them, sometimes read to them and write letters for them, but our nursing was restricted in many areas. The orderlies did the heavy work.

"The wounded of both armies were cared for together. Of all those I nursed, I only knew of one southerner who was uncivil. Both his arms were off and as a friend of mine was feeding him one day he looked up at her with a sneer and said 'we wouldn't let our ladies do this at home. This is what one of our niggers would do.' Well, Lizzie set down that bowl of soup and with the words: 'Get one of your niggers to do it for you now,' she walked out of the room. I don't know whether he ever found anyone else to feed him that day, or the next, but I heard he was reprimanded for his rudeness. I do know none of us girls ever served him again and that an orderly was assigned to him."

Twelve year old MARY ELIZABETH MONTFORT's diary:

"I met a soldier who is only 16 years old. He kept asking for mush and milk. We don't have any cornmeal to make mush, or I would have made it.

"Another soldier kept asking me for pickles. We didn't have any but I knew that Mrs. Wagner had a whole shelf full in her cellar. She gave me some and I gave them to the soldier who hid one under his pillow so he would have it to eat later on. I left the pickle jar beside his bed."

NELLIE AUGINBAUGH:

"After the battle, both Confederate and Union sympathizers came to town. A lot of the Reb wounded resented taking the oath of allegiance before being permitted the freedom of the hospitals. Some refused and bitterness increased. Others did it.

"I never will forget a young girl from a northern state who came searching for her sweetheart. She made the rounds so often and at so many battlefields without success, she was bone tired when she got to Gettysburg. All the others were a disappointment, but she decided to remain here and help other girls with the nursing since she'd failed everywhere else. Well, she and I became quite good friends. One day the surgeons called on me to assist with an operation. It was a lung wound and they're the worst kind. I was holding a basin of water for the surgeon when everything began to get black before my eyes. Never had such a thing happened before...the surgeon saw the basin wavering and called for the orderly, 'Here, help Miss Auginbaugh out of the room, she's going to faint.' With the help of the man I managed to get to the door without falling and this girl happened to be passing by. I thrust the pan at her as I sank into a chair. 'Go in and help the surgeon. I'm sick and can't.'"

"She went in and the patient turned out to be her sweetheart that she'd been looking for for so long. He lived but a few days longer, but long enough to get to know her. She and I were friends a long time.

"My, but the white went quickly. None of us had any white petticoats as it was all cut up for bandages."

A NURSE'S STORY:

"I attended a young Englishman, a color bearer of a New York regiment. He had come to this country an orphan, and volunteered at the outbreak of the war. He had carried the colors of his regiment through all of the battles fought by the Army of the Potomac and, until now, had escaped injury. All this he told me in broken sentences, and added that there was one on whom all his hopes centered, and much more too sacred to repeat.

"To her, at his request, I wrote a letter, telling of his sad condition and that, although he had lost his leg, he had saved the regimental colors, and his life might be spared. This was surely enough to make any true woman feel proud, particularly as I added, at his demand, that his thoughts were all of her.

"Not long after, as I attended him, I saw lying beside him on his pillow a letter directed in a lady's hand. I felt all would be well. Yes, the letter was delicately directed, delicately written and delicately worded...but its meaning was not to be misunderstood.

He handed me the letter to read, with a look of fixed despair, buried his head in the pillow, and wept. It was a cool, calm regret that she could no longer be his; to which was added the fear that the loss of his leg might affect his prospects in life. The blow had been sudden but sure. When he looked up again, his face bore the pallor of marble, and I saw there was no hope. He died, and his last words were, 'Tell her I forgive her.'

"Such an incident was the exception rather than the rule. For the most part the wives and mothers and sweethearts, north and south, endured suffering and privation with the greatest loyalty."[6]

ALBERTUS McCREARY, Baltimore Street:

"At the extreme end of our lot there was a large barn which was used as a prison for Confederate soldiers; there were 400 in it at one time. The barn and yard around it was full of men. For food, they gave them boxes of hardtack and water from our pump. This was all they had. One poor fellow came up to the house with his head tied up and said he had a bullet wound in the back part of it, and that his head was so sore he could not eat hardtack. My sister made him some broth, and he was allowed to sleep on a bench in the yard by the house. The next day, the men were moved away to some northern prison; but they did not take the graybacks (lice) with them. The barn was so alive with them that no one dared go into it until it had been thoroughly whitewashed inside and out.

"One day shortly after the battle, as we were walking over the field, we came to a squad of soldiers who had opened a trench where some of the dead had been hastily buried. They were taking up the bodies and placing them in coffins to be buried in the National Cemetery. The sight became so horrible that we could not endure it and quickly left the spot.

"A man came to the town with patent coffins, and many a poor fellow took his last journey in one of them. The lid had a box in which ice was placed, thus making it possible to take bodies any distance.

"There were a number of hospitals within a block of us. The Presbyterian Church just across the street, the Catholic church a few doors above, the United Presbyterian church back of our lot, and the German Reformed at the end of High street, were used as hospitals; two schoolhouses, half a block up High street, and the Courthouse, a short distance down Baltimore street, and many private residences nearby were all turned to the same account. We were saved much annoyance by having a red flag put up at our door to show that the house was a hospital.

"All our beds were occupied and we boys slept on the floor and ate at the Sanitary Commission for weeks. We thought hard-tack and bacon fried together a great treat. The provisions we had in the house were soon consumed and had it not been for the Commission, we should have starved to death. Their wagon stopped every morning with supplies of meat and bread and anything they had to distribute. We not only cooked for the patients in the house, but sent quantities of food to those in the church across the street. The pews in the church were covered with boards, and then straw and blankets were spread on them to make beds for the wounded. There were many cases of severe wounds and many deaths in that church. The dead were buried in trenches behind it. One day I was watching them bury the dead in this trench when men with a stretcher brought out a body covered only with a sheet. They drew back the sheet and disclosed the form of a young man perfect in every way, with only a small black hole in his breast."

Coming Home

AMELIA HARMON's home, west of the town, was overrun by the armies in the initial stages of the battle, and then was torched by the Rebels. She returned to it on July 5th: "When we reached the site of our home, a prosperous farm house five days before, there appeared only a blackened ruin and the silence of death."

The irony of Miss Harmon's plight is that her home was built by the Reverend C. G. McLean, an uncle-by-marriage of the famous Confederate General, the late "Stonewall" Jackson.

NATHANIEL LIGHTNER had stayed with the Signal Corps on Power's Hill during the battle to watch his property in the valley below:

"On the third day after the battle I got down to my house. There was not a board or rail of fencing left on the place. Not a chicken, pig, cow or dog to be found. The government mules had eaten up the orchard of four year old trees down to the core. The garden was full of bottles and camp litter. There stood the bare (carpentry) shop, the house full of wounded men, and the old barn, where General Slocum had made his headquarters.

"In front of the barn sat a weary-looking lone officer in blouse coat, drying himself at a fire made of pieces of rails. That officer was Major General Slocum[7] himself. Not an orderly was in sight. He looked dreary enough.

"I found Colonel Bebel in charge of the house and asked him when I could have my house again. He said he had no idea when he could vacate. We came back about a week later and lived, gypsy-like, in the shop for six weeks.

"Six weeks later they took the last of the wounded away, and permitted us to live in it, but it made us all sick. Toward spring, I got a chance to take a stocked farm on shares, so I moved away and gave it to an old Dutchman, who did not seem to mind the smells and filth."

CAPTAIN NOBLE DELANCE PRESTON of the 10th NY Cavalry, found his friend, photographer CHARLES TYSON, among a group of refugees returning to their homes via the Baltimore pike:

"When we reached his (Tyson's) house I dismounted and went in with him. He was agreeably surprised to find things in as good order as they were. The Confederates had made a fire in the center of the parlor carpet, scattered clothing about the house, selected some things with the evident intention of taking them away, but probably left them because of the suddenness of their departure. Remembering that he had secreted a barrel of flour behind the cellar door, Mr. Tyson looked to see if it had been taken, but found it just as he had left it, the door opening so as to conceal it. We made a hurried visit to the photograph gallery,[8] which was found locked, no one having entered it during his absence.

"In the front wall of the building, a 3 inch rifle shell was half buried."[9]

TYSON continues:

"My secretary was ransacked and the contents scattered over the room. In the parlor we found a small heap of ashes, the residue of burned letters and papers, the forms of the envelopes still preserved on the top of the pile. Upon removing the ashes, we found the carpet uninjured and after the carpet was swept, no trace of the fire could be found.

"We found several bundles put up, ready to be carried off, but which were left behind. All my clothing was taken and several Rebel suits left in place. With this exception, we missed very little, indeed, outside of the cellar and pantry, which was pretty well cleaned up. Your recollection of the barrel of flour is correct to a fraction. We entered the house in the rear...the front door being locked just as I left it. Or did I unlock it and enter from the front? Indeed, I would not be sure about that. But the door was locked and the front parlor windows open. We found the gallery undisturbed. The wife of lawyer Wills claimed to have prevented the men from going into the gallery by telling them it was dangerous. They, however, entered the cellar and emptied a barrel of 95 percent alcohol. I had a gross of 8 ounce bottles there also and they were seen carrying these bottles out filled with alcohol.

"A minie ball passed through the back window, which was raised, passing through both panes of glass, putting a round hole through the first pane, without cracking the glass. The next pane the hole was much larger and the glass cracked. The ball then passed through an inch pine partition and lodged on its side on the opposite side of the room, half embedded in another partition. I covered this with a glass case."

THE COLORED MAIDSERVANT. West of town:

"When we got back to Mrs. Hartzell's, we found everything either thrown out of the house or all broken up, and the garden all tramped and mashed down. She had relatives who give her some things so we got fixed up after a while.

"Near us was a brick tavern,[10] and in this here tavern a company of soldiers put up after the battle. We used water from the tavern well, but it got so ugly and smelt so bad we could hardly drink it. The soldiers was sick, and we was sick. They thought there was dead frogs down in the well, and so one day they pumped and pumped to clear it out, and by and by, here comes up a little piece of a wrist and thumb. They'd been cookin' with that water and so had we; and now that they knew what was the matter, there was a lot of gaggin' done among 'em...but what was down they couldn't git up. We didn't use that well no mo' and to this day I couldn't drink a drop out of it just for the thoughts of what was found in it so long ago.

"I knew of another well that was half filled with dead soldiers. That was an easy way to bury 'em."

Among CHURCH CLAIMS presented to the government by F. G. Coldren, Esq. ... an attorney of Washington, DC in a hearing held on August 23, 1907. Wm. H. Lamar of the Justice Department representing the Government.

"St. Mark's Church: Doors were taken off for amputation tables. Pews were taken out and cut up for bunks for the wounded. Stable boards were used to make bunks, leaving a skeleton frame. The Church was full of wounded, the floor was bloody, plaster came down. The building was occupied for five weeks. Cleaning bill: $350.

"St. Francis Xavier: $880.04. Asked rental (all did).

"Trinity Reformed Church: No cost record. Many wounded, benches covered with blood. On the first floor, holes were drilled in the floor to let the blood drain through. Pews covered with boards on which the wounded were placed. Walls were smattered with blood and carpets were used for any purpose.

"St. James Lutheran Church: Wounded occupied the whole church. Everything was appropriated for hospital purposes. No cost record."

Although no financial claim was mentioned, the Chairman of the Faculty of the Lutheran Seminary, S. S. Schmucker, filed a report to the Seminary's Board of Governors on August 11th, 1863, detailing damage done to its buildings and its use as a hospital:

"The injury done to the property of the Institution is considerable. The house I occupy was most damaged. The rebels, having driving the occupants out on the first day of the battle, took possession of it themselves and their batteries being also planted in its immediate vicinity, it was unavoidably shattered by the Federal artillery from Cemetery Hill. Thirteen cannon balls or shells pierced the walls, and made holes several of which were from 2 to 3 feet in length and nearly as broad; window frames were shattered to pieces, sash broken and the greater part of the glass in the house destroyed. The fences around the yard and garden were nearly all leveled with the ground, as well (as) those around the entire Seminary lands. The Seminary edifice was perforated by several balls, and large portions knocked out of the N. East gable corner. There being also a crack in the wall extending over two stories, the question arises, whether that portion of the gable end must not be taken down and rebuilt from the foundation. Dr. Krauth's dwelling also received some injury, though not of a very serious nature.

"The fences around all the fields as well as those along the Seminary Avenue were destroyed, many of the rails and boards incorporated with the breastwork, others broken and others burned.

"Soon after the Seminary was occupied as a hospital, I called on the commanding officer, Colonel Alleman, and received from him the positive assurance that it should be vacated in two weeks. Subsequently, the medical board decided to retain it as a regular hospital; but on my calling on them they assured me that though necessity had led them to retain it for this purpose it should be vacated four weeks before our next session commences. I accordingly sent a notice to our church papers, that the exercises of the Seminary would be resumed at the regular time, Sept. 24.

"Still, as the officers in charge have recently been changed and sundry evidences seem to indicate a desire on the part of the authorities to make themselves at ease in the possession of the eligible and healthy Seminary edifice, I recommend that a communication be addressed to the supreme medical authority at Washington urging the reasons why the interests of the Seminary should not be unnecessarily sacrificed to the convenience of these medical officials."

Apparently, the faculty was getting 'restive.'

Dr. S. S. Schmucker, Chairman of the Faculty, Lutheran Theological Seminary. *Courtesy Special Collections, Gettysburg College.*

When Professor Charles Krauth and his family returned to their home on the campus of the Lutheran Theological Seminary, they found it had been used as a hospital for Confederate wounded. It was in shambles and the furniture and floors stained with blood. Townsfolk say that Mrs. Krauth found her good china scattered all over the front lawn. Miraculously, not a single piece of china was broken. *Courtesy Abdel Ross Wertz Library Archives, Lutheran Theological Seminary, Gettysburg, Pennsylvania.*

As The Dust Settles

A few days after the battle, MARY McALLISTER was revisited by some of the grateful men who had sheltered in her home on Chambersburg Street:

"Someone came in and said there was a man on horseback, wanted to see me. Here was (Judge) David Wills with a man on horseback. He said, 'Miss Mary, don't you know me?'

"I looked at him a little and I said, 'No-o! You do look a little like Colonel Morrow, but the Rebels took him.'

"'Why,' he said, 'God bless you, I am Colonel Morrow, safe and sound, and I called for my diary. I am going on to join the army. They are going on toward Frederick and I want to catch them.'

"I said, 'Tell me how you got away from them.'

"Well, they took him to the college and took away his sword and everything, but he said he found a surgeon's sash and tied it on, and went among the soldiers. He went among the wounded and attended to them. When it came night, he thought he would come to our house, but he got lost and came to the square to the Wills house and they hid him, and after the battle he came to see me.

He said, 'Now you know I had no coat and no sword.'

"'I have a sword here and it belonged to General Archer. You can have that one. It is a pretty sword.'

"That was a bad way to keep a trust.

"'But,' I said, 'you must promise me if ever you meet this man [Dennis B. Dailey, who originally captured Archer and took the General's sword], you must promise to give it to him.'

"'Yes,' he said, 'on the honor of a soldier and a gentleman, I promise to give it to him.' So he buckled on this sword and went away.

(Two days later) "here came another man. I did not know him at all. He was carrying a gun and had an old hat on. Martha looked at him and said, 'Why look here, you were taken prisoner!' It was Dennis Burke Dailey, 2nd Wisconsin. Well, I was scared. The sword flashed on my mind at once.

"He said, 'I have come for the sword.'

"I said, 'I thought you were in Libby Prison and maybe they would come back and take me, and I gave it to Colonel Morrow.'

"Well, he did not seem to blame me, but he looked so disappointed. Then Martha said, 'Come in and we will give you something to eat.'

"He said, 'Yes, I will. I am hungry. I had nothing to eat since that piece of bread you gave me. They took me to the mountain and they all were tired out, and they came around and gave each of the prisoners a little flour, but we had nothing to cook it with, and I took out my piece of bread and ate a little.'

"Well, he said he watched the guard and after a while his gun sank down and the man went to sleep. Dailey said he rolled over once to see how it would work. He said he never heard so many sticks crack in his life. Then he rolled a little more, over rocks and briars. He rolled and rolled until he came to a big log and there scraped up the leaves. He said he would have given anything for water, but he ate a little bread and there, under the leaves, he went to sleep. In the morning, he could hear nothing, but was afraid to move. He laid there all the next day. He knew those troops had gone on, but he first heard firing and then rumbling. That night, he passed further off.

"The second day he came to a stream and there he got water and that was so good. That night, he got into a wheat field and lay there all the next day and was afraid to go out for fear he would be captured, and had nothing to eat but dry bread. He was nearly famished. He said, 'I met a man when I got into the country where I could trust people. This man had been wounded and he said our men had all gone toward Frederick to get ahead of the Rebels at the Potomac River.'

"After I told Dailey I gave the sword to Colonel Morrow, I said, 'What else did you give me?'

"'I gave you my pocketbook,' he said.

"'Now, while you are eating, I will hunt for it,' I said, 'but I know no more about it than you do.'

"I hunted until I was worn out.

"'Now,' he said, 'don't worry. You will find it, maybe, sometime; and I will come back when the war is over.' Martha went out to the kitchen and pulled the dresser away. The pocketbook was there, all mouldy. Then he got ready and, with that old musket, he started off. In a few days, I got a letter from him. He had got General Archer's sword from Colonel Morrow."

While the wounded were attended, an army of fit, uninjured Union soldiers remained stationed at Gettysburg. As usual, that meant trouble for JOHN WILLS:

"The Yanks were so boisterous after the battle that an officer came to the hotel and ordered me to close the bar, lecturing me about selling too much whiskey to the soldiers. I proceeded to tell him that if I didn't sell it, they'd take it...and if he didn't want them to drink to put a guard on the door to help keep them out. From the way he looked at me before he left I knew I'd better make myself scarce the rest of the day, so I stayed away from the hotel until 5 P.M. I saw Father and Neely[11] coming back. They said there'd been a group of Union guards looking for me.

"In the evening, there was more drinking. Things got disorderly, and we were ordered to close up. Still, thinking the orders were coming from the Republican headquarters, Eagle Hotel, I sent out a spy to see if other hotel bars were having problems. No, they were open, so we reopened.[12]

"The next morning, there is much drinking. Officers come in and say we can't sell liquor to anyone but commissioned officers. I went to complain to the Provost who told me, 'Sell no liquor to anyone, but by my order and signature' again. I thought all the soldiers had a provost order and signature and again I was taken to his office, but I brought along the order and signature and he shouted 'That's not my signature', and he gave me an order and his signature to compare all others to, and that put a stop to that trick. I figured, 'what the hell', went back to get my stash from the second floor closet where we'd secreted the fine wines and whiskey that had never been found. I told Lawyer Neely that it was for him and his prominent Union Officers and friends, and since he was my benefactor, I wanted to repay his kindness. Word got out and in they came in squads of six.

"Eventually, they offered me money, saying this is too much for kindness alone. I thanked them, said don't mention this belongs to Mr. Neely and his friends, and you're

Some notes from the press.

After the battle, there was serious criticism of the town, particularly of its men folk. Most vocal was the New York Times' Field Correspondent, L.L. CROUNSE, who wrote in an editorial:

"Let me make it a matter of undeniable history that the conduct of the majority of the male citizens of Gettysburg, and the surrounding county of Adams, is such as to stamp them with dishonor and craven-hearted meanness. I do not speak hastily, I but write the unanimous sentiments of the whole army – an army which now feels that the doors from which they drove a host of robbers, thieves and cutthroats were not worthy of being defended. The actions of the people of Gettysburgh (sic) are so sordidly mean and unpatriotic, as to engender the belief that they're indifferent as to which party was whipped..."

Crounse charged male residents of Gettysburg with running away at the time of the battle, leaving their women and children to the mercy of the enemy. Furthermore, when they returned, he wrote:

"Instead of lending a helping hand to our wounded, and opening their houses to our famished officers and soldiers, they have only manifested indecent haste to present their bills to the military authorities for payment of losses inflicted by both armies.

"When the Army of the Potomac votes the citizen's gallant, generous and patriotic," Crounse concluded, "then I shall believe it. Not before."

Subsequently, he was trounced, point for point, in an editorial in the Gettysburg Sentinel on July 21st. When Crounse returned on July 4, 1865, to cover ceremonies marking the battle, there was some talk of running him out of town. The city council passed a resolution of admonishment instead.

In reporting the ceremonies, Crounse wrote that he "came near receiving considerable attention at the hands of the citizens." He said, however, that he was able to learn that the people who had treated the soldiers well, and at great risk to themselves, during the battle were in the majority and that their actions far outweighed "the disreputable conduct heretofore complained of..."

You can picture his mischievous grin when you read his words.

But Crounse was not alone in such criticisms, which were based in large part on the complaints of Union officers.

On July 14th, 1863, the Baltimore Daily Gazette wrote:

"There are some of the most intensely mean persons in this neighborhood that the world produces.

"On Thursday, a bill of $1700 was presented to General Howard for damage to the cemetery during the fight.

"One man presented General Howard a bill for 37¢ for bricks knocked off the chimney of his house by our artillery.

"Our wearied, and in many instances, wounded, soldiers found pumps locked so that they could not get water."

Reporters occasionally wrote private letters to their editors as background for editorials...revealing more than they did in some of their official dispatches.

Since much of the fighting took place over miles of farm fields or in woods, the reporter usually could see only the smallest segment of action, relying on eyewitness descriptions, instead. Often, it was not easy to reconcile the differences among the various accounts.

According to one writer, his sources were: "Weak kneed, watery-eyed young quartermaster clerks, sick or disabled soldiers, returned prisoners, Union officers, intelligence contrabands (slaves), deserters and reliable gentlemen."

Philadelphia Inquirer reporters wrote that there were: "Three general categories of army news...1, based on orders made known at HQ...2, chin news: somebody told him something he got from somebody who knew the person who heard from a reliable sources...3, cook house news: consisted of such impossible exaggeration that no one but a cook would have been capable of spreading it."

As they returned to print, the local newspapers waded into the biggest and longest running story they would ever report.

STAR-BANNER, July 9, 1863:

"In consequence of the terrible excitement to which we were subjected last week, we were compelled to suspend the publication of our paper. Just as we were ready to go to press on Wednesday, the most terrific battle of the war commenced, and in a few hours after the Rebels had possession of Gettysburg, and held it until Saturday morning. During that time they had possession of our office and freely used our type and press to print their army blands. In order that our subscribers may not be the losers by this unfortunate occurrence, we this week issue what we call a double sheet."

UNIDENTIFIED PUBLICATION (Adams County Sentinel?):

"July 20, 1863: We learn that on Thursday night last, a number of Rebels who were connected with the hospitals in this place, managed to get hold of Federal uniforms, arms and horses and, in this disguise, made their escape toward Dixie. Whether they succeeded in reaching their destination or not is a matter of considerable doubt. We hope they may be 'gobbled up'.

P.S. We understand they have been caught."

STAR BANNER:

"July 29: One day last week, among the relics of the dreadful fight, there was picked up by a soldier and presented to a lady or our acquaintance a small paper which contained two separate locks of hair attached thereto, directed to Mr. Wellerford from Louisiana by his wife in a beautiful handwriting. Below one lock was Fanny Wellerford. Below the other, Richard Wellerford. And below both, 'Our Darlings'. These tender mementos of his home and children had been sent on to him by his attached wife to cheer his heart in the far distant land to which the fortunes of war had brought him; and probably he wore the tender testimonials near his heart when the fatal missile of death separated him from those he loved in his far-off southern home. Strangers now possess the tender relic and he rests beneath the clods of a northern valley, his grave probably unmarked and undistinguished from hundreds around him who met with death on the bloody fields of Gettysburg. And his wife and children look in vain for the return of their beloved husband and father."

And, there is also this story:

Sam Wilkeson, of the New York Times, was one of the few reporters who did not hurry off to the railroad telegraph to file stories after the battle. He stayed to find his son.

When Wilkeson arrived in Gettysburg three days earlier, he knew that his eldest boy, 19 year old Lieutenant Bayard Wilkeson, was there as commander of Battery G, US Artillery. He learned on the night of July 1st that the battery had been advanced to a little knoll north of town, east of the Carlisle Road, and that early in the first encounter with the enemy the youth had been wounded in the leg.

It wasn't until the battle ended that Wilkeson learned what happened.

His son's leg had been badly crushed, and he amputated it himself on the spot, while continuing to direct his battery. Then he was taken to the Almshouse on the eastern edge of town for hospitalization. However, the surgeons left when the Rebels overran the town and the boy died on July 2nd because the Rebel doctors had no time to tend him.

One report says Sam Wilkeson wrote his 6th of July account of the battle while sitting beside the body of his dead son.

welcome to all I have. This apparently made enough friends among the officers' corps that we noticed a somewhat lower level of harassment over the next few days and weeks.

Besides the harassment, apparently instigated by their Republican enemies, complaints were filed with the Provost Marshal against the Wills, charging them with "harboring Confederates" during the Rebel occupation.

"We knew we were censured for entertaining Confederates; why! it was our business and we entertained them the same as we did the Union soldiers before and after the battle or any other people who had the money to pay for it and they paid us in U. S. Government greenbacks and gold and they had plenty of it.

"Now there were four hotels other than the Globe Hotel in town and they could have entertained the Confederates as well if they had wanted to, so the only reason I could assign for their not doing so was because they hated them, as those hotels were conducted by Republicans."

Coping

SARAH BROADHEAD. Chambersburg Street:
"(Thursday) July 9 – Rain began to fall early this morning, and so violently that it produced quite a flood, which prevented me from getting to the hospital. I visited, with what supplies I had, some of those in town. I found the wounded in them much better situated, some attention having been paid to them, by the citizens near, during the battle. All had plenty to eat, though very few had beds to lie on and rest their wounded bodies. Nearly every house is a hospital, besides the churches and warehouses, and there are many field hospitals scattered over the country near the scene of the battle. A man called to-day, and requested me to take into our house three wounded men from one of the field hospitals. I agreed to take them, for I can attend to them and not be compelled to leave my family so long every day as I have done. I am quite anxious to hear the condition of that man at the Seminary whose wife I sent for. I was thinking of her when the cars, for the first time since the destruction of the Rock Creek bridge, came into town, the road having been repaired. The Government can now forward supplies in abundance, and the poor fellows can be better provided for in every way. I talked with some wounded Rebels at one of the hospitals, and they are very saucy and brag largely. They are very kindly treated, and supplied, in all respects, as our men are. The spirit manifested by those I met was so vindictive that I believe they would, if they could, requite all the kindness shown them by murdering our citizens. The merciful work of the Sanitary and Christian Commissions, aided by private contributions, was to be seen at every hospital. Without the relief they furnished, thousands must have perished miserably, and thousands more have suffered from want of the delicacies, food and clothing their agents distributed, before the Government even could bring assistance. They are God's blessed agencies for providing for the needy soldier. No one knows the good she has done, in making bandages and clothing, and in contributing dainties and provisions, until she sees the operations of these agencies in distributing her gifts to the wounded and sick soldiers. Whoever aids them is engaged in the noblest work on earth, and will be amply rewarded even here, to make no mention of hereafter."

MARY CUNNINGHAM BIGHAM. Father's farm on Emmitsburg Road south of Seminary Ridge:
"Cassie baked all the bread that the brick oven could hold for six weeks every day. Every wounded man who could walk found his way to the house when the odor of baking bread floated from the oven. They stood in lines and took the hot loaves as soon as Cassie drew them out. There was plenty of government hard tack, but this ration was unobtrusively conveyed to the pigs. All of Father's 25 barrels of flour in the barn were used. As Cassie would bake one barrel, a hospital attendant rolled out another. The remnant of the crop of '63 was cut with a reaping machine and every Confederate who could crawl to the barn doors was there to watch. Most had never seen one before.

SARAH BROADHEAD:

(Friday) "July 10 – This morning I again visited the Seminary, and was rejoiced to see the improvement that had been made in the arrangements of the patients. Nearly all have been provided with beds and clean clothing, and a more comfortable look pervades the whole building. I miss many faces that I had learned to know, and among them the man whose wife I had written to. A lady stayed with him until he died, and cut off a lock of his hair, which she gave me for his wife. At 5 o'clock our men were brought to our home and I prepared them as nice a supper as I could, and they appeared quite cheerful, notwithstanding their dirty persons, having been lying in a field hospital three miles from town, without a change of clothing since before the battle, and with very imperfect attendance."

As the need grew, more and more private homes received soldiers in need of convalescent care. SARAH BROADHEAD's home on Chambersburg Street was among them:

(Saturday) "July 11 – This day has been spent in caring for *our* men. We procured clean clothes from the Sanitary Commission, and having fixed them up, they both look and feel better, though their wounds are very painful. Our town, too, begins to look more settled, and more like its former self. The atmosphere is loaded with the horrid smell of decaying horses and the remains of slaughtered animals, and, it is said, from the bodies of men imperfectly buried. I fear we shall be visited with pestilence, for every breath we draw is made ugly by the stench. The proper officers are sending off the wounded Rebels, left in our hands with only a few surgeons by their inhuman commanders, as fast as their condition will admit of the journey. All day ambulances filled with them have been padding our door on their way to the depot. Though they are our enemies and saucy, I pity them."

TILLIE PIERCE, Baltimore Street:

"The friends and relatives who came to minister to the wounded were, on account of the crowded condition of the hotels, compelled to ask accommodations from private citizens. In this manner, quite a number were taken into our home. Most of their time was spent at the hospital, some coming back to us in the evening and leaving as soon as possible the next morning.

"I was frequently invited to accompany these visitors, and in this way often found myself by the bedside of the wounded.

"One lady who was stopping at our house (was) a Mrs. Greenly. Her son lay suffering at the hospital and in company we frequently visited him.

"One day when he was very low it was concluded that by amputating his limb his life might be spared. After the operation had been performed, her son sank rapidly. At last came the words: 'Mother! Dear Mother! Good bye! Good..! Mother!' And all was over. Her darling boy lay before her in the embrace of death; but a mother's tender love had traced a peaceful smile upon his countenance."

SARAH BROADHEAD:

(Sunday) "July 12 – To-day the lady I sent for came to see her husband. I never pitied anyone as I did her when I told her he was dead. I hope I may never again be called upon to witness such a heartrending scene. The only comfort she had was in recovering the body, and in tears she conveyed it to the resting-place of her family. I had some satisfaction from the fact that I had marked the grave, without which she might not have recovered it. Many persons have called to-day wanting lodging, but we cannot accommodate all. The town would not hold all who, from various motives, visit the battlefield, even if there were no wounded in it. Our house has been constantly full, and every house I know of has been, and is, full. One who called told me that he had sat on a chair in front of a hotel last night, and was glad to get even such quarters. This is Sunday, but since the battle we have had no Sunday. The churches have all been converted into hospitals, and the cars come and go as on other days, and the usual bustle and confusion reigns in the streets, and there is nothing but the almanac to remind us of the day of rest. One of my patients grows worse and worse, and is gradually sinking to his long home. There has been some difficulty in securing proper medical attendance, the surgeons not liking to quit their hospitals and run from house to house, and our own physicians are overwhelmed with business."

MARY McALLISTER, Chambersburg Street:

"One morning when we went out just at daylight, there was a woman leaning against one of the trees. She was weeping. I said, 'What is the matter?'

"'Oh,' she said, 'I got a dispatch my husband was dying and I came here last night, in the night time, and every place was shut up and I could not get in, everything was so full, and they know nothing about my husband.' She thought if she could just get him home, she could cure him.

"'Oh,' I said, 'come to the house and we will give you some breakfast and we will help you try to find out something.'

"Some soldiers that saw me talking to her said, 'He died soon after the dispatch was sent and he is buried and it will be almost impossible to find him.' The Governor had given free transportation to all Pennsylvanians to take their dead away. She said she had spent all her money coming. Well, she sobbed and cried.

"They, the soldiers, said they had dug a trench and laid them in rows in the old grave yard. Finally they told her they had found her husband and then the employees around the depot paid her way back."

SARAH BROADHEAD:

(Monday) "July 13 – This day has passed much as yesterday and the day before. The town is as full as ever of strangers, and the old story of the inability of a village of twenty-five hundred inhabitants, overrun and eaten out by two large armies, to accommodate from ten to twelve thousand visitors, is repeated almost hourly.[13] Twenty are with us to-night, filling every bed and covering the floors. To add to my trouble and anxiety, the nurse has just informed me that our sickest man will die soon. It is sad; and even we, who have known him so short a time, will miss him. What our soldiers are in the army, I cannot say, but when they are wounded, they all seem perfect gentlemen, so gentle, patient, and kind, and so thankful for any kindness shown them. I have seen many of our brave sufferers, and I have yet to meet the first who showed ill breeding. This, too, is the opinion of all whom I know, who have taken care of any, and the invitation and remark is common, 'Come and see our men; they are the nicest men in the army;' and the reply generally follows, 'They cannot be better than ours.'"

MARY CUNNINGHAM BIGHAM, Father's farm on Emmitsburg Road:

"One day the surgeon in charge came to the house and told Mother that a Union soldier lying in a tent in the orchard would die if his leg was not cut off, but he would not consent to the operation. So Mother went to see him and petted and coaxed, and finally promised that if he would submit to the amputation she would have him brought to the house and nurse him herself.

"So Frank Clarke submitted to the knife and Mother kept her promise. It was not a light promise to give, for long before Frank's wound had healed, Father and Mother had followed two little coffins to the old Marsh Creek burying ground. Lizzie had succumbed to a heart ailment and Willie, a boy of 5, had contracted blood poisoning from being about the wounded men.

"Frank Clarke got well, or at least well enough to be moved...against his vehement protest...to the general hospital near town. So when the surgeon's back was turned, he hobbled away on his crutches and hitchhiked back to the farm.

"He finally recovered and went back to his widowed mother in Michigan, but he was mindful of his amputated leg and asked Father, when the bodies of the dead were to be moved to the National Cemetery later, to try to find it. When the graves were opened, Father searched, but could find no extra leg.

"Until after the surrender, no letters could be gotten through the Confederate lines, but Father notified the families of all the Union wounded who were brought to his place. Among many others, the sister of one badly wounded man, Ellen Howard of Merriden, NH, started at once for Gettysburg. And on the train a stranger engaged her in conversation, asking if, should she find her brother dead, she had money enough to bring the body home. She said she had not, and he opened his purse and handed her 40 dollars. The brother had died before her arrival."

SARAH BROADHEAD, Chambersburg Street:

(Tuesday) "July 14 – It is now one month since I began this Journal, and little did I think when I sat down to while away the time, that I would have to record such terrible scenes as I have done. Had any one suggested any such sights as within the bound of possibility, I would have thought it madness. No small disturbance was occasioned by the removal of our wounded to the hospital. We had but short notice of the intention, and though we pleaded hard to have them remain, it was of no use. So many have been removed by death and recovery, that there was room; and the surgeon having general care over all, ordered the patients from private houses to the General Hospital. A weight of care, which we took upon us for duty's sake, and which we had learned to like and would have gladly borne, until relieved by the complete recovery of our men, has been lifted off of our shoulders, and again we have our house to ourselves."

Politics

Some incidents still rankle partisans. In the immediate aftermath, officers and enlisted men were taken anywhere space could be found. The town itself became an overflowing hospital, and some claim that not all patients were treated equally. CHARLES McCURDY, Chambersburg Street:

"One evening a few days after the battle an ambulance, in charge of two Union soldiers, stopped in front of our house. Father was on the porch and he learned from the men that it contained a wounded Confederate officer who had been ordered sent to Fortress Monroe. The evening trains for Baltimore had gone and the men were unwilling to return with their charge to the farm house from which he had been removed. To relieve their embarrassment, Father offered to care for the prisoner during the night, and he was carried on his cot into the parlor and made as comfortable as possible. The men promised to return the next morning and send him on his way.

"The day passed and as they did not return he was taken upstairs to a properly furnished bedroom.

"The prisoner proved to be Major General (Isaac R.) Trimble, a distinguished engineer officer of Lee's army, who had lost a leg during the engagement. The room adjoining the one in which he was placed was occupied by a young officer of our own army whose arm was badly shattered. The poor fellow would not permit the surgeon to amputate and afterwards died from the effects of his wound.

"General Trimble proved to be a delightful and appreciative guest. He was an elderly man, fond of children and my little sisters were frequent visitors to his room and helped to relieve the tedium of his confinement.

"One day General Trimble had a distinguished visitor in the person of Senator Cameron, who had been Secretary of War in Mr. Lincoln's Cabinet[14] and who was an old acquaintance. But in spite of my father's protests he would not receive him and Father had to inform Mr. Cameron that the General was indisposed. Probably, wounded and a prisoner, he felt that an interview with a prominent enemy, even if the call was made with the kindliest interest, would not be pleasant.

"My mother ministered to both the wounded men with the best she could offer but certain citizens were displeased at the idea of a Rebel receiving such care and complained to the authorities. After a stay of two weeks, their efforts to have him removed were successful, and against the repeated protests of the indignant General, he was removed to the General Hospital in the Theological Seminary."[15]

JENNIE McCREARY was a neighbor of the McCurdy's. She says that when Trimble was moved out of the McCurdy house, there was a commotion. According to Jennie, the conversation went like this:

"A surgeon came to the house and (told) the General: 'My orders are to take you.'

Resting as a prisoner and a patient at the home of Robert McCurdy, General Isaac Trimble had plenty of time to reflect on the last three days. Trimble, CSA, had been so outraged on the evening of July 1st when General Ewell failed to take Culp's Hill before the Union occupied it that he is reported to tossed his sword and swore to serve no further under such a general. General Lee ignored him. On July 2nd Trimble was ordered to replace the mortally wounded Major General William Pender. On the afternoon of the 3rd, while leading his division in Pickett's Charge, a wound cost Trimble a leg. Of the fifty or so Confederate generals who accompanied Lee into Pennsylvania nine others had been wounded, and six: Armistead, Barksdale, Garnett, Pender, Semmes, and Pettigrew, had been killed. *Courtesy Massachusetts Commandery of the Military Order of the Loyal Legion of the United States and the US Army Military History Institute, Carlisle, PA*

Brigadier General James Kemper, 40, was a former Virginia legislator, who had been serving under General Lee since the war began. He was leading the advance of his troops in Pickett's Charge when a bullet knocked him from his horse. The wound was near his spine and he was partially paralyzed. Kemper was among several Southern Generals, including Trimble, who had been moved by rail to Baltimore.

     The Star-Sentinel, August 25, 1863, noted: "General Kemper was very indignant at being removed from comfortable quarters. Well attended by female sympathizers he growled at everything on his way to Baltimore." *Courtesy Massachusetts Commandery of the Military Order of the Loyal Legion of the United States and the U.S. Army Military History Institute, Carlisle, Pennsylvania.*

"The General replied, 'It'll be certain death if I go there.'

"'I have my orders, Sir.'

"'Well,' said the General, 'give me a week to stay yet.'

"'I'm ordered to take you now, Sir.'

"'Give me four days.'

"'Sir, you've been in the army long enough to know that orders must be obeyed.'

"'Tomorrow? I'll obey tomorrow.'

"'General, the ambulance is at the door and you must go now.'

"'Well, is General Paul to be moved?'[16]

"'He is comfortable where he is, Sir.'"

Biased or not, Trimble moved. Paul didn't.

Later, General Trimble went even farther:

STAR-SENTINEL, August 25th, 1863:

"On Friday, August 22nd, several wounded Rebel officers were removed from the Seminary hospital by rail to Baltimore. Amongst them, Major General Trimble, Brigadier General Kemper, Captain Leaphart, and Lts. Shurler and Grogan.

General Kemper[17] was very indignant at being removed from comfortable quarters, 'well-attended by female sympathizers', and growled at everything on his way to Baltimore."

THE STAHLE CONTRETEMPS is illustrative of the political divisions in Gettysburg: During the first day of the battle, a wounded Colonel W. W. Dudley, of the 19th Indiana Volunteers was brought to the house of Henry J. Stahle, editor of the Gettysburg Compiler, the town's Democratic newspaper. Dudley was delivered on a stretcher by several of his men. He had a severe leg wound and was in need of a surgeon. Stahle decided to risk going out on the street, which was then being combed by Rebels in search of Union troops. He met and talked with a Rebel officer, explaining his needs, and was sent to a nearby hospital, where he found a Doctor. The Doctor told Stahle to use cold water treatment and to have a barber shave hair from around the wound. The newspaperman went to a barber past the neighboring Buehler home and returned alone, were he was arrested and charged with consorting with the enemy.

Stahle later claimed that his actions were deliberately misconstrued by political enemies.

Colonel Dudley later issued a statement saying he was in the Stahle house for three days and nights and never heard words or saw acts which led him to suspect disloyalty.

Later, Stahle's COMPILER reported the story:

"July 20: The Stahle arrest was made at the instigation of a citizen soldier who delivered an affidavit from a wounded soldier in the David Buehler home. He's accused of, at the heat of battle, coming outside and saying to a Reb officer that 95 Yanks are hiding in a house.

"Stahle had a wounded Union Colonel and his two attendants in his house at the time. Would he have deliberately gone out and told on others if he was caring for them? Stahle is now suffering banishment from his home, his family and friends simply for his political opinions...he is a Democrat. We can assure our readers that he will continue to suffer anything that it may be in the power of his enemies, the enemies of liberty, to put upon him...rather than yield one principle of his faith."

Henry J. Stahle, 40, had come to Gettysburg from York where he worked for the Gazette. He bought the Gettysburg Compiler in 1844, married Louisa Doll from Frederick City, Maryland, two years later, and they had their first child, Thomas, in 1847. Five other children followed.

     Stahle was a Democrat and so his editorials frequently rubbed the old Republican guard the wrong way. Compiler circulation was estimated at between 1,000 and 1,300. From 1858 to 1862 "Adams Countians" vacillated between Republican and Democrat majorities in their voting patterns. However, in 1862 there was a strong surge of strength by the Democrats. It was enough to put Democrats in control of the town council and make Republican Congressman Edward McPherson a lame duck. *Courtesy Adams County Historical Society.*

The paper subsequently reported that copies of the charges were given to General Patrick, the Provost General, on the morning of Stahle's arrest, but that Patrick had not looked them over when he faced Stahle. Patrick said the charges seemed trivial, but that he would investigate and release Stahle the next morning if they were political, as he suspected.

Referring to copies of the charges, Stahle identified the "citizen soldier" in the Buehler home as David McConaughy, an attorney who was considered one of the town's radical Republicans. Before the June invasion, McConaughy offered to work for the government and was assigned to intelligence services. Apparently, he had considered Stahle's movements to be part of his job.

Opportunity Knocks, But Never Without a Price

With their town swollen to a size no one ever dreamed of, business opportunities presented themselves everywhere, particularly to ambitious boys like ALBERTUS McCREARY:

"At the time of the war, lead was very scarce and we could get 13 cents a pound for it, so all the boys hunted lead bullets. We would go along Culp's Hill, poke among the leaves, and sometimes find what we called pockets...a lot of bullets in a pile...8 or 10 pounds; as it took only 8 of a certain kind to make a pound, I gathered many pounds myself in this way. The large shells were full of bullets and we found many of them that had not exploded; we would unscrew the cap-end and, if we were careful, fill the shell with water before we undertook to extract the bullets.

"Sometimes boys became careless. A schoolmate of mine, with others of us, had been hunting bullets on Cemetery Hill. He found a shell and, the contents not coming out fast enough for him, he struck it upon a rock upon which he was sitting and made a spark that exploded the shell. We carried him to his home and the surgeons did what they could for him, but he never regained consciousness and died in about an hour. With all my familiarity with horrors, I nearly fainted when I saw the surgeons probing his wound.

"Almost every boy had a can of powder hidden in the house or barn, with rifles or carbines to shoot it off in. We would go to Brick-Yard Lane, a favorite resort of the boys, load the rifles good and strong, leaving the ramrod in, and then shoot into the air. We never knew where the ramrods went. Another trick was to go to the woods, place five or six large Wentworth shells among dry leaves and sticks, set fire to the pile, and run off

David McConaughy, 40, was a member of one of the county's most prominent families. In 1860 he had been a member of the National Convention which nominated Abraham Lincoln for President. A lawyer, and what some called a "radical" Republican, McConaughy had differences with David Wills, another Gettysburg attorney, who led the more moderate faction of the party. McConnaughy also had a long-going feud with Compiler editor Henry J. Stahle.

McConaughy was instrumental in the formation of the Adams Rifles, a local militia in which he served as a Captain. When the Confederates invaded Pennsylvania, McConnaughy offered his services to the Federal Government and was immediately assigned to the secret service. It is believed that McConnaughy remained in the vicinity during the battle, but tried to keep out of sight, avoid capture, and provide intelligence. *Courtesy Adams County Historical Society.*

Charles H. Buehler, 38, Captain of the Gettysburg Independent Blues, 165th PA Volunteers, was David's brother and a local merchant. *Courtesy Adams County Historical Society.*

to a safe distance and wait for the explosion. It made a racket that put the Fourth of July in the shade.

"The only other accident that I witnessed happened a year after the battle. I was passing along High street, and had reached Power's stoneyard, when I heard a terrible explosion behind me. I turned back to see what had happened. There, I saw a young schoolmate lying on his back with his bowels blown away. He looked at me for a second, then closed his eyes in death. Near him was a man almost torn to pieces, his hands hanging in shreds. He was promptly cared for and, although badly wounded, losing both his hands and one leg, he lived. He was a stranger in the place and was there to visit the battlefield. He was trying to empty a shell he had found on the field. A lady in a house opposite had seen the boy come out of the stoneyard and say to the man that hitting the shell on a stone was a very dangerous thing to do. Just as he spoke, down came the shell on the stone and exploded.

"Visitors soon began to come to see the battlefield, and all wanted relics. We were always on the lookout for bullets and pieces of shell...in fact, anything that could be easily handled, to sell to them. We found that a piece of tree with a bullet embedded in it was a great prize and a good seller. Every boy went out with a hatchet to chop pieces from the trees in which bullets had lodged. I found several trees with bullets in them that had met in mid-air and stuck together. These were considered a great find. Lamps were made of round shells. The caps were taken out, a tube for a wick was placed in them, and the shell was fastened to a square block of wood, thus making a very useful and convenient relic. The guidebooks that soon came out were another source of revenue to the boys, and continue so."

NATHANIEL LIGHTNER, out the Baltimore Pike:
"A man came along from New York a few days after the battle and told the children he would buy any relics they could pick up. They got together some bullets, buckles, canteens, and the like and when he came back, I dickered with him for them and sold him

Robert Goodloe Harper's father founded the first Adams County newspaper the "Centinel." Harper's newspaper, which received support from the Buehler's and McConnaughy, reflected Republican views. The paper contended that unreasonable secessionists were completely to blame for the outbreak of violence. Harper supported Lincoln, and affirmed that the maintenance of the Union was more crucial than the outcome of the slavery question. Harper's whereabouts during the battle of Gettysburg are not known. Understandably, many townsfolk with outspoken views on the war either fled town or remained in hiding until Lee's army had left the vicinity. *Courtesy Adams County Historical Society.*

This photograph of a couple seeing the sights at Spangler's Spring was taken within days of the battle. Almost as soon as the outside world learned of the Battle of Gettysburg it seemed that many began making their plans to visit the battlefield and this spring that had provided water to both sides.

Families desperately seeking to know whether a loved one was alive or dead competed for space with the curious and the cons. At times, the town took on the atmosphere of a macarbe carnival. *Courtesy Massachusetts Commandery of the Military Order of the Loyal Legion of the United States and the U.S. Army Military History Institute, Carlisle, Pennsylvania.*

two or three dollars' worth of things. Soon after, a Colonel Blood, the meanest man in the world, came down to gather up government property, and he had me arrested. I told him how it was, that we had no idea of doing anything unlawful; but he was determined to make me all the trouble he could. He put me to considerable expense, but my neighbors got me off after a few days.

"That arrest is the only thing of it all that made me mad, and I am mad about it yet."

But good businessmen always find the right opportunity. DANIEL SKELLY found his on July 5th:

"On this morning, my friend, Gus Bentley, met me on the street and told me that down at the Hollinger warehouse where he was employed they had a lot of tobacco. 'We hid it away before the Rebs came into town,' he continued, 'and they did not find it. We can buy it and take it out and sell it to the soldiers.' (They were still in their lines of battle).

"We had little spending money but we concluded we would try and raise the cash in some way. I went to my mother and consulted her about it and she loaned me ten dollars. Gus also got ten, all of which we invested in the tobacco. It was in large plugs – Congress tobacco, a well known brand of that time.

"With an old-fashioned tobacco cutter, we cut it up into ten cent pieces and each of us took a basket full and started out Baltimore street to the cemetery, the nearest line of battle. Reaching the Citizen's Cemetery, we found as battery of artillery posted there (brass guns), two of the guns across the road, one on the pavement, and the other in the middle of Baltimore pike. The soldiers stopped us and would not let us pass, their orders being not to let anyone out of the town.

"We went back into the town as far as the Presbyterian church and went up High street to the jail, where we turned into a path leading down to the old Rock Creek 'swimmin' hole'. On the first ridge we saw the first dead Confederate soldiers lying right on the path (two of them side by side) and they were buried there afterward until the Confederate bodies were taken up years later and shipped to Richmond for burial.

"We kept to the path down to the spring then turned over towards Culp's Hill, ascending it at one of its steepest points. There were all kinds of debris of the battle scattered over the hill, but no dead or wounded soldiers, they having already been removed.

"The breastworks were formidable-looking, about three feet or more high, built of trees that had been cut down by the soldiers for the purpose of throwing up these fortifications. A shallow trench was dug in front of the works and the ground thrown up on it.

"The soldiers helped us over the breastworks with our baskets and in a short time they were empty and our pockets filled with ten cent pieces. The soldiers told us to go home and get some more tobacco, that they would buy all we could bring out. We made a number of trips, selling out each time, and after disposing of all of our supply, and paying back our borrowed capital, we each had more money than we ever had before in our lives."

On the far side of the field, MARY CUNNINGHAM BIGHAM:

"After the battle, a group of the retreating Confederates stopped in a strip of woods a little way beyond Grandmother Scott's to prepare breakfast. They had killed a sheep and had preparations well under way when the pursuing Federals began dropping shells uncomfortably near; so it appeared wiser to the pursued to go, and go breakfastless. Two farmers of the vicinity, learning of the uneaten food, went out to take cognizance. They found much more than they could carry away...among other things, a bag of salt. Salt had grown scarce and both men wanted it. They concluded to go home and come back with their wagons. In the meanwhile, a woman of the neighborhood whose husband was in the army learned of the bag of salt and sent a boy with a wheelbarrow to get it.

"The two farmers came back with their teams and each noted that the salt was missing. Each man thought his neighbor had double-crossed him and, for years these two men eyed each other with suspicion and dislike."

Pride

J. F. CROCKER, Portsmouth, Virginia, was a Lieutenant of the 9th Va. Infantry, C.S.A. ... and a graduate of Pennsylvania College (Gettysburg), 1850. He was wounded during Pickett's Charge and was taken to the 12th Corps hospital at the rear of the left end of the Union line.

Professor Martin Luther Stoever of Pennsylvania College paid a visit to the hospital and accidentally ran into his former student. Professor Stoever and Lieutenant Crocker reminisced about college days.

Soon after Stoever's visit, the Sisters of Charity came in to tend to the troops. One sister quietly took Crocker aside and slipped a packet of money to him "from a friend." Dirty, shabby and in need of a bath, Crocker saw the money as the route to a new suit of clothes. Here, he takes up the narrative:

"Colonel Dwight honored my request to leave the hospital and go into town to buy a suit. Amazingly, without escort. They provided me a free pass. I went alone, unattended. They conferred on me a great honor – the honor of personal confidence, absolute confidence.

Lt. James Frances Crocker was born in 1828 in Isle of Wight County, Virginia. He graduated Pennsylvania College in 1850. He was a classmate of Robert Goodloe Harper, Jr. Crocker returned to Virginia where he taught private school and studied law. He was admitted to the Virginia Bar in 1854, was elected to the General Assembly, and served on the Portsmouth, Virginia, City Council. *Courtesy The Confederate Veteran Magazine.*

Colonel William Colvill's 1ˢᵗ MN Regiment, which suffered 80% casualties in turning back Wilcox near the Wheat Field on July 2ⁿᵈ and defending against Pickett's charge on July 3ʳᵈ was among those soldiers brought to the James Pierce home. James daughter Tillie returned from the Weikert farm only to find her own house being used as a hospital:

TILLIE PIERCE: "A few days after the battle, several soldiers came to our house and asked mother if she would allow them to bring their wounded Colonel to the place, provided they would send two nurses along to help wait on him, saying they would like to have him kept at a private house. As we had a very suitable room she consented.

"The wounded officer was carried to the house on a litter, and was suffering greatly. After they got him up stairs, and were about placing him on the bed, it was found to be too short, so that the foot-board had to be taken off and an extension added. The Colonel was a very tall man and of fine proportions. He had been severely wounded in the right ankle and shoulder, the latter wound extending to his spine. The surgeons wanted to amputate his foot, saying it was necessary in order to save his life; but the Colonel objected, and said that if his foot must go he would go too.

"Mother waited on him constantly, and the nurses could not have been more devoted. He was highly esteemed by all his men, many of whom visited him at the house, and even wept over him in his suffering and helplessness. They always spoke of him as one of the bravest men in the army. Before long his sister came, who with tender care and cheering words no doubt hastened his recovery.

Several months elapsed before he was able to be removed; when, on a pair of crutches, he left for his home in St. Paul. As he was leaving the house he could hardly express fully his thanks and appreciation for all our kindness; and on parting kissed us all, as though he were bidding farewell to his own kith and kin. We, on our part, felt as though one of our own family were leaving. He promised that whenever able he would come back to see us.[1] *Courtesy Massachusetts Commandery of the Military Order of the Loyal Legion of the United States and the US Army Military History Institute, Carlisle, PA*

Just have the pass signed by the Provost office before returning, said the Colonel. They somehow knew my honor was more to me than my life.

"On the way to town, I called at the 11th Corps hospital where I understood General Armistead had been taken. I found that he had died. They showed me his freshly made grave, and I was told his leg wound shouldn't have been fatal, but his proud spirit chafed under his imprisonment and his restlessness aggravated the wounds.

"In Gettysburg, I had the pass countersigned and now had absolute freedom of the city. It must have been a queer, incongruous sight, seeing a Rebel Lieutenant in gray mingling in the crowd apparently at home, shaking hands with many old friends.

"I finally made it to the tailor's and left measurements for that suit. This experience in Gettysburg taught me that the hates and prejudices engendered by the war were national, not individual, that individual relations and feelings were but little affected in reality and that personal contact was sufficient to restore kindliness and friendship.

"I remember those in Gettysburg like Colonel Dwight, Professor Stoever, Professor Jacobs, the College President, all my other old friends, including the women of the town, like Mrs. Broadhead, who showed their kindness."

CHARLES McCURDY, Chambersburg Street:

"One of Father's Baltimore friends whose sympathies were with the South, hoping to afford some solace to the forlorn wounded of the Southern Army, sent him a quantity of smoking tobacco and a number of pipes of various designs for distribution among them.

"Probably Father did not approach the proper officer for permission to distribute them, for he was not allowed to use them as the donor had directed. As he did not feel warranted in giving them elsewhere, the pipes and tobacco failed in their humane mission, and gradually were distributed by myself and companions to very different owners than those for whom they were intended. None of us had learned to smoke, we were far too young – but we were proud to be the owners and dispensers of such an imposing and manly outfit."

And remember the young Rebel who begged MRS. HARRIET BAYLY to hide him from any more war? She writes:

"He is now living on a farm near the battle field and the size of his family indicates that he has been more successful in peaceful pursuits than those of war."

NEWSPAPERS IN THE MONTHS FOLLOWING

STAR-SENTINEL[18]
"September 8, 1863: Mr. Michael Crilly, trying to unload a shell which exploded. He lost three fingers. Crilly is a poor man with a family dependent upon his for support."

ADAMS COUNTY SENTINEL.
February 2, 1864
EDITORIAL:
"There appears to be considerable feeling in and around Gettysburg that a place be set apart for the burial of the Confederate dead who are now buried promiscuously over the battlefield, or in the vicinity. The recent rains have washed the places where they are buried and the bones are exposed. Besides which, in a short time the land will be put under cultivation and no trace of their last resting place will be left. Common humanity would dictate a removal to some spot not in or about our own National Cemetery, but the purchase of ground somewhere, where southern friends may, when the rebellion is crushed and all is peace, make their pilgrimage here. Our state should not make the purchase, nor should it be expected; but if southern people should express their desire and could carry it to completion, we should say let it be done for the sake of our common humanity."

STAR-SENTINEL, February 9, 1864:
"28-thousand muskets have been gathered upon the field of Gettysburg. 24-thousand were found loaded, 12-thousand containing two loads and 6-thousand from three to ten loads each. In some cases, half a dozen balls were driven in on a single charge. In some other cases, the former owner had reversed the order, placing the ball at the bottom of the barrel and the powder at top."

"March 1, 1864: Several boys, about 15 years old, playing with a gun found on the field, 'shooting mark, we believe'. The contents of one of the discharges entered the head of a little colored girl who was near the spot, inflicting a mortal wound. She died on Wednesday, aged about 7 years."

"June 21, 1864: Adam Taney Jr., of Fairfield, tried to open a shell from the fields which exploded. It struck him in the feet and may leave him a cripple."

GETTYSBURG COMPILER:
"October 11, 1887: Captain Wynn, who commanded the Sumpter Light Guards, was killed at Gettysburg. The day after the battle his wife, living in Americus, Ga., entered her parlor and saw that a portrait of her husband had fallen from the wall, the face, pierced by a chairpost. She immediately believed her husband had been killed. Sure enough, word came that he had died. The chair pierced the picture in the precise spot on the face where Wynn had been shot."

STAR-SENTINEL:
"November 15th, 1905: The Confederate dead in the battle have been interred on the field following the retreat of General Lee's army, two physicians named Weaver...father and son...residents of Gettysburg...gave diligent personal attention and saw that the graves were marked, or otherwise indicated, looking to the ultimate removal of the remains. After the war, many of the dead were taken away by relatives.
"In 1872 and 73, the younger Weaver (father then deceased) began sending the remains to points in the south under agreements with Confederate memorial associations and the work was completed during the years stated. Colonel Peters says Dr. Weaver's efforts were a labor of love for which he was never fully reimbursed or compensated. About 3-thousand was the number of Confederate dead cared for by the two doctors, chiefly by the son, who stated that all the Confederate dead were removed except about 40 buried in Sherfy's peach orchard."

STAR-SENTINEL:
"December 29, 1863: Mr. Branson, a young man of this place, is another who went out to meet the Rebels, when here, and behaved valiantly. He was not wounded, and that is probably the reason why he did not receive the notice that our old friend Burns did. 'Better late than never.'"

Aftermath, Part Two

Binding the National Wounds

With public support a "sometimes thing," Abraham Lincoln waged war from an almost solitary, certainly lonely, pinnacle until Gettysburg. Prosecuting the war was his duty as President, but as a man he grieved deeply over its collective death and suffering. Trusted aides report that Lincoln paced the White House late at night in a "recurrent melancholy" which today would probably be diagnosed as depression.

But then came July 4th, 1863, and newspaper readers awoke to learn that troops assigned to George Gordon Meade had sent home those under command of Robert E. Lee, and that on the same day Ulysses S. Grant had broken the siege of Vicksburg. The public's view began to brighten.

That autumn in Gettysburg, two men searched for closure.

David McConoughy formed a group to preserve the great battlefield and David Wills started to lay the foundation of a National Soldier's Cemetery. Both were important citizens whose causes and opinions were hard to ignore.

The scars of the firestorm were still visible; businesses, farmers and churches sought reparations; some citizens complained of a lingering stench of death in the cool fall air.

The need for some ameliorating gesture was clear, and plans moved forward.

The ground was prepared and Union soldiers' bodies were moved from shallow temporary graves on the battlefield to permanent interment. Confederate soldiers were left in the shallow graves on the battlefield to which they were consigned after the battle.19 Some monuments were erected. Then, Wills' cemetery committee invited one of the nation's great orators to deliver the dedicatory address, and he accepted. Edward Everett, 69 years old, was a former President of Harvard University, a former Senator from Massachusetts, and had served a year as President Millard Fillmore's Secretary of State.

An invitation was also sent to the President of the United States, asking him to say a few words following Mr. Everett's address.

Abraham Lincoln accepted.

ALBERTUS McCREARY:

"It was a great day for the boys when he arrived. We all wanted to see him, and my strongest wish was to shake hands with him. I saw him several times, and was thrilled with patriotic enthusiasm every time. He stopped at a house at York Street and the corner of the Diamond,[20] and I got close to the open door and had a good view of him walking up and down the hall. He seemed very tall and gaunt to me, but his face was wonderful to look upon. It was such a sad face and so full of kindly feeling that one felt at home with him at once. I was fascinated and kept going up to the steps a step at a time until I was at the very door and very near to him. He did not look up, but kept walking up and down, no doubt thinking over the great speech he was about to deliver. I watched him until he turned into the parlor and the door was shut."

CHARLES McCURDY:

"During the evening he was serenaded by one of the bands in attendance and by a company of young women of the town who sang, 'We are Coming Father Abraham', and other patriotic songs. A great crowd gathered about the (David) Wills residence on the public square and in response to their calls the President appeared in the doorway, standing for a few minutes, but not speaking.

"When Mr. Lincoln re-entered the house the crowd surged around the corner to the residence of Mr. Robert G. Harper[21] on the public square where Mr. Seward[22] was stopping, and called loudly for a speech. Mr. Harper was a gentleman of the old school, and held certain views touching the proper entertainment of a distinguished guest, which now are somewhat difficult of execution. After a short interview, the two gentlemen appeared in the doorway.

Rufus Weaver, who graduated Pennsylvania College in 1862, and went on to study medicine, picked up where his father left off in helping the dead of both sides to a final resting place. Samuel Weaver had played a major role in the reinterment of the Union dead in Soldiers National Cemetery and was also involved in resolving the problem of what to do about the southern dead until his own death in 1870. At that time his son Rufus, now a Philadelphia physician and professor took up his father's work. He and Dr. J.W.C. O'Neal were the leaders in this effort. Dr. O'Neal personally walked the battlefield and recorded the location and identity of as many Confederate graves as he could find. After the war, the battlefield was visited almost daily by relatives and friends from the south who had lost someone at Gettysburg. Many sought ways of recovering the bodies and having them shipped back home. Several southern memorial societies were organized expressly for this purpose. Weaver assumed responsibility for exhuming and shipping south the bodies and skeletons of an estimated 3,000 Confederate dead. *Courtesy Special Collections, Gettysburg College.*

The Gettysburg Railroad Passenger Depot, Carlisle Street at Railroad Street, is where President Abraham Lincoln arrived on November 18th and departed on November 19th, 1863 when he came to Gettysburg to assist in the dedication of the National Soldiers Cemetery. *Courtesy Adams County Historical Society.*

"Mr. Seward began his remarks with a curious blunder. But the grace with which, on a word from Mr. Harper, he quickly sought to correct it, showed his skill as a public speaker. The fact that the battle had been fought and won on Northern soil was impressive and gave particular cause for rejoicing. But he located it elsewhere.

"He began: 'Fellow citizens of Maryland' – 'Pennsylvania, Pennsylvania', whispered Mr. Harper – 'and the States adjacent thereto', he continued, with a comprehensive gesture."

Contrary to legend, Mr. Lincoln's speech was not scribbled on the back of an envelope during the railroad journey to Gettysburg. He made a first draft in his office on White House stationery. He put the finishing touches to it at David Wills' home the night before the dedication, writing in pencil on a legal pad.[23]

At one point in the evening, he followed a body-guard to Mr. Seward's lodgings, perhaps to get his opinion of the speech, certainly to tell Seward that he had received word that

This is the home of Republican attorney David Wills and his wife Jennie. It is located a block from the Railroad Depot, on the square. President Lincoln stayed here. It is said he retired to his room early after dinner to work on the final draft of his Gettysburg Address. The next morning there was a throng outside the house waiting to accompany the President and dignitaries to the new National Soldiers Cemetery south of town. *Courtesy Adams County Historical Society.*

one of the Lincoln's sons was ill, although improving. But the President confined himself primarily to the Wills home that evening. He had a great deal to consider.[24]

On the morning of November 19th, Abraham Lincoln rose early and wrote a new draft, making some changes that added about thirty words.

At 10 A.M., he and David Wills joined the officials for the ceremonial procession to Cemetery Hill.

DANIEL SKELLY was among the crowd waiting in the street:

"I stood in our center square in front of the old McClellan House[25] in company with my boyhood and lifelong friend, Dr. J. C. Felty.

"Our town was filled with people who had come in during the several previous days for the dedication of the cemetery. We had but four ordinary sized hotels of a capacity such as a town of 2300 people would require for the entertainment of visitors during ordinary occasions. These were filled to overflowing and all private houses were also filled to capacity by friends of the families and as many other visitors as could be accommodated. I was up until after midnight on November 18th and there were many people walking the streets, unable to get any accommodations for the night.

"The procession was formed on the four principal streets, all centering at the square: Chambersburg street from the west, York street from the east, Carlisle street from the north and Baltimore street from the south, which led to the cemetery.

"The square was occupied by Colonel Ward Lamon's bodyguard for Mr. Lincoln and was drawn up in an oblong formation, open order.

"When Mr. Lincoln came over from the Wills house on horseback and took his position in the center of his bodyguard, the procession started and I was separated from my friend. I followed the column on the west side of Baltimore street, remaining on the outside of the curb as the pavement was crowded with people.

"I recall very vividly my impressions of Mr. Lincoln as I walked close to him out Steinwehr Avenue. His face, lined and sad, bore traces of the tremendous worry the ordeal of war had brought to him. His expression was benign and kindly, and the strength of his character seemed to me to be evidenced in the pronounced features; a high forehead, a prominent nose and a decided chin jutting below firmly-set lips. His countenance seemed to reflect the tragedy of war and the significance of his visit to Gettysburg on that day.[26]

"When I reached the top of Baltimore Hill I caught up with Mr. Lincoln's position and kept alongside of him up what is now called Steinwehr Avenue,[27] to the junction of the Emmitsburg and Taneytown roads, going almost to the rear entrance of the National Cemetery, at which point the procession turned directly to the east, where I lost my

Attorney David Wills could trace his family history back to 1578 in Ireland. He graduated Pennsylvania College in 1851, read for the law, and later became a judge. After the battle he was instrumental in creation of the National Soldiers Cemetery while his political rival David McConaughy was the power behind the preservation of the battle field. *Courtesy Adams County Historical Society.*

The United Presbyterian Church, on the east side of Baltimore Street's southern corner with East High Street, is where President Lincoln attended a memorial service while in Gettysburg. John Burns was among the members of this church. *Courtesy Adams County Historical Society.*

These people have gathered along Baltimore Street in hopes of getting a glimpse of President Lincoln astride a horse as the November 19th parade passes en route to the new Soldiers National Cemetery. You can see the parade has reached High Street at the crest of the Baltimore Street hill. This photograph was taken just north of Catherine Snyder's house and the Wagon Hotel. *Courtesy Gettysburg National Military Park*

place at the President's side, but managed to get through the crowd and reach the platform (upon) which the exercises were to be held.

"It was erected at or near the position now occupied by the United States monument, facing a little to the north of west. I succeeded in getting close up to the north side of it and held my position until the preliminary exercises were over and the Honorable Edward Everett had commenced his oration, when I climbed up on the side of the platform, with my feet on the floor of it, and left arm over the railing. I kept that place all through the exercises.

"Mr. Everett's oration was quite long, lasting perhaps an hour and a half or longer, but I listened to it attentively, for it was interesting, historical and classical, with a resume' of the battle which no doubt was received from some of the prominent participants.

"When Mr. Everett had finished his address there was some music..."

Then, Abraham Lincoln rose slowly, straightening his papers and adjusting his eyeglasses while looking over an audience of some 15,000. It is doubtful his piping voice carried to the far edge of the crowd, but that did not matter. The ages were listening:

> Four score and seven years ago our fathers brought forth on this continent a new nation, conceived in liberty and dedicated to the proposition that all men are created equal.
>
> Now we are engaged in a great civil war, testing whether that nation, or any nation so conceived and so dedicated, can long endure.
>
> We are met on a great battlefield of that war. We have come to dedicate a portion of that field as a final resting place for those who here gave their lives that that nation might live.
>
> It is altogether fitting and proper that we should do this. But in a larger sense, we can not dedicate – we can not consecrate – we can not hallow this ground. The brave men, living and dead, who struggled here have consecrated it far above our poor power to add or detract.
>
> The world will little note, nor long remember, what we say here, but can never forget what they did here. It is for us, the living, rather, to be dedicated here to the unfinished work which they who fought here have, thus far, so nobly advanced. It is rather for us to be here dedicated to the great task remaining before us – that from these honored dead we take increased devotion to that cause for which they gave the last full measure of devotion – that we here highly resolve

that these dead shall not have died in vain; that this nation shall have a new birth of freedom; and that this government of the people, by the people, for the people, shall not perish from the earth."

In contrast to Edward Everett's speech, Mr. Lincoln's statement was just about 270 words long. It took less than three minutes to deliver.

Witnesses say the President only glanced at his paper once or twice. In point of fact, the Gettysburg Address was finished so quickly that the official photographer barely had time to adjust his camera and a proper image of the moment was lost.

DANIEL SKELLY:

"As I remember it, (it) was received with very little, if any, applause. This will not seem strange if you consider the character of the audience and the occasion that brought them here.

"The war had been going on for two years and quite a number of the battles had been fought with terrible losses in killed and wounded, and at that time there seemed no prospect that there would be any letup in the fighting until one side had been decisively victorious. There were present fathers and mothers who had lost sons in the war, brothers and sisters who had lost relatives, and sweethearts whose lovers had been killed or maimed since the war began. Could there be much applause from such an audience?

"It was a prophecy and promise to the northland and to the southland ...and the latter part of it a notice to the nations of the world...some of whom had been just waiting for a favorable opportunity to recognize the southern confederacy...that 'this nation shall not perish from the earth'."[28]

He had said everything the moment...and the nation...required.

When the ceremony was over, the President took time for the small things...and people.

Twelve year old MARY ELIZABETH MONTFORT:

"As Mr. Lincoln came down the steps I looked up into his face. He held out his hand and said, 'Hello, young lady, who are you?' I took his hand and said, 'I'm Mary Elizabeth.'

It was the greatest moment of my life."

SUE KING BLACK:

"When my turn came, he clasped my hand and smiled his wonderful, kind smile, but he did not say anything."

This photograph was taken during the dedication ceremony. Unfortunately, no photographs exist that show President Lincoln delivering his Gettysburg Address. Rising above the crowd on the far left is the Gatehouse to Evergreen Cemetery. Whether Elizabeth Thorn, who gave birth to Rosie Meade Thorn three months after the battle, watched the proceedings from her windows, or elected to join the crowd on this day isn't known. *Courtesy Library of Congress*

ALBERTUS McCREARY:

"In the evening, there was a meeting in the Presbyterian church, and it was reported that Mr. Lincoln was to be there. The church was so crowded that many were turned away. I managed to work myself past the guard at the door and about halfway down the aisle; the aisle was blocked with others unable to get seats. I looked every way for the sight of Mr. Lincoln, and by the time the services were nearly over, I felt sure he was not there.

"As the people arose to leave, I turned around to leave also, and there was Mr. Lincoln in the pew just at my side. I held my ground until he was in the aisle near me, when I put out my hand and said, 'Mr. Lincoln, will you shake hands with me?'

"'Certainly,' he said, and gave me a good strong grasp.

"He moved on and was soon lost to view, but I was a proud boy, and to this day feel a thrill of pride to have pressed the hand of one of the greatest men the world has known."[29]

THE COMPILER, August 3, 1863:
"The Honorable Thaddeus Stevens of Pa., who advocated in one of his speeches the burning of every Rebel mansion, has had to take some of his own medicine. The Rebels have destroyed his extensive iron mills near Gettysburg, and stolen all his horses. His personal loss is said to exceed 50-thousand dollars."

ADAMS COUNTY SENTINEL, March 7, 1865:
"George Patterson, one of those taken prisoner after the battle, was jailed in Salisbury, NC. He was only one of six taken at the time who have been exchanged or paroled. Guinn, Trostle, Codori and two Harpers are still in the hands of the Rebels, but William Harper died in Salisbury a few weeks ago. Shortly after Patterson's capture, his wife died and, on the very day of his return, his aged mother was buried."

March 14, 1865: "George Codori Sr. returned home last night."

ADAMS COUNTY SENTINEL, Mar 21, 1865: "Guinn, Harper, Pitzer, Trostle, Bushman and Doll have returned."

LANCASTER EXAMINER March 3, 1904 obituary:
"Mrs. Abrev Kamoo, born in Tunis, 1815. Daughter of a triplet, a triplet herself, and twice gave birth to triplets.

Mrs. Kamoo came to this country with Commodore Perry.

In 1862, disguised as a man, she enlisted as a nurse in the northern army under the name of Tommy Kamoo. Later became a drummer. Her sex was never discovered. She was shot in the nose."

NOTES

1. Many of the horses and mules sold for 25 cents apiece. The "colored farmhand" and his story may be found in Johnson's *Battlefield Adventures*.
2. Excerpt from Bell Wiley's *Johnny Reb and Billy Yank.*
3. A similar incident led to the founding of a Soldier's Orphans Home in Gettysburg. Gettysburg resident, Peter Beitler, found a dead Union soldier clasping a picture of his three children. Dr. J. Francis Bourns of Philadelphia borrowed the picture and circulated it widely, leading to identification of the soldier and his family. He was Sgt. Amos Humiston of the NY Volunteers – his children were Frank, Frederick and Alice of Cataraugus County, NY. The story received nationwide publicity and an organization grew from public donations. It's reported that the Humiston children attended the school.
4. At the Seminary.
5. Sadie and the man who saved her on the battlefield were reunited some 30 years later in San Francisco when Dr. Benjamin Lyford spotted a newspaper article about her exploits. Ironically, although Lyford had looked for the girl during that time, they had been living only a few miles apart – he in San Francisco, she in Oakland.
6. Although it clearly does not apply in this case, according to Gettysburger, Liberty Hollinger, "Many romances bloomed in the hospitals."
7. Major General Henry W. Slocum, USA
8. The gallery was located at 9 York street, down the street from Tyson's house on Chambersburg Street.
9. Tyson later reported that the shell was still there years later.
10. Probably Herr Tavern, some three miles out Cashtown Road, east of Marsh Creek.
11. Attorney J. Cassat Neely.
12. Once again, here's an example of the political division...not only in Gettysburg, but throughout the nation at the time. Wills is convinced that his political enemies in the Republican party are painting him as a Rebel sympathizer to Union military authorities. Wills makes clear that he and his father, Charles, saw themselves merely as businessmen.

13. The town was quickly overwhelmed by sightseers and by families who rushed to the scene to search the hospitals for sons, husbands or brothers. Too often, they were told to look among the gravestones or on the battlefield itself. Another contingent that quickly descended on the town: embalmers, who set up shop near the hospitals and soon had more business than they could handle.

14. Simon Cameron, former Secretary of War, Senator from Pennsylvania.

15. McCurdy reports that sometime later, Trimble sent Mrs. McCurdy a silver soup ladle, inscribed: "General Trimble to Mrs. McCurdy. The tribute of a grateful heart."

16. Brigadier General Gabriel Paul, USA, also wounded.

17. Brigadier General James L. Kemper, CSA, Pickett's Division.

18. A small broadsheet, normally in the business of distributing advertisements. It was not in the category of the Adams County Sentinent or the Gettysburg Compiler when it came to journalism, but it appears to have risen to the occasion when "major national news" dropped in its lap.

19. In the weeks leading up to the dedication ceremony (November 19th) for the new cemetery, Pennsylvania Governor Andrew Curtin asked Gettysburg attorney David McConaughy how much it would cost to correct the exposed condition of the Confederate dead on the field. McConaughy saw to it before the arrival of the reporters and crowds. However, several years passed before the Confederates not immediately claimed by their families after the battle were located for more proper reburial. Dr. O'Neal had gone to the field and made careful note of their location, records which were turned over to the southern reburial committees when the time came.

20. Home of David Wills.

21. Robert G. Harper was one of the town's leading Republican politicians and publisher of the Adams Sentinel.

22. Secretary of State William Seward, who accompanied the President to Gettysburg.

23. Both of these copies can be seen today at the Library of Congress. Neither contains the exact language of the dedication speech. The copies in the Library of Congress were given by Mr. Lincoln to associates. The commonly-accepted "as delivered" text is presented here as recorded by Charles Hale, a reporter of the time for the Boston Advertiser. Regarding the story about the speech having been written 'on the back of an envelope'; it may have been started by Liberty "Libby" Hollinger, who was among the crowd outside the Wills house on the night before the speech. She wrote that when Mr. Lincoln came to the window to acknowledge the crowd, he was carrying something that looked like an envelope. She connected the object with the speech, and yet another legend may have been born.

24. The notice that his son was ill is all the more interesting in light of a report that Lincoln himself was stricken during his return to Washington. Author Burke Davis writes in his *Our Incredible Civil War* (Holt, Rinehart & Winston, 1960) that Lincoln lay down in his rail car with a wet cloth on his forehead. Davis claims there is evidence that Lincoln had "a mild case of smallpox."

25. Later the Hotel Gettysburg.

26. We have taken an editorial liberty here: We moved this description of Mr. Lincoln by half a page from its location in Mr. Skelly's account to better fit the flow of the proceedings.

27. Skelly: "In those early days of my life I was around horses daily and rode horseback a great deal, and to me, Mr. Lincoln was the most peculiar looking figure on horseback I had ever seen. He rode a medium-sized black horse, and was dressed in black and wore a high silk hat. It seemed to me that his feet almost touched the ground, but he was perfectly at ease, indicating he was at home on horseback."
A lifelong resident of Gettysburg, Mr. Skelly wrote these memoirs in 1932. He was 18 at the time of the battle.

28. In fact, the speech was received very poorly by most newspapers of the day. One called it "silly." Later, it was pointed out that it was doubtful that all of the reporters could hear Lincoln's piping voice. It was also noted that since oratory like Edward Everett's was the current style, critics did not get what they expected from Mr. Lincoln. More probably, since Lincoln was not popular in the press anyway, he got the reviews he expected. Nevertheless, it was Mr. Everett who was among those who immediately understood the import of the President's remarks. He wrote to Lincoln: "I should be glad if I could flatter myself that I came as near the central idea of the occasion in two hours as you did in two minutes." Lincoln presented a 272 word handwritten copy to Everett.

29. Albertus McCreary's narrative was in McClure's Magazine of July 1909.

Caption Notes

1. Three years after the war, Colonel William Colvill did return to the Pierce residence for a visit. TILLIE PIERCE: "I was standing on the front pavement one day, when a carriage suddenly stopped at the front door. A gentleman alighted, and kissed me without saying a word. I knew it was the Colonel by his tall, manly form. He ran up the front porch, rang the bell, and on meeting the rest of the family, heartily shook hands, and greeted mother and sister with a kiss.
"We were all glad to meet each other again, and we earnestly desired him to stay. He, however, said his time was limited, and his friends were waiting in the carriage to go over to the battlefield. So we were forced to again say farewell."

Epilogue

In later years...

Charles Tyson sold his property at 216 Chambersburg Street in 1867, leaving behind the Brussels carpet which withstood "uninjured" a fire the Confederates set on it to burn his personal papers.

Tyson gave up the photography business he and his brother, Isaac, operated in Gettysburg when he moved to Flora Dale, Pennsylvania, to buy a plant nursery. Some of his photographs appear today in publications dealing with the battle of Gettysburg.

Daniel Skelly lived in Gettysburg the rest of his life, writing the memoirs quoted in this book in 1932. He remained with his beloved Fahnestock Store, eventually taking over its operation.

James Fahnestock, along with Gates and the rest of the family, moved to Philadelphia in 1865. After several years, Daniel Skelly managed to purchase the Fahnestock store. Once the store was purchased, Edward Fahnestock moved to South Dakota and became a Speical Investigator for the US Interior Department in 1880; brother Henry joined him in 1887. However, in 1891 Edward left South Dakota for Minnesota where he was in the insurance business.

Harriett Bayly was one of the strong women of Gettysburg who pitched in quickly to aid the fallen soldiers of both sides. So far as the Confederate soldiers were concerned, it appears that her greatest contribution was to feed them, perhaps as a way of keeping them from damaging her family's farm, but just as likely because of a compassionate, loving heart.

Mrs. Bayly had a delicious sense of humor, which can be found in her accounts. Complemented by the descriptions furnished by her then-13 year old son, Billy, her narratives lent a welcome touch of humanity to an otherwise dark episode in American history.

William Bayly, "Billy," went on to attend Pennsylvania College, from which he graduated in 1871. He became a lawyer.

Henry Eyster Jacobs became one of the first to publish a citizen's description of the great battle and is one of the most quoted.

Eighteen years old at the time, Henry followed his father's footsteps into academe, eventually becoming the Reverend Dr. Henry E. Jacobs, dean of the Lutheran Theological Seminary in Gettysburg.

John W. C. O'Neal, MD was 42 at the time of the battle. He continued to practice medicine in Gettysburg, well into his 80s, becoming one of the citizens that newspaper reporters and other writers sought out when they were looking for a human interest story or an "anniversary piece on the great battle."

The talk about Dr. O'Neal's "southern sympathies" was either highlighted or ballooned by his service during and after the battle. O'Neal circulated among the Rebels and then treated their wounds with the same concern he treated his Yankee patients. He is further remembered as a person who took careful notes of the places where the Confederate dead were hastily buried, a service which later helped in their proper burial and commemoration.

John Wills continued at the famous Globe Hotel until his father sold it in 1864. He remained in Gettysburg, enjoying his reputation as a raconteur and, probably, a rascal.

Wills and his family were considered southern sympathizers, leading to no end of trouble for him during the time of Gettysburg's military occupation. As a hotel and innkeeper, he was in a choice position to spot and point out the people he described later as spies or scouts for the Rebel army who frequented the town in the days and weeks before the battle.

Several months after the battle, John Wills married Martha Martin whose older brother Robert was the town Burgess.

Twenty-five years old at the time of the battle, Wills was 80 when he died in 1918.

Sallie Myers met and, five years later, married Reverend Henry Ferguson Stewart, the brother of Alexander Stewart, one of the soldiers Miss Myers nursed in her home after the battle.

Reverend Stewart died a year later, but the marriage produced a son, Henry, who became a doctor. Characteristically, his mother would sometimes assist Henry in his medical practice.

After the death of her husband, Salome Myers Stewart returned to Gettysburg and resumed teaching. But her destiny was larger: she was actively involved in many service organizations, including Chatauqua, and the Sons of Union Veterans. In 1901, she was named to the National Association of Army Nurses of the Civil War. And the GAR elected her National Treasurer in 1903. She held that office until her death in 1922.

William McLean lived his life as an attorney in Adams County. He rose to serve as President Judge of the county. He and his wife Fannie had three children. William died in 1915.

Rufus Weaver, who was instrumental in the reinternment of Confederate dead at Gettysburg, was an 1862 graduate of Pennsylvania College. He made his home in Philadelphia and had a distinguished career as a professor of medicine. Weaver was praised by colleagues, in 1888, for "dissecting and mounting the entire human cerebro-spinal nervous system – the only specimen of its kind."

Lieutenant James Francis Crocker, born in 1828, returned to the tidewater area of Virginia after the war. There he married and resumed his law practice. He became a Judge in Portsmouth.

William and Maria Meals lived out their lives in Adams County. Their oldest son Louis Henry became a partner in the family stone cutting business.

Charles McCurdy lived out his life as a resident of Gettysburg. By 1886 he was a teller at the bank founded by Alexander Cobean in 1813.

Sarah and Joseph Broadhead eventually returned to her native New Jersey, where Joseph was in the coal business.

After Joseph died in 1903, Sarah lived with their daughter, Mary, in Rathmill, Pennsylvania, where she died on May 21, 1910. She is buried in Pleasantville, New Jersey.

Sarah was not a nurse, but rose to that service during the battle. Perhaps as a token of her esteem for the work performed by the United States Sanitary Commission, she presented 75 copies of her diary to the Commission to be used in fund-raising. An additional 125 copies went to "the kindred and nearest friends of the writer."

Tillie Pierce was 15 at the time of the battle. She wrote and published her account of it in 1888. In the meantime, she married attorney Horace Alleman in 1871, moving with him to Selinsgrove, Pennsylvania. The Allemans had three children.

Tillie died in 1914.

Becky Weikert, a friend of Tillie Pierce, later married her soldier friend, Lieutenant George Kitzmiller of the Pennsylvania Reserves.

And still, there were others. Their tale, but not their memory, ends here.

Jacob.A. Kitzmiller, had left high school to learn blacksmithing, but enlisted in the army in 1862. He returned home by the end of the war and within three years married Anna Garlach. Kitzmiller became a lawyer. He and Anna had two children.

Bibliography

ACHS = Adams County Historical Society
NMPA = National Military Park Archives
NFI = No Further Identification

Alleman, Tillie Pierce. *At Gettysburg or What a Girl Saw and Heard of the Battle.* New York: W.L. Borland, 1889. ACHS.

Aughinbaugh, Nellie. Narrative. ACHS.

Barlow, Francis, General, USA. Letter to his mother. Massachusetts Historical Society. ACHS.

Bayly, Harriet. Narrative. NMPA.

Bayly, William H. Narrative. NMPA.

Bigham, Mrs. J. Paxton. Narrative. ACHS.

Black, Sue King. Letter. ACHS.

Broadhead, Sarah. *A Diary of a Lady of Gettysburg.* ACHS.

Crocker, J.F., Lt., 9th Virginia Infantry. Narrative. ACHS.

Dustman, Henry. Narrative. ACHS.

Fahnestock, Gates D. Narrative. ACHS.

Garlach, Anna. Narrative. ACHS.

Gilbert, Mrs. Elizabeth. Narrative. ACHS.

Hill, C.M. Narrative. ACHS.

Jacobs, Henry. Narrative. ACHS.

Johnson, Clifton. "The Black Servantmaid" (NFI). *Battlefield Adventures.* 1913. NMPA.

_____. "The Colored Farmhand." (NFI). *Battlefield Adventures.* 1913. NMPA.

_____. "Mr. Benner." (NFI). *Battlefield Adventures.* 1913. NMPA.

_____. "Samuel Bushman." *Battlefield Adventures.* 1913. NMPA.

Kendlehart, Joyce Ann. Term Paper. Gettysburg College.

King, Sarah Barrett. Gettysburg Compiler. July 4, 1906. ACHS.

Lightner, Nathaniel. Gettysburg Compiler. July 6, 1910. ACHS.

McAllister, Mary. Narrative. ACHS.

McCartney, Margaretta Kendlehart. Narrative. ACHS.

McCreary, Albertus. ACHS.

McCreary, Jennie. Narrative. ACHS.

McCurdy, Charles M. NMPA.

McLean, William. Narrative. ACHS.

Minnigh, Captain N.N., 1st PA Res. Narrative. ACHS.

Myers, Salome "Sallie". NMPA.

Panebraker, Lydia Meals. Narrative. ACHS.

Plank, Lizzie R. Beard. Narrative. ACHS.

Powers, Alice. Narrative. NMPA

Pratt, F.F. Letter to his parents, July 4, 1863. ACHS.

Rupp, John. Narrative. ACHS.

Rupp, John. Narrative. NMPA.

Schick, Lawrence. Narrative. ACHS.

Sheely, Aaron. Narrative. NMPA.

Simpson, William. *Recollections of a Drummerboy*. NMPA.

Skelly, Danial A. *A Boy's Experiences During the Battle of Gettysburg*. 1932. ACHS.

Smith, Thomas. Letter to Henry E. Jacobs. ACHS.

Snyder, Catherine. Narrative. ACHS.

Stoever, Dr. M.L. Narrative. ACHS.

Thorn, Catherine Elizabeth. Narrative. ACHS.

Tyson, Charles. Letter. January 16, 1884. ACHS.

Tyson, Charles. Letter. ACHS.

Tyson, Charles. Recollections of a relative. NMPA.

Unidentified College Student's Diary. ACHS.

Veil, Charles. Letter. September 1864. NMPA.

Wade, Virginia. File. NMPA.

Warren, Leander H. Narrative. ACHS.

Watkins, Horatio James. ACHS.

Weikert, Jacob. Thesis. May 1930. ACHS.

Wills, Ruth. Narrative. ACHS.

Young, Anne. Narrative. ACHS.

Young, Annie. Letter. July 17, 1863. ACHS.

Ziegler, Lydia C. Narrative. NMPA.

Books and Periodicals

Adams County Sentinel.

Alleman, Tillie Pierce. *At Gettysburg, or What a Young Girl Saw and Heard of the Battle.* Borland, New York: W. Lake, 1889.

Andrews, J.C. *The North Reports the Civil War.*

Andrews, J.C. *The South Reports the Civil War.*

The Atlantic Monthly. November 1865.

The Baltimore American. June-July 1863.

Bennett, Gerald R. *Days of "Uncertainty and Dread."* 1994.

Berger, Meyer. *The Story of the New York Times.*

Bigham, James L. *Traditions Recalled by a Descendent.* c. 1975.

Broadhead, Sarah M. *A Diary of a Lady of Gettysburg, Pennsylvania.* June 15 to July 15, 1863.

Butts, Joseph T. *A Gallant Captain: Frederick Otto von Fritsch.*

Centennial Alumni Publication. University of Georgia, 1901.

Civil War. Fairfax Press.

Civil War Times Illustrated. *Gettysburg!*

Coggins, Jack. *Arms and Equipment of the Civil War.*

Commanger, H.S. *The Blue and The Gray.* Volume 2.

The Confederate Soldier in the Civil War. Fairfax Press.

Confederate Tales.

Crapster, Basil L. *The Family of Dr. J.W.C. O'Neal & The Battle of Gettysburg.* ACHS.

Crozier. *Yankee Reporters in the Civil War.*

Daily Transcript. September 16, 1901.

DC Chronicle. July 9, 1863.

Dictionary of American Biography.

Dictionary of National Biography, 20th Century. 1901-1911.

Douglas, Henry Kyd. *I Rode With Stonewall.*

Eaton, Clement. *History of the Southern Confederacy.*

Fite, Emerson. *Social & Industrial Conditions in the North During the Civil War.*

Flemming, George T. *The Homecoming of Wes Culp.*

Generals in Blue.

Generals in Gray.

The Gettysburg Compiler.

The Gettysburg Times. December 4, 1952.

Harper's Pictorial History of the Civil War. Fairfax Press.

Harper's Weekly. July 1863.

A History of Cumberland and Adams Counties, Pennsylvania. 1886.

A History of Gettysburg College.

A History of the Weikert Family. ACHS.

Hollinger, Liberty Augusta. Narrative. *Pennsylvania History.* 5(3). July 1938.

Horan, James D. *Matthew Brady: Historian with a Camera.*

Jacobs, Henry. "Gettysburg 50 Years Ago." *The Lutheran.* July-August 1913.

Jaquette, Henrietta Stratton (ed.). *South After Gettysburg. Cornelia Hancock Letters.*

Johnson, Clifton. *Battlefield Adventures.* California 1913. NMPA.

Klees, Frederic. *The Pennsylvania Dutch.*

Knightly, Phillip. *The First Casualty.*

The Lancaster, Pennsylvania Intelligencer. November 1902.

Long, E.B. *The Civil War, Day by Day.*

Lord, Walter. *Civil War Collector's Encyclopedia.*

Lord, Walter (ed.). *The Fremantle Diary.*

Matthew Brady's Illustrated History of the Civil War. Fairfax Press.

McCreary, Albertus. *Gettysburg: A Boy's Experience of the Battle.* ACHS.

McLaughlin, Jack. *Gettysburg: The Long Encampment.*

"Miss Jane Smith's Diary." *Adams Star & Sentinel.* July 2, 1913.

Montgomery, J.S. *The Shaping of a Battle: Gettysburg.*

The New York Times. June-July 1863 and July 1, 1913.

North American Review. February 1891.

Nevins, Allan. *The War for the Union.*

Nichols, E.J. *Toward Gettysburg: Biography of General J.F. Reynolds.*

Oates, Stephen. *With Malice Toward None.*

Philadelphia Evening Bulletin. July 2, 1938.'

The Philadelphia Inquirer. June-July 1863.

Philadelphia North American. June 29, 1913.

Philadelphia North American. Sallie Meyers Interview. July 4, 1902.

Philadelphia Public Ledger and Daily Transcript. September 16, 1901.

Philadelphia Weekly Times. March 29, 1884.

Pierce, Matilda. *A Girl at Gettysburg.* NMPA.

Powers, Alice & Byrle F. MacPherson. *Volunteer Nurse in the Civil War.* ACHS.

Quarrels, Benjamin. *The Negro in the Civil War.*

Rodgers, Sarah Sites. *The Ties of the Past.* Thomas Publications, 1996.

Roland, Charles P. *The Confederacy.*

Ross, Fitzgerald. *Cities and Camps of the Confederate States.*

The Savannah Republican. June-July 1863.

Simpson, William. *Recollections of a Drummerboy.* NMPA.

Skelly, Daniel Alexander. *A Boy's Experiences During the Battle of Gettysburg.* 1932. ACHS.

Starr, Louis. *Bohemian Brigade.*

Stoever, Sue Elizabeth. Adams Compiler. June 24, 1903.

Stories of Adventure.

The Times of London (England). June-August 1863.

Tucker, Glen. *High Tide at Gettysburg.*

Turner, Justin and Linda. *Mary Todd Lincoln: Her Life & Letters.*

Two Views of Gettysburg. Chicago, Illinois: The Lakeside Press/R.R. Donnelly & Sons, 1964.

Washington Star. June-November 1863.

Weisberger. *Reporters for the Union.*

Wheeler, Richard. *Voices of the Civil War.*

Wiley, Bell. *The Life of Billy Yank.*

Williams, William G. *Days of Darkness: The Gettysburg Civilians.* New York: White Mane Publishing/Berkley Books, 1986.

Wills, John. *Three Days at the Globe Hotel.* NMPA.

Yoseloff, Thomas. *Battles and Leaders of the Civil War.* Vol. III.

Index

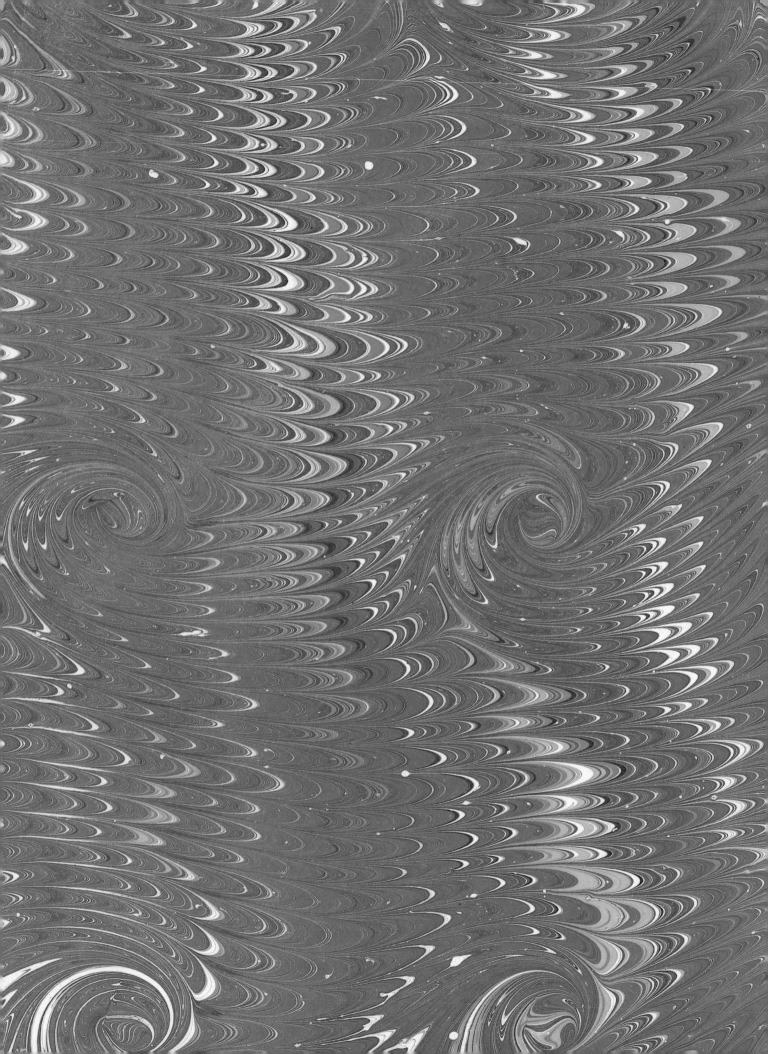